day trips® from
raleigh-durham

help us keep this guide up to date

We would love to hear from you concerning your experiences with this guide and how you feel it could be improved and kept up to date. Please send your comments and suggestions to:

editorial@GlobePequot.com

Thanks for your input, and happy travels!

day trips® series

day trips® from raleigh-durham

fourth edition

>>> **getaway ideas for the local traveler**

james l. hoffman

gpp®
travel

Guilford, Connecticut

All the information in this guidebook is subject to change. We recommend that you call ahead to obtain current information before traveling.

To buy books in quantity for corporate use or incentives, call **(800) 962-0973** or e-mail **premiums@GlobePequot.com**.

Editor: Kevin Sirois
Project Editor: Heather Santiago
Layout: Joanna Beyer
Text Design: Linda R. Loiewski
Maps: Design Maps Inc. © Morris Book Publishing, LLC.
Spot photography throughout © www.visitkure.com

ISBN 978-0-7627-6007-7

Printed in the United States of America
10 9 8 7 6 5 4 3 2 1

for bonnie

—james l. hoffman

contents

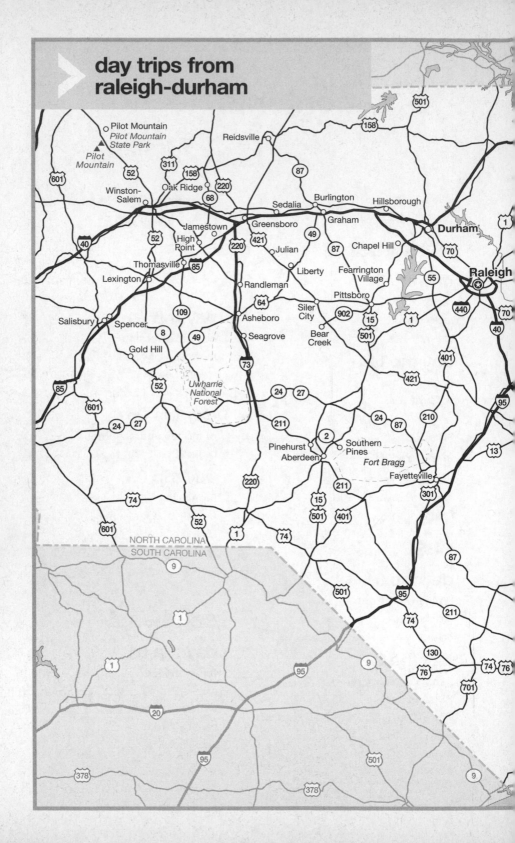

day trips from raleigh-durham

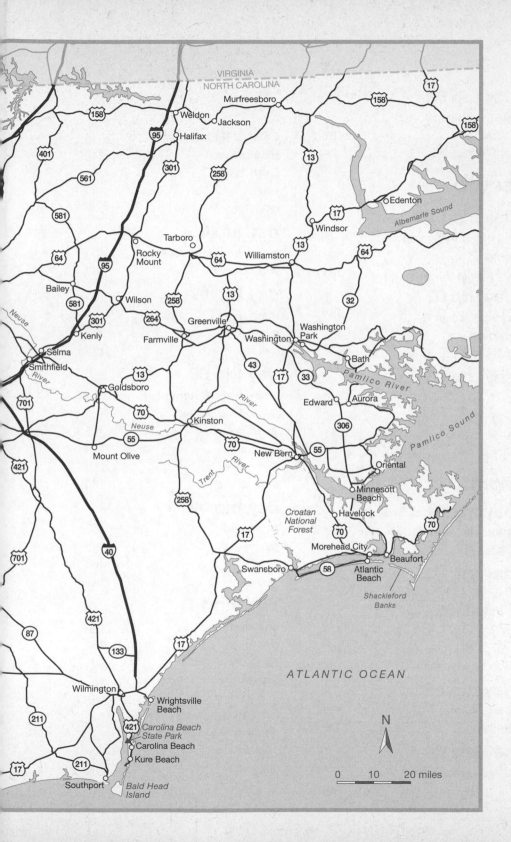

about the author

James L. Hoffman is a lifelong resident of North Carolina. He is a freelance writer and marketing director for Daniel Stowe Botanical Garden in Belmont. Hoffman has also been a newspaper reporter and editor and worked in marketing and public relations at Charlotte's Discovery Place science center. He is also the author of *Fun with the Family North Carolina*, also published by GPP Travel. Hoffman lives in Gastonia with his wife, Bonnie. They have five children.

introduction

North Carolina automobiles once bore license plates that displayed the tagline "Variety Vacationland." Those words have since been replaced with "First in Flight," in honor of Wilbur and Orville Wright, two brothers who on December 17, 1903, launched the age of human flight from Kitty Hawk, North Carolina. Still, North Carolina remains a variety vacationland, and our 80,000 miles of blacktop that the state maintains (second among all states) put our state's varied attractions within driving distance for all.

Raleigh-Durhamers are particularly blessed. Within about a two-hour drive, they can reach country and coast—and even the edge of the mountains on the western end of our state. Nearly every type of tourist diversion beckons to capital-area travelers seated behind the steering wheel.

To the east, day trippers can point their cars toward the more than 301 miles of coast edging the Atlantic Ocean. Dotting these shores are exquisitely charming fishing villages and islands where local residents, descendants of English settlers, sound as though they just stepped off a boat from Britain. A day trip to the North Carolina coast can be not only culturally enlightening but also invigorating for mind and spirit. Be sure to breathe in deeply the salt air and sea spray from the Atlantic Ocean.

Your taste buds needn't go unrewarded as you travel the blacktop. Point your car in any direction, and you're bound to find a memorable meal. As you leave Raleigh, US 70 east is known as the "Barbecue Highway." We've scoped out the best of the barbecue joints for you, so be sure to leave home with a full tank and an empty stomach.

A little farther inland, good roads will lead you to our colonial past, which lives in perpetuity in towns like New Bern. There, stately Tryon Palace, although rebuilt in the 1950s, looks much as it did when it was home to two royal governors in the 1770s. Nearby Bath, settled in 1705, boasts North Carolina's first church and the three historic homes that compose the historic site at "North Carolina's First Town." Pardon the pun, but you'll want to immerse yourself in the history of Bath and other towns that reflect our heritage and our eventual break with the British Isles.

Heading northeast takes you to Halifax—where the Halifax Resolves, signed several months before the Declaration of Independence, represented the first movement toward independence in our nation—and to Edenton, another of the three colonial capitals from which the king's appointees once ruled the Carolinas. You'll learn a great deal about who we once were and who we have become on day trips to these destinations.

Heading south and southeast from Raleigh puts you in golf country—North Carolina claims to be the birthplace of American golf. The sand hills that make for such good golf courses also are home to one of the world's largest military complexes, Fort Bragg, where the nearby Special Operations Museum is a must-see. The sand meets the sea in the coastal city of Wilmington and, a little farther to the south, charming Southport. Are you beginning to get our point about North Carolina's being the variety vacationland?

Going west takes you, young or not, to the college town of Chapel Hill, to the colonial town of Hillsborough, and to the Moravian village of Old Salem—with lots in between. For example, marvel at the world's largest Duncan Phyfe chair in Thomasville. It rises 18 feet above its base and has seated President Lyndon B. Johnson as well as several Miss Americas. Or stand beneath what was once the world's largest coffeepot, erected by two Moravian tinsmiths in 1858 and measuring 16 feet in circumference and 12 feet in height. It's located on the north side of Old Salem.

Wherever your journeys may lead, a taste from the fruit of the vine is not far away. A burgeoning wine business over the past decade has given a big boost the state's tourism business and provides numerous tasty stops along the road for the day-tripper. We'll take a look at that business and give you some tips for enjoying North Carolina wine.

All of this, however, is only a sample of what's ahead of you as you get behind the wheel to travel the scenic ribbons of road that traverse the Old North State. Remember always to enjoy the journey: It can be just as rewarding as the destination. And remember too to permit yourself to be detoured now and then. One of our own said it best. "You can travel the interstate highways and miss the whole country," said Wilmington-born Charles Kuralt. "I always choose the back roads whenever possible." It is there, passing through farmland and forests, towns and cities, that you will find what is best and true of our great state.

>> using this travel guide

Highway designations: Federal highways are designated as US or as an interstate (I-85). State roads are indicated by SR. There are no county-maintained roadways in North Carolina.

Hours: Hours of operation have been included when possible but are subject to frequent changes. Addresses, phone numbers, and Web sites appear for obtaining up-to-date information.

Restaurants: Restaurant prices are designated as $$$ (expensive; $20 or more for an entree), $$ (moderate; $10 to $20), and $ (inexpensive; $10 and under).

Accommodations: Room rates are designated as $$$ (expensive; over $150 for a standard room), $$ (moderate; $100 to $150), and $ (inexpensive; under $100).

The prices and rates listed in this guidebook were confirmed at press time. We recommend, however, that you call establishments before traveling to obtain current information.

travel tips

carry a road map

Don't leave home without one! Two, in fact. For your glove compartment, pick up the free State Transportation Map, published by the North Carolina Department of Transportation (NCDOT). Order one by calling (800) 847-4862 or pick up one at offices operated or approved by NCDOT, such as the Driver's License office. The second map that we wouldn't leave home without is the exotically named *DeLorme North Carolina Atlas & Gazetteer*. Retailing for $19.95 and available at bookstores and online, this 88-page reference with lists of campgrounds, natural features and more will become well worn from use over the years. While the increasingly ubiquitous GPS will probably get you where you need to go, you might end up missing all the simple pleasures the great state has to offer.

follow the rules of the road

It may seem to be common sense, but keep your eyes on the road. In 2009, the latest year for which figures are available, of the 223,678 crashes reported in the state, a third involved drivers who were drowsy, distracted, or on their cell phone. In fact, in 2009 it became illegal to text while driving in North Carolina.

Don't speed. It's the leading violation in fatal crashes.

Obey the law. In 61 percent of all crashes in North Carolina, at least one driver was in violation of a traffic law.

Choose your travel times carefully. Fully 77 percent of all crashes occur between 7 a.m. and 7 p.m. Sunday is the lowest crash day, with only 11 percent of all crashes.

Don't drink. Nearly a quarter of highway fatalities are the result of alcohol violations.

The North Carolina Governor's Highway Safety Program provides information to help keep you safe behind the wheel. For more information call (919) 733-3083 or www.ncdot.org/secretary/GHSP.

watch out for wild animals

Deer are an increasingly severe problem on the state's highway, causing 9.2 percent of all reported North Carolina driving accidents in 2008, according to a University of North Carolina at Chapel Hill study. Eastern counties showed the highest rates overall, with nearly 80 percent occurring between 6 p.m. and 6 a.m. The state's Wildlife Resources Commission estimates North Carolina's deer population at just more than one million. Keep your eye out not only for deer but also for bears (abundant in eastern North Carolina), raccoons, opossums, and livestock. North Carolina ranks as the ninth most dangerous state, by the way, for wildlife/automobile accident frequency, according to the Insurance Information Institute.

On the other hand, these are animals to look for, as opposed to look out for: the cardinal (state bird), the channel bass (state fish), the honeybee (state insect), the box turtle (state reptile), and the gray squirrel (state mammal). We even have a state dog, the Plott hound.

plan accordingly

Our day trips are designed to be just that: trips that can be done well within one revolution of the clock, including travel to and from Raleigh-Durham. Should you want to linger, however, some trips will require an overnight stay. If you prefer a long weekend, look for day trips that can be combined.

sleeping away from home

We've listed hotels and bed-and-breakfasts, should you decide to spend a little more time away from home. The North Carolina Division of Tourism, Film and Sports Development publishes North Carolina: The Official Travel Guide both in print and online. Call (800) VISIT-NC (in Raleigh, 733-8372) or visit www.visitnc.com. Also, North Carolina Bed & Breakfasts and Inns publishes a brochure listing more than 150 small lodging establishments across the state. Call (800) 849-5392 or log on to www.bbonline.com/nc/ncbbi.

northeast

>>>

day trip 01

northeast

>>> **rocky road:**
rocky mount, tarboro

What was first discovered by aboriginal hunters and first known as "Rocky Mound" wouldn't become Rocky Mount until 1816, but the name would stick. The name, however, is about the only thing that would remain the same. Just an hour on SR 64 East takes the day-tripper to an area that's rediscovering itself in the 21st century. Economic staples of cotton and tobacco have given way to growing technological industries, so left for the local traveler are the history of those changes and new cultural opportunities.

Further east, still on SR 64, get those peds pumping in the small, charming town of Tarboro. The entire area is rife with history, but this is especially true along the tree-lined streets of Tarboro. Its name is attributed to the Tuscarora Indian word "taw" meaning "river of health."

rocky mount

Following the original discovery of this fertile land, Tuscarora Indians would farm, hunt, and fish here until the late 17th century when colonization by white settlers began. Nash County formed in 1777 and when the postal service needed a name for the area in 1816, Rocky Mount was born. Today the city straddles Nash and Edgecombe counties. What would become Rocky Mount Mills was the state's second cotton mill which began production soon after the city's founding and stayed in operation until 1996. It is now on the National Register of Historic Places.

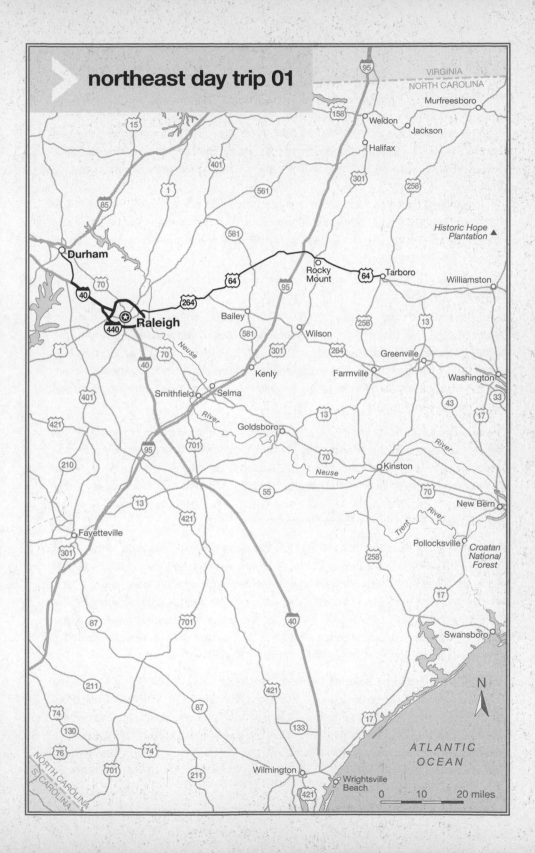

northeast day trip 01

Although the mill made the area strong economically, drawing a route of the Wilmington to Weldon Railroad line, its history was turbulent, even being ravaged by fire during a raid by Federal troops in 1863. In the 20th century, tobacco became king and the area became the largest brightleaf tobacco center in the world. While some agriculture still exists, local workers now depend on companies like Honeywell, pharmaceutical giants, and food distributors.

Day-trippers come to trace those historical steps and enjoy a cultural renaissance. Both new construction and renovated tobacco factory buildings make up the innovative Imperial Centre in downtown Rocky Mount. The complex includes an art center, a science museum, and a theater.

where to go

Train Station. 100 Coast Line St.; (252) 972-5080 or (800) 849-6825; www.rockymount travel.com. The Train Station is where you will find the **Nash County Visitors Bureau.** The original Romanesque building was constructed in 1903 with two stories added by 1916. Alongside the transportation center are several refurbished train cars for visitors to peruse. You can also stop in at the Rocky Mount Fire Museum across Church Street or stop in at one of the downtown shops.

The Arts Center. 270 Gay St.; (252) 972-1163; http://arts.imperialcentre.org. In addition to being a local resource for arts education, The Arts Center features a permanent collection of works primarily by North Carolina artists. Temporary exhibitions in wood, glass, fibers, metal, and other media focused on craft are on display. The center also includes ten working galleries where artists work and sell their wares. Open Tues through Sat 10 a.m. to 5 p.m. and Sun 1 to 5 p.m. Admission is free.

Battle Park. 1308 Falls Rd.; (252) 972-1151. This expansive park is located at the "Great Falls of the Tar River," where aboriginal hunters once roamed, and the Tuscarora hunted and fished. It ties into Tar River Trail and paths that lead to the original "rocky mounds," and the site of that first Rocky Mount post office. The park includes scenic overlooks of the Tar River, fishing piers, and a boat ramp. Hikers will also find a cemetery with markers dating before the Civil War. The Confederate Monument on the edge of the park was unveiled in 1917 in memory of Nash County soldiers known as "The Bethel Heroes."

Children's Museum and Science Center. 270 Gay St.; (252) 972-1167; http://museum .imperialcentre.org. Children up to age six can experiment with sound, color, light, and more in exhibits designed especially for them. Children and adults can explore animal life and the elements that support them in the Live Animal Gallery. A space exhibit and planetarium gives guests an opportunity to explore worlds we can't so easily touch. Open Tues through Sat 10 a.m. to 5 p.m. and Sun 1 to 5 p.m. Admission is $4 for adults, $3 for children ages three through fifteen and is free for children under three. Admission is free for everyone on Sundays. Admission to the planetarium is an additional $3.50.

Performing Arts Center. 270 Gay St.; (252) 972-1266. The performing arts center is the home of Rocky Mount's fifty-year-old community theater. Productions include everything from Shakespeare to Disney, well-known holiday classics, and choral presentations.

where to shop

Shehedah Antiques. 401 South Washington St.; (252) 985-3355. While many area antique shops are flea markets or consignment operations, Shehedah offers standard antiquing offerings. In addition to furniture, it typically offers a large selection of affordable art.

301 Craft & Flea Mall. 108 South Wesleyan Blvd.; (252) 442-5225. Rocky Mount has developed a reputation as an area that offers more than just traditional antiques. Collectibles, unusual, hard-to-find items, and more than one or two good deals are available at the Craft and Flea Mall.

where to eat

Central Cafe. 132 South Church St.; (252) 446-8568. Central Cafe is a Rocky Mount institution. It's a little small, but you can't beat the burgers. $.

Gardner's Barbecue. 301 North Wesleyan Blvd., (252) 442-0531; 841 Fairview Rd., (252) 442-5522; Westridge Shopping Center, (252) 443-3996. With three locations you'll find the Gardner operation hard to miss. The barbecue is tops in the state, but the buffet at the 301 North site is convenient and hard to beat. $.

tarboro

Incorporated in 1760, Tarboro is a beautiful, small town with a forty-five-block residential historic district. Stroll the tree-lined streets and restored neighborhoods of this town located on the Tar River. A thriving river port throughout the 18th and 19th centuries, Tarboro was once a candidate to become North Carolina's capital city.

where to go

Blount-Bridgers House. 130 Bridgers St.; (252) 823-4159; www.edgecombearts.org/bbh .htm. This federal-style plantation house was built around 1808 by Thomas Blount, a prominent Edgecombe County businessman and United States congressman. "The Grove," as it was known then, occupied a 296-acre tract of land purchased in 1795. Today the home serves as a museum and art gallery. The first floor displays a collection of 19th-century furniture, furnishings, and Edgecombe County memorabilia. The second floor houses the

Hobson Pittman Memorial Gallery and a living museum to Pittman (1899–1972), the artist who lived here in Edgecombe County and gained some international prominence during his lifetime. Included in the gallery are oils, pastels, drawings, and watercolors of 19th century local artists. A guided walking tour of Historic Tarboro departs from the house on Saturday morning or you can get a self-guided map from the Rocky Mount Tourism office. Open Wed through Sat 10 a.m. to 4 p.m. and Sun 2 to 4 p.m. Admission is $2.

Town Common. Albemarle Avenue, Wilson Street, Panola Street, Park Avenue. Tarboro's lush and stately Town Common is one of two remaining original town commons in the United States. The other is 700 miles north in Boston. Totaling fifteen acres of oak-shaded lawn, it's a gateway to the historic district. Here, you can stroll past stately homes built between 1890 and 1910. The Common was established by Tarboro's founding fathers in 1760, originally designed for the common grazing of livestock, community outings, and military drills. It is now listed on the National Register of Historic Places. Among granite statues that grace the grounds is the Wyatt Fountain, named for Henry Wyatt, the first North Carolina casualty of the Civil War. The property also includes herb gardens, and the nature walk along McBryde Trail.

where to stay

Lady Ann of Tarboro Bed and Breakfast Inn. 1205 Main St. North; (252) 641-1438. This elegant Italianate-style Victorian home is just around the corner from the historic Blount-Bridgers House. Call after 5 p.m. for reservations or more information. $$.

Little Warren Bed and Breakfast. 304 East Park Ave.; (800) 309-1314. This large and gracious family home, renovated and modernized with spacious rooms is located in a quiet neighborhood of the historic district. Originally built in 1913, the home has a big wraparound front porch that overlooks the Town Common. Full English, American Southern, and continental breakfasts are elegantly served. Patsy and Tom Miller purchased the home in 1984 after twenty-four years of living in Africa, the Orient, England, and several parts of the United States. Fresh flowers, fluffy towels, terry cloth robes, and electric blankets are among the guest room amenities. $$.

day trip 02

northeast

>>> **back in time:**
williamston, windsor, edenton

Dig down to the roots on this day trip that takes you to three 18th-century towns, including North Carolina's first colonial capital, Edenton. Stop first in Williamston, on US 64 east out of Raleigh. Founded just three years after the signing of the Declaration of Independence, Williamston has two National Register Historic Districts that highlight 19th- and early 20th-century life. Along the town's tree-shaded streets, you'll walk past well-preserved 19th-century structures to get a feel for this charming town.

Pick up US 13/17 north to Windsor, the next stop on this trip, founded nearly a decade earlier than Williamston. Windsor has a scenic boardwalk that borders the waterfront of what was once a busy port. A customs house and a branch of the State Bank served West Indian and coastal water trade. Just outside town is Historic Hope Plantation, dating from the 1720s.

Continue north on US 17 to the old colonial capital of Edenton. You'll have traveled 140 miles from Raleigh to the town that bills itself as the "Prettiest Town in the South," and upon arrival you will likely agree that the drive was worth the trip. Edenton certainly is picturesque, but what makes this visit so special is the town's well-preserved and well-presented history. Established in 1712 and incorporated in 1722, Edenton was a political, cultural, and commercial center.

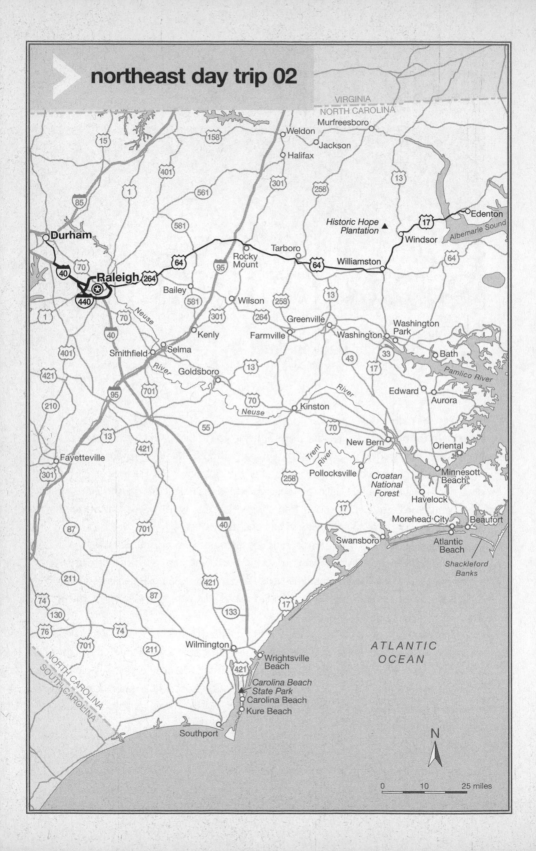

northeast day trip 02

williamston

William Williams migrated to North Carolina from Wales in the early 1700s. He settled on the south bank of the Roanoke River in the upper end of what is now Martin County, and bought and operated large plantations in the northwestern part of the county. The first incorporated town in Martin County, Williamston was founded in 1779 as the county seat. The town was named in honor of Williams's son, Colonel William Williams II, who was a delegate to the Hillsborough and Halifax Conventions in 1776 and was elected colonel of Martin County's militia when it was organized. He was elected as the county's first state senator in 1777.

The Civil War saw both Confederate and Union soldiers marching back and forth across Williamston and Martin County. Union soldiers occupied the 1810 Williams-Knight House after the capture of Williamston in July 1862. Across Main Street another home, the Hassell-King House, was used by Union soldiers to slaughter livestock.

Following Reconstruction, the railroad and tobacco plantings revitalized the town as a commercial market. With the bridging of the Roanoke River in 1922, Williamston became the hub of a system of major highways and roads, including US 17 ("the beach highway," as it is known locally), running north–south, and US 64, running east–west. The town is a featured site on the Historic Albemarle Tour Highway. For more information about this tour, see www.historicalbemarletour.com.

where to go

Martin County Travel and Tourism and Visitor's Center. 100 East Church St.; (800) 776-8566; www.visitmartincounty.com. The visitor center is in the circa 1831 Asa Biggs House. The former home of this Senator, forced out of it by invading Union Troops, is located downtown behind Town Hall in a picturesque residential neighborhood. Now owned by the Martin County Historical Society, it is open for tours Mon through Fri 8 a.m. to 5 p.m. but closes for lunch from 1 to 2 p.m.

Commercial Historic District. Pick up a map at the visitor center for a self-guided tour through the business district, composed of parts of seven city blocks with Main Street as its primary thoroughfare. Be sure to pop into the post office at 121 East Main St. to see the 1940 Wright Brothers First Flight mural.

Fort Branch. Fort Branch Road, off SR 125 North, Hamilton; (800) 776-8566; www.fort branchcivilwarsite.com. 12 miles north of Williamston off SR 125, Fort Branch is the best-preserved earthwork Civil War site east of the Mississippi. Eight of the fort's original twelve cannons and other artifacts are on display at this privately-owned center. The fort is open to the public Sat and Sun 1:30 to 5:30 p.m. from Apr through the first weekend in Nov, when an annual battle reenactment is held. There is also a Fort Branch Christmas event the first Sat in Dec.

Senator Bob Martin Eastern Agricultural Center. 2900 SR 125 South; (888) 792-5802; http://ncagr.gov/markets/facilities/agcenters/eastern. Schedule your daytrip here during one of the many events at this state-run center. Among the offerings are ATV and motocross races, truck pulls, circuses, boat shows, concerts, and some of the state's top equestrian events.

St. James Place Museum. (252) 795-3591. Located on the corner of Outerbridge Street and Business US 64 in Robersonville, 12 miles west of Williamston, this restored Primitive Baptist church serves as a museum of Southern folk art. Included are the original pews and pulpit, more than one hundred North Carolina quilts, and hundreds of pieces of North Carolina pottery. Open by appointment. Call the library for information Mon through Fri 9 a.m. to 5 p.m. and Sat 9 a.m. to noon. Free.

where to eat

Cypress Grill. 1520 Stewart St., Jamesville; (252) 792-4175. 10 miles from Williamston on US 64 east, Cypress Grill serves lunch and dinner seasonally, during the annual herring run on the river, usually mid-January to mid-April. The restaurant specializes in herring and seafood. $$.

Deadwood's Smokehouse Grill. 2302 Ed's Grocery Rd., Bear Grass; (252) 792-8938; www.deadwoodnc.com. The only late-night menu in town, this western-style opry house features live music weekend nights. Menu includes appetizers, sandwiches, great steaks, and baby back ribs. There's also a miniature-golf course and arcade, all in a western-style setting, about 5 miles southwest of Williamston. Open 5 to 9 p.m. Thurs, 5 to 10 p.m. Fri, noon to 11 p.m. Sat, and noon to 9 p.m. Sun. $$–$$$.

The Filling Station. 7309 US 64, Robersonville; (252) 795-3496; www.fillingstationnc .com. The menu is as eclectic as the decor in this restaurant that was never really a service station, rather a pack house and grocery store. For breakfast and lunch you'll find country cooking and then steaks and seafood for dinner. Check out the mid-century murals high on the walls. $–$$$.

La Casetta. 109 East Academy St., Robersonville; (252) 795-6699. Subs, salads, pasta and pizza offer a little variety in a locale where the mainstays are largely country cooking. The staff at this Italian restaurant is just as friendly as the locals you will meet. $.

The Moratoc. 101 East Blvd.; (252) 792-1323. Located in the Holiday Inn, Moratoc offers home-cooked chicken, pastries, collards, corned backbone, and a variety of steaks and seafood, plus vegetables daily. Open daily for breakfast, lunch, and dinner. $–$$.

Sunnyside Oyster Bar. 1102 Washington St.; (252) 792-3416; www.sunnysideoyster barnc.com. Listed on the National Register of Historic Places, Sunnyside serves up shrimp and shucking oysters (with a bowl of hot melted butter) the way this popular restaurant has done it for sixty years. Dinner is served from 5 p.m. $$.

where to stay

Big Mill Bed & Breakfast. 1607 Big Mill Rd.; (252) 792-8787; www.bigmill.com. Situated on 200 acres of woods, farmland, and landscaped gardens, Big Mill offers four rooms, continental breakfast, private entrances, and baths. The B&B overlooks a pond, an orchard of grapes and blueberries, and ninety-year-old pecan trees that proffer the luscious pecans used in making breads for guests. $$.

Roanoke River Paddle Camping Trail. US 64 at Gardner's Creek between Williamston and Jamesville; (252) 792-0070; www.roanokeriverpartners.org. A series of camping plat-forms situated just above the water in the tributaries of the Roanoke River allows you to wake up in the swamps of Devil's Gut, Three Sisters, the Cashie River or any number of other stopping points from the town of Weldon to the Albemarle sound. Watch for bald eagles during the day, and listen for owls during the night. The Roanoke River Canoe Camping Trail meanders through what The Nature Conservancy calls "one of the last great places," part of the largest intact and least disturbed bottomland hardwood and cypress-tupelo forest ecosystem remaining in the Mid-Atlantic region. $.

windsor

Created by the Colonial Assembly in 1768, New Windsor was established on the site for-merly known as Gray's Landing, where William Gray offered one hundred acres for a town. Today Windsor's National Register Historic District encompasses that same area.

where to go

Freeman Hotel. 102 North York St.; (252) 794-4277; www.albemarle-nc.com/windsor. Pick up maps here at the home of the Windsor Chamber of Commerce and the Windsor Visitor's Center for the self-guided walking tour through the historic district. Constructed in the 1840s as a hotel and renovated for offices in the 1980s, the Freeman Hotel is a Greek Revival building with double portico and fanlighted gables; two of its first-floor rooms have original tin walls and ceilings. It's listed on the National Register of Historic Places.

Historic Hope Plantation. 132 Hope House Rd.; (252) 794-3140; www.hopeplantation .org. Located in southern Bertie County on the edge of Roquist Pocosin, 4 miles west of Windsor, adjacent to US 308. Hope Plantation was a grant in the 1720s from the Lords Proprietors of the Carolina colony to the Hobson family. Hope was a self-contained planta-tion, with a water-powered gristmill, a still, a sawmill, a blacksmith shop, a cooper's shop, and houses for spinning and weaving. Farmlands produced wheat, corn, oats, rye, flax, and cotton. The King-Bazemore house and the Hope mansion represent a continuing agrarian culture during the colonial and federal periods in northeastern North Carolina.

Built on an "aboveground" basement, the Hope mansion's design is Palladian with some neoclassical elements. The five-bay facade has a pedimented double portico, and the widow's walk atop the hipped roof is surrounded by a Chinese Chippendale balustrade. The floor plan is adapted from Abraham Swann's The British Architect.

The first-floor rooms are entered from the front hall. On the second floor are a large drawing room and a library, which once housed 1,400 volumes. In addition to the main stair, a service stair runs from the basement to the attic.

Moved 4 miles from its original site, the 1763 King-Bazemore house is now one of only two gambrel-roofed houses in North Carolina with brick end walls. Evidence indicates that the house is similar to the 18th-century Hobson House, which first stood at Hope.

Open Apr through Oct Mon through Sat 10 a.m. to 5 p.m. and Sun 2 to 5 p.m.; and Nov through Mar Mon through Sat 10 a.m. to 4 p.m. and Sun 2 to 5 p.m. Closed Thanksgiving Day and Dec 21 through Jan 2. Admission is $8 for adults, $7 for seniors, and $3 for children ages eighteen and under.

Roanoke-Cashie River Interpretive Center. 112 West Water St.; (252) 794-2001; www .partnershipforthesounds.org. The center focuses on the vast floodplain and bottomland swamp system of the lower Roanoke basin. Historic items on the property include an "in situ" brick vault, a 150-year-old grave marker, and an outbuilding from a historic home that houses various artifacts. Also on display are special exhibits on migratory songbirds, a native wild turkey exhibit, and an active beehive exhibit. The center is open Tues through Sat 10 a.m. to 4 p.m. Admission is $2 for adults and $1 for children age six and up. Canoes are also available for rent beginning at $10 per hour.

Roanoke River National Wildlife Refuge. 114 West Water St.; (252) 794-3808; www.fws .gov/roanokeriver. Established in 1989 to protect the natural habitat, the refuge is home to deer, otters, beavers, muskrats, black bears, nesting ducks, raptors, osprey, and a total of nearly 200 species of migratory birds. Informal trail systems are open to the public for hiking and bird-watching. Some of the trails are accessible by boat. Open daily during daylight hours. Free.

where to eat

Bunn's Barbecue. 127 North King St.; (252) 794-2274. Located in historic downtown Windsor in a former Texaco station, Bunn's serves home-style northeast North Carolina barbecue made from the proprietor's secret recipe. Daily specials. $.

Little Mint of Windsor. 103 West Granville St.; (252) 794-3468. Mouthwatering chicken is served a variety of ways, either for take-out or for dining in. If you want to go to the Mint on the weekend, be prepared for a big crowd and don't be in a hurry $.

where to stay

Gray's Landing Bed and Breakfast. 401 South King St.; (252) 794-2255; www.grays landing.com. Located in one of the oldest homes in Windsor (ca. 1790), the Gray's Landing B&B is furnished with period antiques and reproductions and features carved fireplace mantels and crystal chandeliers. Each of the five spacious sleeping chambers has a private bath, cable TV, and a fireplace. The common areas include parlor, ballroom, and screened porch. A complimentary full breakfast is served. $–$$.

edenton

Alongside the north shore of the Albemarle Sound, Edenton was established in 1712 and incorporated in 1722. A leading center for political, social, educational, and industrial activity, the town served as the first colonial capital until 1743. As the seat of the provincial and colonial governments, the town had a citizen who signed the Declaration of Independence and another who signed the U.S. Constitution.

Edenton was home to two early North Carolina governors, U.S. senators, and an associate justice of the U.S. Supreme Court. Artisans in Edenton and the surrounding Chowan and Roanoke River Basins were leaders in building and cabinetmaking. A prosperous port in the 18th and early 19th centuries, Edenton cleared more than 800 ships for trade with Europe and the West Indies between 1771 and 1776.

Edenton's prosperity as a shipping center, however, began to decline by the end of the 18th century. Roanoke Inlet was closed by a hurricane in 1795, and the construction of the Dismal Swamp Canal, completed in 1805, further diverted shipping to Norfolk, Virginia.

Having escaped destruction during the two major wars fought in this country since its founding, Edenton is famous for its history and architectural qualities, primarily because of its colonial past. Today the town provides fine examples of Jacobean, Georgian, Federal, Greek Revival, and Victorian architectural styles spanning a period of more than 250 years.

Edenton's historic district includes two structures that are designated National Historic Landmarks and numerous buildings listed on the National Register of Historic Places. The waterfront has been given over to parks, with vistas across Edenton Bay, and to transient slips for dockage. The heart of the community is a quaint and viable downtown lined with shops and businesses that cater to both residents and visitors.

where to go

Historic Edenton Visitor Center. 108 North Broad St.; (252) 482-2637; www.visiteden ton.com. In addition to a fourteen-minute audiovisual program, exhibits, a gift shop, and visitor information/orientation, the visitor center offers well-conducted guided tours of five properties. Hours are Mon through Sat 9 a.m. to 5 p.m. and Sun 1 to 4 p.m. Admission to the center is free, but tours cost $10 for adults, $3.50 for school-age children and are free for pre-school children. Tours cost $20 for families. On Sat trolley tours are offered at a cost of $10 per adult and $2 for students.

The Barker House. 505 South Broad St. Built in 1782, this was the home of Thomas and Penelope Barker. On October 25, 1774, Penelope orchestrated the famed Edenton Tea Party: Fifty-one women met for a party but refused to drink tea. The group had penned a letter that expressed dissatisfaction with Parliament's Tea Act of 1773: "We the ladyes of Edenton do hereby solemnly engage not to conform to ye pernicious Custom of Drinking Tea or that we, the aforesaid Ladyes, will not promote ye wear of any manufacture from England, until such time that all Acts which tend to enslave this our Native Country shall be repealed."

Chowan County Courthouse. East King Street. In November 1712, the colonial assembly passed an act "to promote the building of a courthouse to hold the assembly in, at the fork of Queen Anne's Creek," effectively establishing the town as the seat of the provincial government. By 1718, the first Chowan County Courthouse was completed; a second building was constructed on the same site on in 1724, and a new courthouse was built there in 1767. That structure, the finest Georgian courthouse in the South, is one of the most important public buildings in colonial America. As the oldest government building in North Carolina, it is a National Historic Landmark. It provided the setting for the roles of Joseph Hewes, Samuel Johnston, James Iredell, and others in their local, state, and national political actions during the 1770s and 1780s.

The Cupola House. 408 South Broad St. A National Historic Landmark, the house dates from 1758–59. The original first-story interior woodwork was removed in 1918 and was carefully reconstructed in the 1960s.

Iredell House Historic Site. 107 East Church St. In 1778, silversmith Joseph Whedbee acquired four lots here for 160 pounds. Whedbee built a house and made considerable improvements on the two western lots, selling them for 800 pounds to James Iredell Sr., a justice on the first U. S. Supreme Court. Covered with beaded weatherboard, the one-bay-by-three-bay house had a single exterior chimney. The side-hall interior, and the fact that the house may have been an expansion of an older residence, might explain the gable's atypical orientation to the street.

Archaeologists who worked underneath the house thought there had been a wing west of Whedbee's original dwelling, which was later replaced with the Iredell wing. This earlier wing may well have been a house that was erected around 1756. The entrance to Whedbee's house is on the west elevation; the configuration of the original porch is unknown.

J. Robert Hendrix Park and Cannon's Ferry Heritage River Walk. 311 Cannon's Ferry Rd., Tyner; (252) 482-8595. Anglers, paddlers and picnic-goers will all appreciate this well-done site along the Chowan River. Created to commemorate the area's rich herring fishing industry, the 250-foot riverfront boardwalk provides an opportunity to view wildlife and learn about the natural history of the Chowan region. It is built on the site of an old fish house where river herring were netted during the fish's spring migration. The boardwalk is lined with interpretive signs that describe the role the fishing industry played in the community during the 19th and 20th centuries before catches declined.

Providence Burial Ground. West Albemarle Street; (252) 482-2637. As the burial ground of prominent and free blacks and military people from the late 18th and 19th centuries, notables buried here include Thomas Barnswell, free black and noted builder; Molly Horniblow, grandmother of Harriet Jacobs, a slave who escaped from Edenton by boat, traveling eventually to New York, where she went to work as a nursemaid for a family of abolitionists; and Jonathon Overton, private of the Continental Line of Captain Jones's Company, tenth regiment.

St. Paul's Episcopal Church. 100 West Church St. This is the second oldest church building in North Carolina and the oldest in regular use. This handsome Flemish bond brick edifice is one of the most important colonial period buildings in Edenton. The parish was organized in 1701 as the first in the colony under the provisions of the Vestry Act of 1701.

where to eat

Chero's Market Cafe. 112 West Water St.; (252) 482-5525. Located within the historic district and near many of the places you are likely to visit, this upscale cafe offers lunch, dinner, and Sunday buffet. It's also located in a charming historic building. $.

The Chicken Kitchen. 809 North Broad St.; (252) 482-4721. This local homestyle restaurant, specializing in southern fried chicken, serves savory, affordable fare that also includes fish. Save room for a hearty slice of apple pie. $.

Edenton Coffee House. 302 South Broad St.; (252) 482-7465. Enjoy gingerbread, cookies, snaps, cakes, and fresh pastry with a variety of delicious coffees and teas. It also offers sandwiches for lunch as well as works of local artisans, including jewelry, prints, and handmade dolls. $.

Kristy's Place. 319 South Broad St. at Gaslight Square; (252) 482-7655. This restaurant serves New York–style pizzas, pastas, wings, and subs. Big storefront windows proffer a view of dough-tossing pizza makers inside. $.

Mac's Back Door Oyster Bar and Grill. 108 Wharf Landing Dr.; (252) 482-2300. You can get more than oysters at Macs, but the oysters, clams, shrimp, and scallops are why patrons come here. Located at Wharf Landing, Macs is open for dinner Mon through Sat and for brunch 11 a.m. to 3 p.m. on Sun. $$.

Waterman's Grill. 427 South Broad St.; (252) 482-3323. This casual seafood restaurant located one block from the waterfront has daily lunch and dinner specials. It's located in a historic building, the former Tynch and Toppin Fish Market. Try the warm pecan pie with ice cream for a mouthwatering dessert. $$.

where to stay

Belvidere Bed and Breakfast. 316 Blue Heron Landing; (252) 482-1622; www.belvidere bandb.com. Located on the waterfront, this B&B offers modest, comfortable accommodations. Have breakfast, enjoy a drink on the deck, or take a walk onto the sound via the observation deck. $$$.

Captain's Quarters Inn. 202 West Queen St.; (252) 482-8945 or (800) 482-8945; www .captainsquartersinn.com. Located in Edenton's historic district, this comfortable and elegant ca. 1907 inn has eight guest rooms. Guests may choose either a continental breakfast delivered to their door or a three-course breakfast served in the Harbor Room. Mystery weekend sailing and golf packages available. $$.

Granville Queen Themed Inn. 108 South Granville St.; (252) 482-5296 or (866) 482-8534; www.granvillequeen.com. The seven guest rooms provide themed accommodations. The Egyptian Queen guest room, for example, invites guests to "experience the everlasting romance of Antony and Cleopatra." Appropriately, the room is adorned with Sphinx-flanked thrones, leopard-skin bed, tomb mural garden tub, and a bust of Queen Nefertiti. A five-course "plantation breakfast" is served on the porch; wine tastings are held on the weekends. $–$$$.

The Pack House Inn. 300 North Broad St.; (252) 482-3641 or (888) 394-6622; www .thepackhouse.com. Formerly the Lords Proprietors' Inn, this lovely inn has eight rooms. A breakfast that includes the guest's choice of eggs Benedict, quiche, and assorted continental breakfast items as well as evening wine and cheese is served daily. $$.

Trestle House Inn at Willow Tree Farm. 632 Soundside Rd.; (252) 482-2282 or (800) 645-8466; www.trestlehouseinn.com. Built in 1972 as a retreat for a winemaker and developer, the five-room inn, surrounded on three sides by water on a wildlife refuge, offers a gourmet breakfast. $$.

day trip 03

northeast

plantation valley:
halifax, murfreesboro

Colonists who found the valley's fertile bottomlands ideal for large-scale farming settled the Roanoke River Valley of northeastern North Carolina in the early 1700s. By the late 18th century, the growth of that plantation system had created a society of merchants, craftsmen, wealthy planters, small farmers, freedmen, and slaves.

On this day trip, you'll travel US 64 east to I-95 north to visit Historic Halifax, a North Carolina historic site that bills itself as the "birthplace of independence."

From Halifax, US 158 wends its way east through a couple of small towns well worth stopping to stretch your legs. The first is Weldon, where the Wilmington to Weldon Railroad terminated (the rail line, the longest in the world at the time, was the lifeline of the Confederacy). The other is Jackson, whose courthouse, built in 1858, is one of the state's few surviving examples of a Greek Revival public building.

The trip terminates in Murfreesboro, a small town with an interesting history and accommodations in this otherwise desolate part of the state. From here, you could head back toward Windsor, 40 miles south (see Northeast Day Trip 01), for an extended weekend.

Should you want to beeline it home, head back on US 158 toward I-95 south, but don't hit the interstate before treating yourself to Ralph's Barbecue, 2 blocks east of the interstate at exit 173.

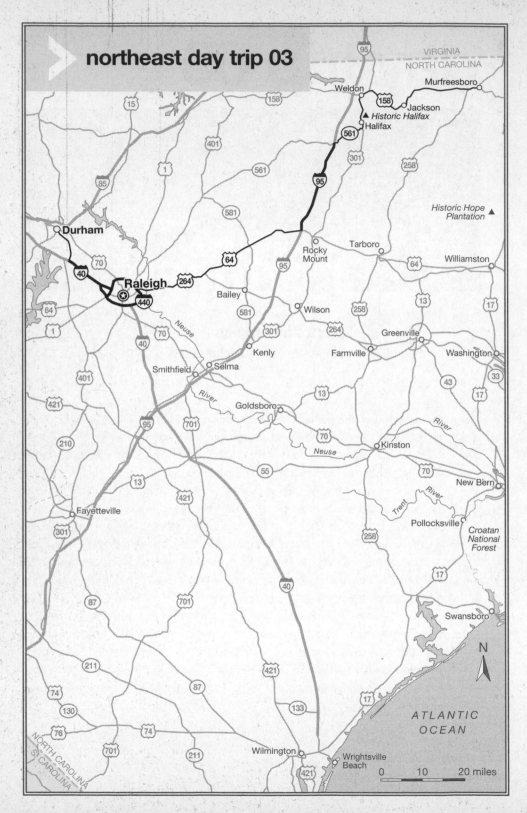

halifax

The town of Halifax was founded on the south bank of the Roanoke River in 1760 and quickly became a focal point for the entire valley. Halifax was a river port, county seat, crossroads, and social center. A farmers' market operated here, and inns and taverns did a brisk business. By 1769 Halifax could boast of nearly sixty houses and public buildings.

During the American Revolution, the town was the scene of important political events: North Carolina's Fourth Provincial Congress met in Halifax in the spring of 1776, and on April 12, unanimously adopted a document later called the Halifax Resolves, which was the first official action by an entire colony recommending independence from England.

The Fifth Provincial Congress assembled in the town late in the fall of that year, drafting and approving North Carolina's first state constitution and appointing Richard Caswell the first governor. Cornwallis briefly occupied the town in May 1781 on his northward march toward Virginia and eventual surrender at Yorktown.

After the Revolution, Halifax and the Roanoke River Valley entered a golden age. Wealth, power, and influence were concentrated here. The society was among the most cultured in the state; planters and merchants built fine homes. Halifax remained prosperous until the late 1830s, when its political power was diminished and when the new railroad bypassed the town. The first eighty-five years of the town's life are preserved at Historic Halifax.

where to go

Historic Halifax State Historic Site. 25 St. David Street; (252) 583-7191; www.visithalifax .com. The home of the Halifax Resolves, the first official action for independence by any colony, Historic Halifax offers an audiovisual presentation, exhibits, guided tours, and displays depicting the history of the town. A guided walking tour takes you into several authentically restored and furnished buildings.

> **The Owens House.** With its gambrel roof, this building dates from about 1760. It is furnished in the style of a prosperous Halifax merchant. Two other buildings within the historic district also are thought to have been built during the 18th century: **Eagle Tavern,** which was moved and converted into a residence during the 1840s, and the **Tap Room,** a smaller tavern built sometime between 1760 and 1810. Both are open for visitors.

> The prosperity of the Roanoke River Valley is reflected in the many federal-style plantation dwellings constructed here between the 1790s and the 1820s. **The Sally-Billy House** is an elegant example of such a dwelling; the tripartite house was constructed about 1808. **The Burgess Law Office** probably dates from the same period, although the roofline and other features of the structure follow the

older Georgian style. Thomas Burgess owned the building in the early 1800s, and it is furnished as his law office and town house.

The same contractor built the two public buildings within the historic district. Both are fashioned of brick and are fireproof. **The Clerk's Office,** built in 1832–33, served as a location for storing valuable court records. One of its rooms is furnished as a court official's office and one as a printer's office, complete with a working press. The jail was built in 1838; two earlier jails at the same location were burned to the ground by escaping prisoners.

Other sites reflect everyday life in Halifax: **Magazine Spring,** long a source of water for townspeople; the cemetery; **Market Square,** which served as the town park, pasture, and marketplace; and the river outlook, near the site of an early ferry landing.

In addition to the historic structures, the **Montfort Archaeological Exhibit,** constructed over the excavation of Joseph Montfort's house, is open for public viewing. Through exhibits and walkways over foundations exposed by the scholar's spade and trowel, the building depicts the lifestyle of this wealthy resident of early Halifax.

Guided tours originate at the **Historic Halifax Visitor Center,** open Tues through Sat 9 a.m. to 5 p.m. Free.

Sylvan Heights Waterfowl Park. 1829 Lees Meadow Rd., Scotland Neck; (252) 826-3186; www.shwpark.com. What is promoted as the world's largest collection of rare and endangered waterfowl is certainly worth the thirty-minute drive from Halifax. Once a private waterfowl breeding facility, Sylvan Heights is now affiliated with the North Carolina Zoo and gives visitors the opportunity to see over 1,500 birds, especially ducks, geese, and swans. It includes more than 170 different species, some of the rarest and most endangered in the world such as the White-Winged Wood Duck from Sumatra. Crane, parrot, macaw, brush turkey, cockatoo, kookaburra, pheasant, and currasow also await the visitor.

where to shop

Although Halifax wasn't always considered to be as such, it has proven itself to be a great spot for antiquing. You could easily spend the better part of your day trip perusing the offerings of even just these few shops:

Hidden Treasures. 15 South King St.; (252) 583-1933. In addition to furniture, shoppers will find glassware and a wide selection of collectibles.

Now & Yesteryears. 13 South King St.; (252) 583-1000. Shoppers get a taste of a wide range of antiques and collectibles.

Peoples General Store.16 South King St.; (252) 583-1338. A blacksmith still works this general store that also offers standard antique selections.

Southern Heritage Woodworks. 10 South King St.; (252) 583-1861. Antique frames and other woodwork are offered here.

murfreesboro

As the northernmost point of navigation on the Meherrin River, Murfreesboro was as far as a seagoing vessel on the Albemarle Sound could penetrate into the large and productive farming area of southern Virginia and northeastern North Carolina.

Congress designated Murfreesboro as an official port of entry in 1790, and customs records indicate a profitable three-cornered trade with New England and the West Indies. The vessels and their cargoes were owned mostly by captains from New England, many of whom put down roots here and impressed their outlook on the new town in ways that remain evident.

where to go

Brady C. Jefcoat Museum of Americana. High Street; (252) 398-5922; www.murfrees boronc.org. Located in the Old Murfreesboro High School, the world's largest collection of washing machines, flatirons, and dairy equipment contains thousands of artifacts and Americana items to total more than 13,000 items. Open Sat 11 a.m. to 4 p.m. and Sun 2 to 5 p.m.

Murfreesboro Historic District. 116 East Main St.; (252) 398-5922; www.murfreesboro nc.org. A twelve-block historic district, listed on the National Register of Historic Places, its guided tour headquarters are at Roberts-Vaughan Village Center (ca. 1790). Tours are conducted continuously from 11 a.m. to 4 p.m. each Sat. The cost per tour is $7 per adult and $5 per student. A self-guided walking tour brochure is available for $5 if you find yourself day tripping during the week. All of the sites are within walking distance of one another.

Originally constructed in 1810 as a store by William Hardy Murfree and his partner George Gordon, the **Wheeler House** was sold in 1814 to John Wheeler, a native of New Jersey who came south around 1790. Wheeler converted the building to a residence, as it appears today. John Hill Wheeler, his son, became famous as a legislator, treasurer of the mint in Charlotte, the nation's first minister of Nicaragua, and the first native historian on North Carolina. The house is authentically furnished with period pieces, some original to the Wheeler family. For visitors interested in the decorative arts, an outstanding and rare example of neoclassical wall coverings is found here.

Built in the late 1870s, the **Winborne Law Office/Country Store** was used as a law office by several generations of the Winborne family, including B. B. Winborne, whose famous History of Hertford County still serves as a primary reference concerning the area and the early families who lived here. Originally located on the town's Main Street, the building was moved to the historic district in 1976. The first floor is furnished as a country store, with hundreds of items such as may have been found in a store of this vintage.

William Rea of Boston was the first of five brothers to make his home in the Murfreesboro area. Arriving here in the 1790s, he became a successful merchant ship owner and, with his brother Joseph, operated a store in the redbrick building that now serves as the **Rea Museum.** The only surviving 18th-century brick commercial structure in North Carolina, the museum presents exhibits on local Native American tribes, agriculture, and river transportation. A room interior moved from the Gatling Plantation to the museum houses a large collection of Gatling family memorabilia and an authentic Gatling gun.

At the **Vincent Deale Blacksmith Shop,** you can see hand-hammered ironware wrought on a full-scale forge typical of those throughout the country in the 19th century. The smithy and his tools were an indispensable part of the village life, keeping wagons and buggies repaired, shoeing horses, and producing implements for household and farm use. You can also tour the **Evans Tin Shop,** originally opened in 1877 or 1878 and moved to this site in the 1990s. The one-room shop includes original tools and patterns for coffee and teapots and other utensils.

Built in the early 1800s by William Hardy Murfree, son of Murfreesboro's founder, the **Murfree-Smith Law Office** was later used by W. N. H. Smith, the first North Carolinian to become chief justice of the Supreme Court. Tradition has it that the building has served variously as a theater, jail, school, and post office. It currently houses the Murfreesboro Historical Association's gift shop.

The **Agricultural Exhibit** has early examples of wheeled vehicles of all kinds, along with a wide range of horse-drawn farming implements. Be sure to see the surry with "the fringe on top" as well as a rare early peanut picker and swing cart.

where to eat

Walter's Grill. 317 East Main St.; (252) 398-4006. Famous for its hot dogs, Walter's Grill offers plate lunches daily, as well as southern fare, chili and homemade soups. A tasty, inexpensive place to grab a bite. $.

where to stay

Barnes House Bed and Breakfast. 308 West Main St.; (252) 398-3676; www.bbonline .com/nc/barneshouse. A popular setting for weddings and receptions, Barnes House also serves as a good place for R&R. The home's peaceful surroundings and historic charm fit well in this town of history. $$.

Piper House Bed and Breakfast. 809 East High St.; (252) 398-3531. This restored 1900s home offers two bedrooms for guests. Guests will begin their day with the wonderful hostess as she serves a delicious breakfast. $$.

east

day trip 01

east

>>> **on the waterfront:**
new bern, oriental

From Raleigh, New Bern is 113 miles east, an easy day's drive there and back, with sufficient time for touring the sites and for soaking up the charm of this historic river town. Traveling US 70 east, the drive is pleasant across the Neuse River Basin, as the road makes its way past tin-roofed farmhouses under broad, leafy oaks sitting in expansive green fields. The highway continues through small towns where folks still shop for groceries at the local Piggly Wiggly.

In New Bern, you'll visit historic Tryon Palace, stroll the pleasant downtown, and drive along the picturesque waterfront, where you will find fine Southern homes with broad, wraparound porches that look out on the Neuse and Trent Rivers. Along the riverfront, be sure to look for the historical marker depicting the birthplace of Bayard Wooten, one of the South's first professional female photographers.

As with many North Carolina towns, New Bern's city center fell into decline in the 1970s, when the sprawl of shopping malls and suburban housing drew citizens away from the business district. But in 1979, a nonprofit corporation of civic leaders was charged with breathing new life into the downtown, and their efforts have been successful in attracting art galleries, specialty shops, antiques stores, restaurants, and other businesses. Still, don't expect New Bern to be bustling. It is a quiet, friendly river town where the slow-paced lifestyle invites leisurely strolls down the charming streets.

A thirty-minute drive east of New Bern on SR 55, Oriental is a charming village that, largely because of its proximity to the Intercoastal Waterway and Pamlico Sound, has earned its place as the sailing capital of North Carolina. On your way back to New Bern

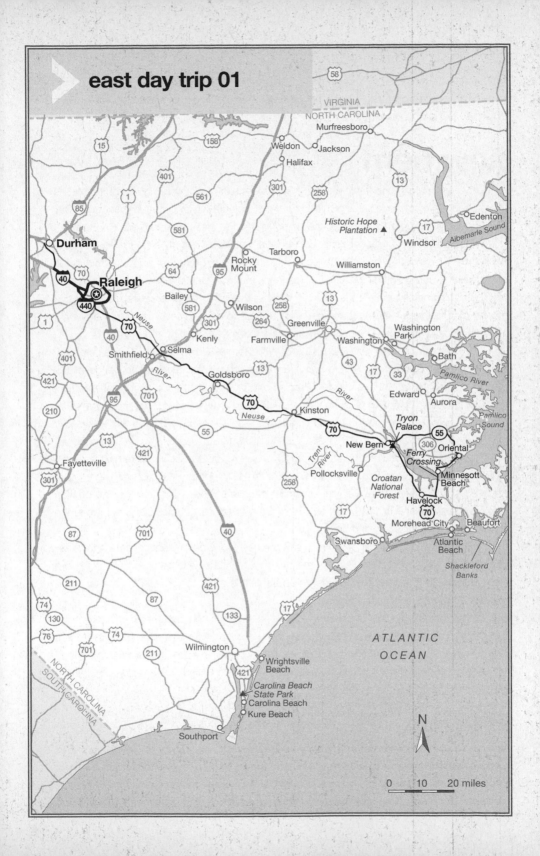

east day trip 01

(or Raleigh), drive along the Pamlico Sound to Minnesott Beach, where the ferry takes you across to Havelock and US 70.

new bern

As North Carolina's second oldest town, New Bern claims many firsts: home of the state's first four-faced clock; originator of the state's first celebration of both Independence Day and George Washington's birthday; and home to the first steamboat in North Carolina.

Other claims have grander historical significance: New Bern is home to the first state capital, the first meeting of the state legislature, the first incorporated public school in the state, the first public school for African-Americans in North Carolina, the first printing press and published newspaper in the state, the first torpedo put into practical use, the first motion picture theater built in the state, and the first postal service in the Carolina colony. The first Pepsi was poured here. Clearly, this is a town worth getting to know.

A Swiss baron settled New Bern in 1710. With German Protestant and Swiss colonists, Christophe von Graffenried pitched camp on a triangle of land at the confluence of the Neuse and Trent Rivers. He named the settlement for Bern, his home in Switzerland. Like the Swiss capital, New Bern's symbol, the black bear, is ubiquitous throughout the town. Another reminder of the town's Swiss heritage is the 1910 redbrick clock tower above City Hall.

The Swiss baron eventually returned to Switzerland, and the British were next to assert their dominion over New Bern. By the middle of the 18th century, the port city had grown in size and importance. The colonial assembly often met here. The colony's first printing press was established in 1749, and two years later, the printer James Davis published the first newspaper, pamphlet, and book.

British Royal Governor William Tryon saw the need for a permanent capital in the growing colony and selected New Bern as the site. Tryon Palace was completed in 1770, but the governor left the lovely Georgian-style palace a little more than a year later, after being reassigned to the New York colony.

In March 1862, 13,000 Union forces captured the town and occupied it until the end of the war. Because of Union occupation, New Bern survived with less damage to its homes and buildings than many other small Southern towns. Thus, in addition to finding more than 150 homes and buildings listed on the National Register of Historic Places, you will find a fair number that date back to the 1700s.

where to go

Craven County Convention and Visitor's Bureau. 203 South Front St.; (800) 437-5767; www.visitnewbern.com. Located in the riverfront convention center, the visitor center is convenient to historic downtown, so you'll want to begin your visit here; there's free parking across the street. Pick up brochures or ask questions of the staff, who will point you in the right direction for walking tours. Before shuffling out the door, spend a moment looking over the large display board listing Craven County firsts.

Historic Downtown District. (252) 637-7316 or (800) 849-7316; www.newberntours .com. For a dose of history and charm, walk the downtown district, then board the New Bern Tours trolley, across from Tryon Palace Visitor Center, for a ninety-minute narrated tour. From the comfortable open-air (but covered) trolley, you will see such sites as the Coor-Gaston House, a Georgian-style home built around 1770. Its most famous resident was Judge William Gaston, the first chief justice of the North Carolina Supreme Court and composer of the state song, "The Old North State." Purchase tickets on the trolley ($15 per adult, $7 for children twelve and under). Departure times vary with season but are typically at 11 a.m. and 2 p.m. Apr through Oct. Also offered on a weather-permitting, seasonal basis, are horse-and-carriage tours. Call for times or to make reservations.

Fans of Nicolas Sparks, the best-selling novelist who bases many of his stories on locales and people of coastal North Carolina, may want to take the **"Walk to Remember Tour."** The visitor center offers a self-guided tour that takes day-trippers on a tour to fifteen landmarks from three of Sparks' most popular books. The center offers suggestions for more traditional tours, too.

Croatan National Forest. 141 East Fisher Ave.; (252) 638-5628. Hike, swim, boat, hunt, fish, camp, and picnic at the 157,000-acre Croatan National Forest, 9 miles south of New Bern just off US 70 east. Look for the rare Venus flytrap, black bears, and alligators. The site of a Civil War battle, the recreation area has been nationally recognized for the quality of its offerings.

A Day at the Farm. 183 Woodrow McCoy Rd., just west of New Bern via US 70 in Cove City; (252) 514-9494; www.adayatthefarm.com. Of interest are the historic dairy barns, milking equipment, and period antiques. For the young and young at heart, the farm offers a pumpkin patch, a peanut patch, a fish and duck pond, a swinging playground, hayrides and of course farm animals! Help make butter or enjoy an ice cream cone to end the day. A Day at the Farm typically serves schools and other groups, but it holds special events throughout the year. Check the Web site or call before heading out.

The Firemen's Museum. 408 Hancock St.; (252) 636-4087. The museum displays century-old hose wagons, an 1884 Button steamer, and an assortment of 18th- and 19th-century firemen's hats, leather fire buckets, and hand-drawn reels. Don't miss the mounted, stuffed (and somewhat macabre) head of Fire Horse Fred, who pulled the Atlantic hose wagon for seventeen years and died answering a false alarm. Open Mon through Sat 10 a.m. to 4 p.m. Admission: $5, $2.50 for children.

Ghosts of New Bern. Departing from Morgan's Tavern at 235 Craven St.; (252) 571-4766; www.ghostsofnewbern.com. These ghost tours are a fun way to learn about New Bern's rich history and heritage. Mysteries, myths, and legends, passed down through the generations (and probably just made up for entertainment purposes) provide an hour-long tour through the streets of the Historic District. Basic tour tickets are $12 for adults and $6 for children under age 12. The tour company can also arrange an overnight at the haunted Harvey Mansion Historic Inn.

Tryon Palace Historic Sites and Gardens. 610 Pollock St.; (252) 514-4900 or (800) 767-1560; www.tryonpalace.org. Completed in 1770, then burned to the ground in 1798, Tryon Palace was rebuilt in the 1950s. That's right, the Tryon Palace you see today is a replica of the original palace. The twenty-seven-room brick Georgian-style mansion and its furnishings were painstakingly reproduced from meticulous records kept by British Royal Governor William Tryon.

In addition to serving two royal governors, the palace was used by four state governors before the capital was moved from New Bern to Raleigh in 1794. Guides in period dress conduct an informative forty-five minute palace tour (daily except Thanksgiving, Christmas holidays, and New Year's Day). You'll learn, among other things, that George Washington not only slept but also danced here.

After you've done the digs, tour the 18th century–style English gardens surrounding the palace on your own. You could easily spend a day at Tryon Palace and its splendidly well-manicured gardens, but two hours or so will suffice. Hours are Mon through Sat 9 a.m. to 5 p.m. and Sun 1 to 5 p.m. The last guided tour begins at 4 p.m. daily. The gardens are open until 7 p.m. in summer. Visitors can purchase tickets until 4:30 p.m. Admission for adults is $15 ($6 for students through grade 12) to tour the palace, buildings, and 14-acre grounds.

John Wright Stanly House. Included with admission to Tryon Palace, this Georgian-style home was built in the early 1780s. On his Southern tour in 1791, President George Washington slept here—twice, as New Bernians are eager to point out. Washington described his overnight accommodation as "exceeding good lodgings." The Stanly House remains one of the finest examples of Georgian architecture in the South.

Robert Hay House. Also part of Tryon Palace, this unimposing house features character interpreters, who greet and respond to you as if it were 1835. Nothing can shake them out of character. We know. We've tried. Ask questions of the staff to learn about what life was like for the early colonists.

New Bern Academy Museum. Nearby, and part of the Tryon Palace complex, New Bern Academy was the first established school in North Carolina. During the Civil War, the building was converted to a military hospital to treat the victims of spinal meningitis, smallpox, and yellow fever epidemics, as well as casualties of war. Now a museum, the building has four rooms that chronicle the history of New Bern: its founding, history, architecture, Civil War, Reconstruction, and education.

where to shop

Antiques Shops. New Bern has a slew of them, all located in the compact town center on Middle and Front streets. Just point yourself in any direction downtown and walk. You'll indubitably land at the threshold of an antiques shop.

Birthplace of Pepsi-Cola. 256 Middle St.; (252) 636-5898; www.pepsistore.com. The restored Caleb Bradham's Pharmacy marks the spot where Pepsi-Cola was invented in 1898. Be sure to see the thirty-five-minute video about the history of Pepsi, narrated by Walter Cronkite. Also offered is a twenty-minute video that chronicles the history of Pepsi through commercials. The store sells fountain Pepsi in a cup (for 60 cents) and Pepsi collectibles, such as T-shirts, drinking glasses, coffee mugs, key chains, and caps. Open Mon through Sat 10 a.m. to 6 p.m. Mar through Dec; it is also open noon to 4 p.m. on Sun.

Mitchell Hardware. 215 Craven St.; (252) 638-4261. A hardware store since 1898, this jam-packed, turn-of-the-20th-century establishment is as much a museum as it is a store. You could spend a good hour browsing the mix of hardware, garden tools, and yard equipment. You might even want to take home one of the store's country hams. An honest-to-goodness hardware store where the locals shop, Mitchell Hardware is open 6:30 a.m. to 5 p.m. Mon through Sat.

Tryon Palace Museum Store/Craft and Garden Shop. 610 Pollock St.; museum store, (252) 514-4932; garden shop, (252) 514-4927. Tryon Palace Museum Store carries New Bern and colonial memorabilia. The Craft and Garden Shop carries just what the name implies: heirloom plants, crafts, gardening books, and more. Both shops are open daily.

where to eat

Captain Ratty's Oyster and Piano Bar. 202 Middle St.; (252) 633-2088. Here you'll find the only palpable nightlife in downtown New Bern, which is not to say a lot, as New Bern is a small town. The best thing hopping is the Imperial pint of Newcastle that you can get here. Captain Ratty's specializes in seafood, serving lunch and dinner. $$–$$$.

The Chelsea. 335 Middle St.; (252) 637-5469; www.thechelsea.com. It's modeled after an English-style pub, thus the friendly bartender at the Chelsea will serve you a Guinness Stout or Bass Ale. The Chelsea's excellent food is fusion cuisine. For an appetizer that won't leave you hungry for dinner, try the Blue Chip Dip, a blend of blue, cheddar, and cream cheeses, bacon, and scallions served hot with homemade chips for dipping ($4.95). Pepsi inventor Caleb Bradham used this building as his second drugstore. $$–$$$.

Morgan's Tavern & Grill. 235 Craven St.; (252) 636-2430. From a bottomless soup and salad to fish or shrimp tacos, you should have no problem finding something to please your palate here. You can also grab a steak or chop before heading out on the ghost tour. $–$$.

Trent River Coffee Co. 208 Craven St.; (252) 514-2030. The locals gather here for coffee and, on occasional weekend nights when it's offered, live entertainment. $.

where to stay

The Aerie. 509 Pollock St.; (800) 849-5553 or (252) 636-5553; www.aeriebedandbreakfast .com. This two-story 1880 Victorian house, located a block from Tryon Palace, has seven guest rooms with private baths, a cozy parlor with player piano, and a library with an extensive Civil War collection. A full breakfast with a choice of three hot entrees is served. Herbal flower gardens cover 1,500 square feet. $$.

Hanna House Bed and Breakfast. 218 Pollock St.; (252) 635-3209 or (866) 830-4371; www.hannahousenc.net. Listed in the National Register of Historic Places and designated a historic home, Hanna House is furnished in fine antiques and Oriental carpets. $$.

Harmony House Inn. 215 Pollock St.; (252) 636-3810 or (800) 636-3113; www.harmony houseinn.com. Purchased by Benjamin Ellis in 1850, Harmony House began as a four-room, two-story Greek Revival home. During the Civil War, Harmony House was occupied by Company K of the 45th Massachusetts Volunteer Militia. The house has seven guest rooms and three suites. Breakfasts include such specialty entrees as orange French toast, egg and bacon casserole, or the inn's unique stuffed French toast. All are served with home-baked coffee cake and breads, fresh fruit, coffee, tea, and juice. $$–$$$.

Hilton New Bern. 100 Middle St.; (252) 638-3585 or (866) 716-8127; www.hilton.com. Billed as both a hotel and an inn, the Hilton faces the scenic Trent River waterfront. The hotel's guest rooms afford spectacular views of the river. The adjacent inn, connected by a breezeway, has cozy guest rooms with an old-time feel, suites, and mini-suites. $$–$$$.

Meadows Inn. 212 Pollock St.; (252) 634-1776 or (877) 551-1776; www.meadowsinn-nc .com. Formerly the King's Arms Bed and Breakfast, the Meadows Inn is located in the heart of the historic district. John Alexander Meadows built the home in 1847, four years after a fire destroyed most of the structures on Pollock Street. The inn was a private residence until 1980, when it became New Bern's first bed-and-breakfast. Each of the nine spacious guest rooms has a decorative fireplace, private bath, TV, and phone. $$.

New Berne House. 709 Broad St.; (252) 636-2250 or (866) 782-8301; http://newberne house.com. This colonial-style bed-and-breakfast hosts Mystery Weekends several times throughout the year. Guests solve these fun, scavenger-hunt whodunits by collecting clues from downtown businesses and attractions. Seven guest rooms are available. $$.

oriental

A quaint sailing and fishing village thirty minutes east of New Bern on SR 55, Oriental is the place to hoist your sails. If you've no time for that, you'll still enjoy breathing in the salty air of this yachting town. After a few hours (or a few days) here, you can return by way of Minnesott Beach, where the year-round ferry will take you to Cherry Branch and US 70. Head west to return to New Bern or Raleigh. Get more information at http://visitoriental.com.

where to go

Whittaker Creek Yacht Harbor. 200 Whittaker Point Rd.; (252) 249-0666; www.whittaker creek.com. If you yearn to get out on the water, here is the place to do it. With four boats in its fleet, Whittaker Creek Yacht Harbor's bareboat charters begin at $800 for three days (minimum) on a 28-foot sailboat.

where to eat

M&Ms Café. 205 South Water St.; (252) 249-2000. M&Ms is both a fine restaurant where you can dine alfresco and the local watering hole where you are likely to bump into a sailor or two. The menu offers salads, quail and a whole lot in between. Open daily except Tues. $$–$$$.

Toucan Grill and Fresh Bar. 103 Wall St.; (252) 249-2204; www.toucangrill.com. The moderately upscale menu includes fried fresh seafood and specialty items, including pasta and ribs. Try the delicious crab cake dinner: two five-ounce crab cakes (no fillers) with a baked sweet potato, salad, and vegetables. Afterward, head up to the Topside Lounge, open nightly from 5 p.m., or outside to the Tiki Bar, open seasonally Wed through Sun. $$–$$$.

where to stay

The Cartwright House. 301 Freemason St.; (252) 249-1337 or (888) 726-9384; www .cartwrighthouse.com. Located on a quiet, tree-lined street in the heart of Oriental, this inn offers a view of the river and is a short walk from the art and craft galleries, shops, restaurants, and the harbor. Begin your day with morning coffee at your door, followed by a generous English breakfast served by the English hosts in the dining room. $$$.

The Inn at Oriental. 508 Church St.; (252) 249-1078 or (800) 485-7174; www.innatoriental .com. The inn's twelve guest rooms are tastefully decorated and feature private baths and cable TV. A full American breakfast of homemade favorites is served in the dining room. $$.

day trip 02

east

>>> **george washington slept here:**
washington, bath, aurora, edward

Head east on US 264 to the wide Pamlico River for this day trip to North Carolina's oldest town. Here you'll get a glimpse into the state's past at North Carolina's first church and the three historic homes that compose the historic site at "North Carolina's First Town."

But before plunging into Bath, linger a little in Washington—the original Washington, as the local residents are fond to point out. As you stroll along on the Historic Washington Walking Tour, you'll learn more about this quaint Southern town, such as the fact that prolific film producer Cecil B. DeMille spent time here as a boy. Washington is a good place to overnight if you're extending your trip.

On the way to Bath, take a short detour through the incorporated district of Washington Park. Your detour will reward you with the sight of beautiful homes facing the Pamlico River, where cypress trees expose their knotty knees along the river's bank.

Travel downriver to Bath on US 92 east to immerse yourself in North Carolina's earliest history, then proceed to the ferry terminal for a thirty-minute journey across the Pamlico River. On the other side you'll make for tiny Aurora, population 652, where you'll have to do some digging at the Fossil Museum to find evidence of a history that predates even Bath. Some of the artifacts you'll discover at the museum are 22 million years old.

From Aurora, it's a short drive to Edward, where you'll visit a winery before driving the flat coastal plain back to Washington on US 33 north. Of course, you could detour toward New Bern, the state's second oldest town, for an extended day trip. Combining Bath with East Day Trip 01 to New Bern provides you with a double dose of history.

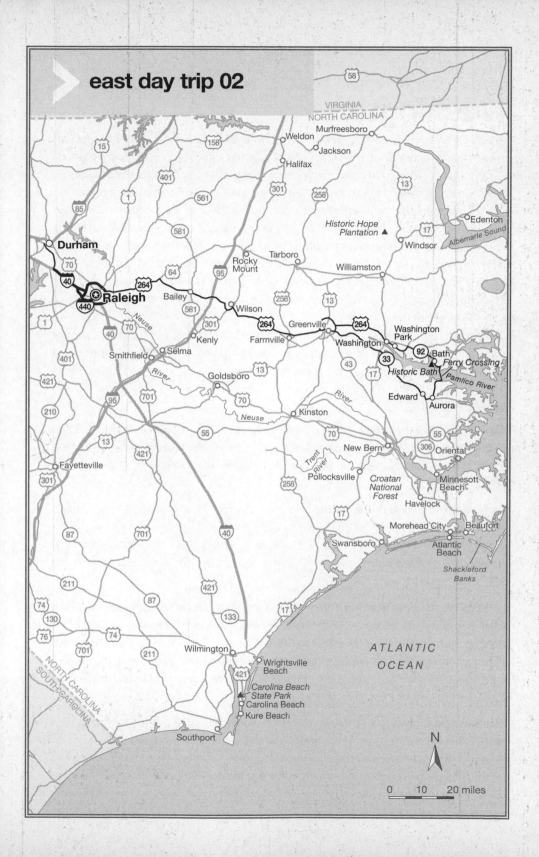

washington

English explorers came here as early as 1585, but the first settlement did not appear until more than a century later. In the 1770s, a farmer started a town on his property, flanked by Pamlico and Tar Rivers. He called the town Forks of the Tar, but in 1776 it was renamed, becoming the first town in the nation to be named after General George Washington.

Washington became a major supply port during the War for Independence, when Savannah, Charleston, and Wilmington were under siege. During the Civil War, federal troops devastated Washington by setting fire to the naval stores they left behind upon vacating the port town. The fire destroyed most of Washington's buildings. Residents rebuilt the town only to watch it burn again in 1900, when a faulty stove flue sparked flames that spread to other buildings in the business district. Downtown today consists of late Victorian commercial architecture.

Movie producer Cecil B. DeMille spent most of his boyhood in Washington with his grandmother and aunt, who lived on the corner of Bridge and Second Streets. A historical marker indicates the spot where the house once stood.

where to go

Washington Visitors Center. 138 South Market St.; (800) 546-0162; www.visitwashington nc.com. Begin your visit to this area by picking up maps for your walking tour of the historic district. There's also a small shop with local memorabilia and souvenirs. It's open daily 10 a.m. to 4 p.m.

Carolina Wind Yachting Center Inc. 411 West Main St.; (252) 946-4653; www.carolina wind.com. This sailboat operation can arrange any number of sailing trips, including week-end and weeklong trips. They've been in business here since 1980. The East Carolina Sailing School also offers sailing classes, beginning with a four-hour introductory offering for $175, that originate here.

Historic Washington Walking Tour. After picking up a map at the visitor center, begin the 1.9-mile self-guided Historic Washington Walking Tour at the old Atlantic Coast Line Railroad Depot on the corner of Main and Gladden Streets. Most of the private homes and buildings are closed to the public, but the walk is pleasant in this quaint waterfront down-town. The downtown and several sites are on the National Register of Historic Places. The tour takes about two hours to complete.

Old Beaufort County Courthouse. 158 North Market St.; (252) 946-6401. Dating from about 1786, this is the second oldest courthouse standing in North Carolina and one of only a handful of surviving federal courthouses in the state. Listed on the National Register of Historic Places, the courthouse is now home to the Beaufort-Hyde-Martin Regional Library, open to the public Mon through Fri 9 a.m. to 5 p.m. The original courtroom may be viewed on the second floor by request at the lending desk. The courtroom contains a portrait of Henry, Duke of Beaufort, the lord proprietor for whom the county was named. The library also houses paintings and sketches of historic buildings in Washington, some of which are no longer standing.

North Carolina Estuarium. 223 Water St.; (252) 948-0000; www.partnershipforthesounds .org. Adjacent to the visitor center, the state's only estuarium presents 200 displays, artwork and aquariums, and a thirteen-minute film that focuses on the scenic beauty of North Carolina's coastal rivers and sounds. Walk a ¾-mile boardwalk along the Pamlico River or make a reservation to tour by pontoon boat. The Pamlico/Tar River Estuary, by the way, is the second largest in the nation behind Chesapeake Bay. Admission is $4 for adults, $2 for children through grade twelve, and no charge for children four and under. There is no additional charge for the roving boat tour. Open 10 a.m. to 4 p.m. Tues through Sat. Allow forty-five minutes to one hour.

St. Peter's Episcopal Church. 101 North Bonner St.; (252) 946-8151; www.stpetersnc .org. Washington has one church for every fifty residents. Imagine what it must sound like to be within earshot of all the clanging bells on a Sun morning. One of the more interesting houses of worship is St. Peter's Episcopal Church, where Cecil B. DeMille's family is buried.

Turnage Theater. 150 West Main St.; (252) 975-1191; www.turnagetheater.com. This former vaudeville theater has been restored and now hosts an ongoing calendar of live events, including musicals, comedy performances, family events, bands, and even movies.

washington park

Now here's a tip that you won't find in any other guidebook. Leaving Washington on US 32 east, turn right on Edgewater Street, then left on Riverside Drive. The drive through Washington Park would still be a pleasant diversion, even if you didn't know that one of America's most beloved journalists lived here. CBS newsman Charles Kuralt lived here when he was five years old. Green Court Apartments are long gone, but not the banks of the river, where Kuralt played with the neighborhood boys. Turn left on Walnut Street to return to US 32, then head east on US 92 to Bath.

where to eat

Backwater Jack's. 1052 East Main St.; (252) 975-1090. Located on the Pamlico River, Jack's offers plenty of cold beer, tasty seafood, and rustic seaside atmosphere. Have a couple of fish tacos or blue cheeseburger and hang out at the Tiki Bar afterward. $–$$.

Down on Main Street. 107 West Main St.; (252) 940-1988. The menu includes lots of sandwiches from which to choose for lunch. For dinner, try steak or seafood, but you'll want to give the fried dill pickles a shot anytime. Open for lunch and dinner. $–$$.

Nana and Papa's Country Kitchen and Grill. 421 Bridge St.; (252) 948-2500. This tiny restaurant with seating for no more than fifty people offers soul food that's completely in character for the atmosphere. For a taste of the south, try the crunchy-sweet fried crabs that are offered Saturdays in warm weather months. Closed Sun and Mon. $–$$.

Pia's of Washington. 156 West Main St.; (252) 940-0600. This is a great choice for deli sandwiches, burgers, and salads for lunch. For dinner, try a fresh seafood dish with Greek or Mediterranean flare. The decor is bright and tasteful. $–$$.

Riverwalk Steaks. 100 North Bridge St.; (252) 975-2125. The menu here offers everything from baby back ribs to fresh salmon, but the specialty is Omaha aged steaks. You are sure to get a visit from owners Larry or Judy sometime during your meal. $$–$$$.

where to stay

Carolina House Bed and Breakfast. 227 East Second St.; (252) 975-1382; www.carolinahousebnb.com. Located two blocks from the waterfront, this four-guest-room home, built in 1880 and listed on the National Register of Historic Places, puts you within walking distance of downtown, the Turnage Theater, and the estuarium. $$.

The Moss House. 129 Van Norden St.; (252) 975-3967; www.themosshouse.com. This four-guest-room 1902 Victorian home, located only a block away from the waterfront within walking distance to shops and restaurants, once belonged to the owner's great-grandfather. The Moss House serves a full breakfast highlighted by traditional Southern favorites and creative turns on classics from across the country. These hearty entrees, accented by fresh juices, freshly ground coffee, seasonal fresh or baked fruit, and an assortment of muffins and breads baked in-house, will prepare you for a full day. $$–$$$.

bath

With easy access to the Pamlico River and to the rest of the world via the Atlantic Ocean—50 miles downriver at Ocracoke Inlet—French Protestants from Virginia decided in 1705 to make Bath their permanent home. Only three years after becoming North Carolina's first town, Bath could boast fifty people and twelve houses.

As the first port of entry into the colony, Bath had a sea trade consisting of naval stores, furs, and tobacco. Ferries plied the Pamlico River, linking Bath to New Bern and Edenton via post roads. The colony's first shipyard and gristmill were established here, as was the first public library. The 1,050 books and pamphlets from England that had been entrusted to a plantation owner found a home in St. Thomas Church, built in 1734, the oldest existing church in the state.

The town struggled through periods of the 18th century with violent rebellions, drought, an outbreak of yellow fever, Indian wars, and piracy but managed to retain its significance. Bath's importance began to fade in 1776 when Washington, 15 miles upriver, was founded. Beaufort County's government moved to Washington ten years later. Today, Bath is a quaint historical village, occupying only a few blocks. Still, allow at least a couple of hours to see the town.

Bath was also the haunt of Edward Teach, better known as Blackbeard. He is said to have married a local girl and briefly settled in the little harbor town around 1716.

where to go

Historic Bath Visitor Center. 207 Carteret St.; (252) 923-3971. Begin your exploration by viewing the free video, "Bath: The First Town," shown every fifteen minutes. You can get a jump on this by viewing the video online at the Bath Historic Site Web site www.ah.dcr.state .nc.us/sections/hs/bath/bath.htm.

You can easily walk from the visitor center to historic sites. Take the guided tours of two historic homes: **Palmer–Marsh House** (1751), which includes an exhibit detailing the history of **Bath and the Bonner House** (1830). The cost is $2 for adults, $1 for students. The **Van Der Veer House** (1790) offers a free self-guided tour. Open Tues through Sat 9 a.m. to 5 p.m.

St. Thomas Episcopal Church. Craven and Main Streets; (252) 923-9141. Inside the state's oldest church, built in 1734, you will find Queen Anne's Bell. Cast in 1750, it is eighteen years older than the Liberty Bell. Also of significance but not on display: a large silver chalice presented by the Bishop of London in 1838, and a silver candelabra reputed to have been given by King George II in 1740.

where to eat

Blackbeard's Slices & Ices. 101 North Main St.; (252) 923-9444. This is a simple pizza place named for the swashbuckler who once called Bath home. Check out the garlic knots to start and stick around for the occasional live music. $.

Old Town Country Kitchen. 436 Carteret St.; (252) 923-1840. Open for breakfast, lunch, and dinner, the Old Town Country Kitchen features country cooking with daily specials. Local seafood, scrumptious fried chicken, and sloppy barbecue sandwiches worthy of finger-licking are served here; you can't go wrong. $–$$.

where to stay

Bath Harbor Marina and Motel. 101 Carteret St.; (252) 923-5711; www.bathharbor.com. You have a choice of four waterfront efficiency units. If you stay here, ask for the $10 guest discount on canoe, kayak, powerboat, and sailboat rentals. $$.

The Inn on Bath Creek. 116 South Main St.; (252) 923-9571; www.innonbathcreek .com. This five-room inn offers Southern charm across the street from the water. Here you are among the oldest buildings in the state where natives and early settlers once roamed. $$–$$$.

aurora

From Bath, head to the ferry landing at Bayview, 15 miles east on US 92. Just follow the signs to the Aurora–Bayview ferry, which departs regularly year-round (call 800-293-3779 for schedules or visit www.ncferry.org). There's no charge for the thirty-minute crossing. At the ferry landing, follow US 306 to Aurora.

where to go

Aurora Fossil Museum. 400 Main St.; (252) 322-4238; www.aurorafossilmuseum.com. An eighteen-minute video describes the great geologic forces that created the coastal plain over millions of years. Explore two rooms of fossilized bones, teeth, shells, and coral. Find your own fossils (some dating back twenty-two million years) or shark teeth by sifting through tons of fossil-bed diggings delivered to the site. Be sure to bring your own tools to dig. A garden trowel, a pair of gloves, a sifter, and small plastic bags for your finds should do nicely. The museum is open Mon through Sat 9 a.m. to 4:30 p.m. and Sun 1:30 to 4:30 p.m. The fossil pile, known affectionately as "the Pit of the Pungo," is open during daylight hours. Free.

where to eat

Wayside Restaurant. US 33; (252) 322-7299. Serving breakfast and lunch, the Wayside has daily specials, meat with choice of vegetables, plus rolls and hush puppies. The food is so good you'll wish they served dinner, too. $–$$.

where to stay

Creekside Cottage Waterfront. 457 Muddy Creek Rd.; (252) 322-4473. Short-term completely furnished housing in a rural setting (one-week minimum stay) is perfect for those enrolled in week-long sailing schools in the region. $.

edward

Named for Josephus Edwards, who built a mill on nearby Durham Creek in 1868, this small town is 22 miles from Washington and 3 miles off the route between the Aurora and Minnesott ferries.

where to go

Bennett Vineyards. 6832 Bennett Vineyards Rd. (Old Sandhill Rd.); (877) 762-9463; www .bennettvineyards.com. Bennett Vineyards is the largest muscadine and scuppernong vineyard in the Carolinas. It lies on a 138-acre parcel of colonial grant land in North Carolina east of US 17 between the Neuse and the Pamlico Rivers. The wine barreled in a converted tobacco barn derives from recipes and techniques that emulate those of the earliest colonists. The winery offers tours and tastings 8:30 a.m. to dusk Mon through Sat and noon to dusk on Sun.

day trip 03

east

barbecue highway:
smithfield, selma, goldsboro,
kinston

The road from Raleigh to Morehead City should be called the Barbecue Highway. That's because the towns that dot US 70 east (rightfully) boast some of the best barbecue in the state. Along this corridor from the capital to the coast, you'll not only visit noteworthy attractions but also sample eastern North Carolina–style barbecue, distinctly different from the style of barbecue found west of Raleigh.

Few topics have inspired such intense debate as North Carolina barbecue. The *New Yorker*'s Calvin Trillin wrote in his book *Alice, Let's Eat* of being "subjected to stern geographical probings" when he mentioned to North Carolina residents that he had sampled barbecue in their home state.

The debate was perhaps best characterized by the feuding between Jerry Bledsoe, who was a columnist for the *Greensboro Daily News* at the time, and Dennis Rogers, formerly of the *News and Observer*. Bledsoe wrote: "In the East, you get all these little things in your mouth and wonder what the hell they are. They're ground up pork skin. That's the only way they have to give the meat any flavor."

Rogers replied in his column: "When I am hankering for a big piece of dead hog meat, I like to follow the advice of my good friend Jerry Bledsoe and head west, where you find lots of it. For some reason, Jerry calls that barbecue."

The difference between the two is as much in the sauce as in the meat, writes author of the *Guide to North Carolina Barbecue,* Bob Garner, a producer for UNC-TV. Garner explains that the pork originally would be seasoned with "an ordinary table condiment of the

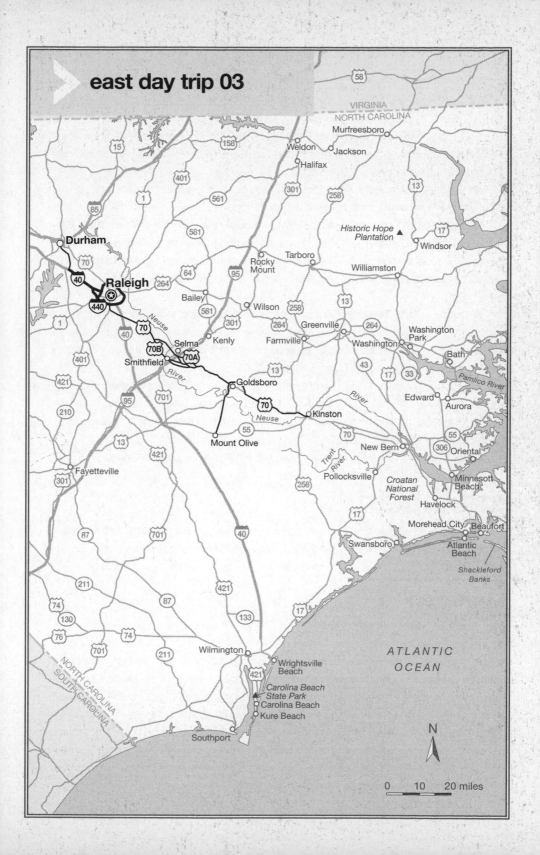

time, which consisted of vinegar, salt, red and black pepper, and oyster juice. Salty vinegar liberally laced with pepper is still basically the same sauce used on eastern North Carolina barbecue today." Still, the biggest and most noticeable difference between eastern barbecue and western barbecue—or Lexington-style, as it is sometimes called—is that ketchup is commonly added to western-style barbecue sauce.

Beyond that, restaurants have their own recipes for augmenting their house sauces and their own time-tested methods for roasting the pig.

In Smithfield the locals gather as they have for nearly five decades at White Swan Barbecue. In addition to sampling Smithfield's mouthwatering barbecue, you'll have the chance to visit the Ava Gardner Museum. Cast in many popular and memorable roles, Gardner was born just 7 miles east of Smithfield. She is buried at Smithfield's Sunset Memorial Gardens on US 70.

While you're in the area, take a short detour north of Selma to Atkinson's Mill, where cornmeal is ground to make the hush puppy mix used at some of the barbecue restaurants you can visit. On the way back to US 70, stop by the American Music Jubilee Theatre to appreciate the music that goes along with good barbecue.

Continue east on US 70 to Goldsboro, home to Wilber's Barbecue, where two U.S. presidents have eaten. Also popular is McCall's Barbecue and Seafood Restaurant, which started as a home-based take-out service. Further east still, in Kinston, stop at King's Restaurant, home of the "pig in a pup."

Should you lose your way, roll down your car window and follow your nose.

smithfield

Only 28 miles east of Raleigh, Smithfield was established on the banks of the Neuse River in 1777, making it one of the ten oldest towns in the state. A classic Southern town, Smithfield's downtown is the heart of this community of just more than 12,000 residents.

where to go

Ava Gardner Museum. 325 East Market St.; (919) 934-5830; www.avagardner.org. Gardner, who rose to fame as a sex symbol in 1940s Hollywood, was married to Mickey Rooney and Frank Sinatra. An incredible collection of items includes childhood memorabilia, film clips, costumes, domestic and foreign posters, black-and-white stills, film scripts, magazine covers, and scrapbooks. Stored and forgotten in a London attic, Gardner's childhood and career keepsakes were shipped to the museum in 2002. Among the items were teenage Ava's scrapbook with dance cards, cotillion invitations, and telegrams from a boyfriend, as well as three scrapbooks completed by Ava's sister that chronicle the actress's career up to 1953. Gardner, who was born near Smithfield, is buried in Sunset Memorial Gardens, 3 miles from the museum. Museum and gift shop open Mon through Sat 9 a.m. to 5 p.m.,

Sun 2 to 5 p.m. Admission for adults, $6; teens up to age sixteen and seniors, $5; children ages three through twelve, $4; children under age three, free.

where to shop

Carolina Premium Outlets. 1025 Industrial Park Dr., #905; (919) 989-8757; www .premiumoutlets.com. The more than eighty factory-direct stores include Liz Claiborne, Nike, Gap, Adidas, Carolina Pottery, Polo Ralph Lauren Factory Outlet, Tommy Hilfiger, Reebok, and Fossil Company Store. Open Mon through Sat 10 a.m. to 9 p.m., Sun 11 a.m. to 7 p.m.

where to eat

White Swan Barbecue. 3198 US 301 South; (919) 934-8913. The White Swan, which has been serving barbecue since 1959, also serves ribs, fried seafood, Brunswick stew, hush puppies, slaw, potatoes, and desserts. Open Mon through Wed 10:30 a.m. to 7:30 p.m., Thurs through Sat 10:30 a.m. to 8:30 p.m., and Sun 10:30 a.m. to 8 p.m. Join the crowd of locals on Thurs nights from 4 to 9 p.m., when barbecue sandwiches are just 99 cents each (regularly $2.25). A handful of White Swan locations are sprinkled throughout Johnston County. $–$$.

selma

Tiny Selma offers more than twenty shops and malls covering 100,000 square feet, all within walking distance in a 1950s small-town setting. Selma also hosts the East Coast Antique Show and Sale each October. It includes dealers, vendors, food, and entertainment. Selma also boasts the very best fine-ground cornmeal around, ground by millstones at the more than two centuries–old Atkinson Milling Company.

where to go

American Music Jubilee Theatre. 300 North Raiford St.; (877) 843-7839; www.amjubilee .com. Offering a touch of Branson and Myrtle Beach in eastern North Carolina, the theater presents evenings of Southern hospitality, American music, and sidesplitting comedy to delight audiences every weekend. The Branson-style variety show entertains visitors with music from '50s rock 'n' roll to classic and contemporary country and gospel. Admission rates vary by season but begin at $16.50 per adult.

Atkinson Milling Co. 95 Atkinson Mill Rd.; (919) 965-3547; www.atkinsonmilling.com. This old gristmill was built in 1757, while North Carolina was still a colony. The mill has been in continuous operation for more than 240 years. Today, Atkinson's Mill is the only water-powered gristmill operating in the area. A wide variety of cornmeal products, including a selection of hush puppy mixes, is available at the gift shop. Open Mon through Fri 8 a.m. to 5 p.m. and Sat 8 a.m. to noon.

Selma Union Station. Railroad St.; (800) 871-7245; www.bytrain.org/istation/iselma.html. Built in the 1920s, the new station serves as a working depot for passengers boarding Amtrak's Carolinian from Selma to Charlotte and Jacksonville to New York. Be sure to see the interpretive exhibits from the days when Selma was a major hub in the state.

goldsboro

Goldsboro is a town with a rich history. Claims to fame include: Sherman's invasion of Goldsboro during the War Between the States; and Andy Griffith's teaching high-school here before going on to become Sheriff Taylor in TV's *Mayberry*. Local legend also has it that barbecue was born here.

where to go

Cherry Hospital Museum. 201 Stevens Mill Rd.; (919) 731-3483. Opened by the state in 1880 for black citizens with mental illness, Cherry Hospital was named in 1959 for R. Gregg Cherry, governor from 1945 to 1949. It has been open to all races since 1965. Patients worked about 3,500 acres of farmland until the 1970s. The museum depicts more than a century of history with photographs, logbooks, and a variety of medical and farming equipment once used at the hospital. Open weekdays 8 a.m. to noon and 1 to 5 p.m. Free admission.

Cliffs of the Neuse State Park. 345-A Park Entrance Rd., Seven Springs; (919) 778-6234; www.ncparks.gov. Located just 15 miles south of Goldsboro off US 111, the cliffs tower 90 feet above the Neuse River. The multicolored cliff face reveals layers of sand, clay, seashells, shale, and gravel, formed when a fault in the earth's crust shifted millions of years ago. The Neuse River followed this fault line, cutting its course over time and resulting in the erosion that eventually carved the Cliffs of the Neuse.

Now a newly approved site on the NC Birding Trail, this North Carolina State Park offers hiking trails, paddling, picnicking, birding, and fishing. Seasonal family camping and swimming are permitted for a modest fee. It's generally open during daylight hours. A small museum is open daily from Mar 15 to Nov 30 and on weekends during the winter months.

Old Waynesborough Historic Village. 801 South US 117; (919) 731-1653; www .waynesboroughhistoricalvillage.com. Visit a 19th-century family home, a medical office, a one-room school, a law office, and a Quaker meetinghouse. Listen to the blacksmith beating upon his iron. Walk down to the Neuse River. Enjoy your day in this tranquil setting and learn more about this faded town, now a living-history museum. Open Tues through Sat 10 a.m. to 5 p.m., Sun 1 to 5 p.m. Free admission.

Willow Dale Cemetery. 306 East Elm St. Visit the Confederate monument, erected in 1883, that marks the site of a mass grave where 800 Civil War soldiers, both Union and Confederate, are buried.

where to eat

McCall's Barbecue and Seafood Restaurant. 139 Millers Chapel Rd.; (919) 751-0072. This popular Goldsboro restaurant began as a home-based operation. Owner Randy McCall roasted pigs at his house on Thurs nights and sold take-out barbecue from his home on Fridays. In 1989, McCall quit his day job and opened his restaurant, which specializes in barbecue, chicken, and seafood. Open 11 a.m. to 9 p.m. daily except Christmas Eve and Christmas Day. $$.

Wilber's Barbecue. 502-A Eastgate Dr. and 4173 US 70 East; (919) 778-1990 or (919) 778-5218. Wilber's claimed *Our State* magazine's Award of Excellence for best barbecue in the state, and *Southern Living* recognized Wilber's as the best barbecue in the South. Since 1962, Wilber's has roasted its chopped barbecue over oak coals. Presidents Bill Clinton and George Bush Sr. have eaten here. Open daily 6 a.m. to 9 p.m. $$.

kinston

At the museums and nature park in Kinston, you'll have plenty of opportunities to burn off the extra calories that you'll ingest at King's Restaurant. Then point your car west on US 70 to head back to Raleigh, or east for the thirty-minute drive to New Bern for an extended day trip. (See East Day Trip 01.)

where to go

Caswell Center Museum and Visitor Center. 2415 West Vernon Ave.; (252) 208-3779. Built in the 1800s, the Stroud House became home in 1914 to the first residents of Caswell Center, the first facility serving people with mental retardation in the state. The museum, which includes a videotape presentation, describes early life at Caswell Center. Free admission. Open Mon through Fri 8 a.m. to 5 p.m.

Caswell No. 1 Fire Station Museum. 118 South Queen St.; (252) 527-1566. Enter the world of the late-1800s fire fighter. The Caswell No. 1 Fire Station was built in 1895 after a disastrous fire destroyed much of the downtown Kinston area. A 1922 LaFrance Pumper is the focus of the museum, along with a collection of helmets, nozzles, ladders, fire extinguishers, and other memorabilia that span a period of one hundred years. Free admission. Open Tues, Thurs, and Sat 10 a.m. to 4 p.m.

CSS *Neuse* State Historic Site and Governor Richard Caswell Memorial. 2612 West Vernon Ave.; (252) 522-2091; www.nchistoricsites.org/neuse/neuse. The *Neuse* is one of only three remaining Civil War ironclads. Designed to ram and sink enemy boats, the CSS *Neuse* had a short life and was destroyed to keep Union soldiers from capturing her. The site includes remnants of the ship. The memorial is a self-guided museum depicting the life and career of North Carolina's first elected governor. Free admission. Open Tues through Sat 9 a.m. to 5 p.m.

Harmony Hall. 109 East King St.; (252) 522-0421. One of the oldest homes in Lenoir County, Harmony Hall has been tastefully restored with authentic 18th-century furnishings. Built in 1772, it was once the home of Governor Richard Caswell. Free admission. Open Mon, Wed, and Fri 10 a.m. to 1 p.m. or by appointment.

Neuseway Planetarium, Health and Science Museum. 403 West Caswell St.; (252) 939-3302. Located adjacent to the nature park is a 4,000-square-foot, century-old building that has been converted into a science center. The first floor houses Lenoir Memorial Hospital's Health and Science Museum, which includes interactive exhibits, a butterfly garden, computers, and a giant bubble machine. The second floor houses a 32-foot planetarium dome and projector. An observation deck with a telescope allows a look at the constel-

pickle festival

I didn't really understand how important pickles are to the state of North Carolina until my daughter enrolled in the North Carolina School of the Arts. I knew the school didn't have a basketball team, but I didn't find out until parent orientation that the school's mascot is the pickle. Mount Olive Pickle Company, the country's largest privately held pickle company, based in eastern North Carolina, is a big supporter of the arts.

*The company not only supported the arts school—in fact, the **Mount Olive Pickle Festival,** which it supports, is widely recognized as one of the best festivals in the state. Held the last full weekend in April since 1986, the festival features appearances by Mr. Crisp and Andyman; activities such as mechanical bull riding, a rock-climbing wall, and a bungee pull; plus a Pickle Pedal Parade and an art show. Children take part in a variety of games, and the court of the NC Pickle Princess Pageant reigns over the festival. Of course, there is a pickle recipe contest and all the free pickles you care to eat.*

To find the festival, travel south on US 117 out of Goldsboro about 16 miles until you arrive in Mount Olive. For more information, check out www.ncpicklefest .org or call (919) 658-3113.

lations, the moon, and even the planets when the time is right. The center is open Tues through Sat 9:30 a.m. to 5 p.m. and Sun 1 to 5 p.m. Free.

where to eat

King's Restaurant. 910 West Vernon Ave.; (252) 527-1661; and 405 East New Bern Rd.; (800) 332-6465; www.kingsbbq.com. King's acclaimed barbecue uses a vinegar and red pepper–based sauce. It's also hand chopped so that the sauce will be properly absorbed. Should you stop at King's, abandon all plans to count calories, and order the "pig in a pup," an oversize hush puppy stuffed with barbecue that goes for $2.50. Top it off with King's famous banana pudding or pecan pie. No time to dine at King's? Order your pork barbecue to be shipped overnight (no kidding). $–$$.

day trip 04

east

>>> **coastal diversion:**
morehead city, atlantic beach,
swansboro

Okay, so the drive to the "Crystal Coast" may be a stretch for a guidebook that purports to highlight destinations within two hours of Raleigh-Durham. Sure, it will take you an additional half hour to make the Atlantic coast, 147 miles from Raleigh, a straight shot on US 70 east, but for the extra effort, you'll be rewarded with a quaint downtown, beautiful beaches, and coastal charm.

The four-lane US 70 becomes Arendell Street as you enter the peninsula that claims Morehead City. You'll pass the Crystal Coast Visitor Center on the way in; stop here for maps and detailed information about the area. Farther on is the bridge to Atlantic Beach, but you'll want to explore Morehead City before crossing.

Beachgoers have been coming to Atlantic Beach since 1887, when a small, one-story pavilion was all that was here—well, that and the beach itself. Back then, visitors stayed in Morehead City and traveled by sailboat to the beach.

Today, you cross a high-rise bridge, then pitch camp in one of the many fine properties along the coast. You'll be joining the 3,000 residents who live here year-round and the 35,000 visitors who come here during the summer months. For the young—or the young at heart—the town center has amusement park rides.

Head back to Raleigh through Swansboro, a quaint fishing village 23 miles south of Morehead City via SR 24, or take the scenic drive down Emerald Isle. Either way, the trip back to Raleigh from Swansboro is 135 miles.

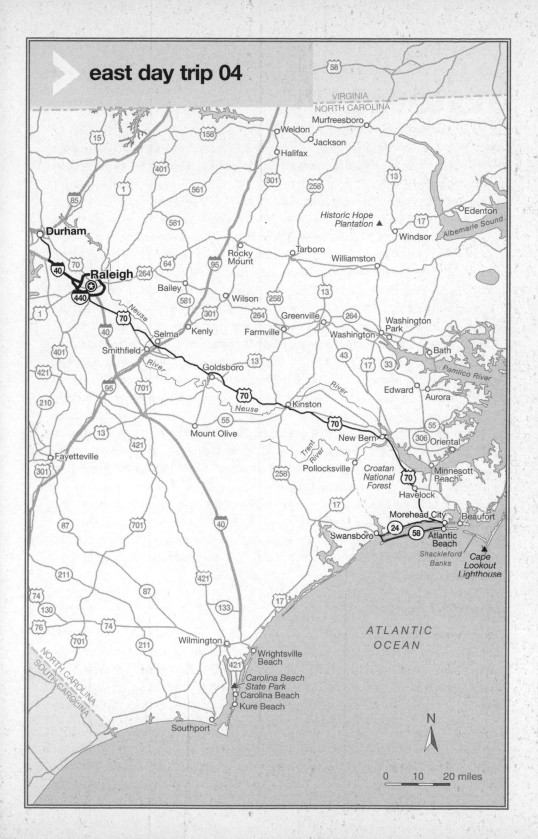

east day trip 04

morehead city

Incorporated in 1861 and named for Governor John Motley Morehead, the site formerly known as Shepherd's Point is located on a peninsula flanked by Bogue Sound and the Newport River. A summer resort, Morehead City is also the state's only deepwater port north of Wilmington.

East of the bridge to Atlantic Beach, from 25th to 3rd Streets, the oldest part of Morehead City skirts both sides of Arendell Street. The noticeable divider along the way is the railroad track that bisects the main street. The train brought passengers from the Triangle a century before there was a Triangle. Now it serves the North Carolina State Port at Morehead City with state exports like wood chips and tobacco.

The two or three streets parallel to the Bogue Sound waterfront make up the more well-to-do residential area of past years. On both sides of Arendell, the renovation of houses and summer cottages has created neighborhoods with lots of architectural character.

One block south on Evans Street between 10th and 4th Streets is the downtown Morehead City waterfront, where the peninsula narrows into single-digit street numbers. Here you'll see that seafood rules. The Gulf Stream charter fishing boat fleet is harbored here next to combination seafood market/restaurants where commercial fishing boats dock.

The smell of hush puppies is in the air by eleven in the morning. Memorials to captains and fishermen invite you to linger on a walk along the waterfront. The captains' memorial is located beside Capt. Bill's Seafood Restaurant at Seventh Street, and the statue of the Core Sounder in Jaycee Park on the waterfront between 9th and 10th Streets remembers the strength required of commercial fishermen.

A walk along the Morehead City waterfront introduces you to the character of this town that has always flaunted its greatest assets: fishing and feeding tourists. At the Sanitary Seafood Market and Restaurant, stop to browse the memorabilia before you exit. The restaurant is filled with comments of visitors since 1938, along with photographs of beauty queens and politicians.

where to go

Crystal Coast Visitor Center. 3409 Arendell St. (US 70 East); (252) 726-8148 or (877) 206-0929; www.crystalcoast.org. Designed after lighthouses of the 18th century, the Crystal Coast Visitor Center is a harbor of information. Find out how to get around the Crystal Coast and learn about attractions, lodgings, and dining. The adjacent rest area is well kept, and a picnicking area cooled by the shade of live oak trees by Bogue Sound. A North Carolina Wildlife launch ramp is available for trailerable boats, but parking is limited on busy weekends.

Cape Lookout Lighthouse. (877) 206-0929; www.crystalcoastnc.org. In 1804 Congress authorized construction of a lighthouse on Cape Lookout, the southernmost tip of the Outer

Banks barrier islands. Completed in 1812, the Cape Lookout light was reconstructed in 1859 to its height of 163 feet, and it is still an acting aid to navigation. It was painted with its distinctive black-and-white diamond pattern in 1873. A new keeper's quarters, constructed at the same time, is accessible to visitors on a seasonal basis. The lighthouse is open for climbing on specific dates four times a year, and reservations are required. There is no access by road to the undeveloped islands of the Cape Lookout National Seashore. The only permanent inhabitants are loggerhead sea turtles—which waddle to shore to bury their eggs—and 7,200 species of birds, including piping plovers, peregrine falcons, and Arctic birds migrating south.

At the point of Cape Lookout, the chilly Labrador Current meets the warm Gulf Stream with such force that it sends plumes of sea mist soaring skyward. These powerful currents wreak havoc on the ocean floor, shifting sand and shoals so that sailors and sea captains can scarcely navigate. For good reason, this region is known as the Graveyard of the Atlantic. More than 600 ships have wrecked along this treacherous stretch of coast since the 16th century.

From Morehead City, Cape Lookout ferry services operate seasonally, generally Easter through Oct. Contact the Crystal Coast Visitor Center for more information or call the national park office at (252) 728-2250.

Downtown Waterfront. Tenth to Fourth Streets on Evans; (252) 808-0440; www.downtownmoreheadcity.com. Seafood, sportfishing, and art galleries come together along this beautiful waterfront area where the smell of hush puppies mixes with the excitement of Gulf Stream sportfishing. The lifestyle, scenery, and heritage of commercial fishing in this Cape Lookout region of the North Carolina Outer Banks are reflected in the art galleries of downtown Morehead City.

The History Place. 1008 Arendell St.; (252) 247-7533; www.thehistoryplace.org. Opened in 2001, The History Place is home of the Carteret County Historical Society and Museum of History and Art. The museum collection includes artifacts of Native American inhabitants of this coastal region, costumes of the 18th and 19th centuries, furnishings, medical displays, and Civil War artifacts. The research library contains a notable genealogy collection, publications, archival manuscript material, and an extensive photography file. Tours are offered Tues through Sat, 10 a.m. to 4 p.m. Free admission.

where to shop

Morehead City has a number of fine art galleries that show the works of local and regional artists. Among our favorites:

Carolina Artist's Studio Gallery. 800 Evans St.; (252) 726-7550. A cooperative representing thirty or more regional and local artists, the sunny gallery rooms display original paintings, pottery, batiks, photography, and other art forms. Open Tues through Sat year-round.

Carteret Contemporary Art. 1106 Arendell St.; (252) 726-4071. Thematically, the North Carolina and Southeastern artists featured in the special exhibits share an appreciation of the coast. Open daily year-round.

Dee Gee's Gifts and Books. 508 Evans St.; (252) 726-3314. A landmark on the Morehead City waterfront where, in addition to best-sellers, greeting cards, and specialty gifts, you will find the complete collection of local nautical charts and every book that has ever been written about the Crystal Coast area. Dee Gee's schedules frequent book signings with state and local writers. Open daily year-round.

where to eat

Bistro by the Sea. 4301 Arendell St.; (252) 247-2777. Located beside the Hampton Inn, Bistro is a favorite with a faithful local clientele for its dinner choices, presentation, and service. You won't go wrong with the mahi mahi or the beef filet. For an appetizer, try the sushi tray. You can also share a song in the piano bar before or after dinner. Open Tues through Thurs 5 to 9:30 p.m., Fri and Sat until 10 p.m. Closed Sun, Mon, and Jan. $$–$$$.

Picata's. 506 Arendell St.; (252) 240-3380. This new kid on the block has quickly become a restaurant row favorite, serving a range of offerings from local seafood to Italian. Open for dinner every day except Sun and for lunch weekdays. $–$$.

Raps Grill and Bar. 715 Arendell St.; (252) 240-1213. Patrons go to Raps as much for the atmosphere as for the food. Longtime area restaurateur Mike Chaanine has gone to great lengths to create a festive place to dine. Dishes range from Southwestern to Italian and several points in between, including North Carolina coastal catches. $$–$$$.

The Sanitary Fish Market and Restaurant. 501 Evans St.; (252) 247-3111. The saying goes that if you haven't been to the Sanitary, you haven't been to Morehead City. After sixty-three years of serving seafood, the Sanitary continues to be a destination as well as a restaurant. The hush puppies are on the table before the chairs are completely pulled in, and all dishes are served with coleslaw and french fries. Lunch and dinner, generally fried or broiled, are served daily. Closed Thanksgiving through Jan. $$.

where to stay

Best Western Buccaneer. 2806 Arendell St.; (252) 726-3115 or (800) 682-4982. The Best Western offers the standard motel accommodations along with a complimentary full breakfast at the on-site Old Anchor Inn Restaurant. $$.

Econo Lodge. 3410 Bridges St.; (252) 247-2940 or (800) 533-7556. The Econo Lodge has comfortable rooms, low mainland rates, an outdoor pool, and complimentary continental breakfast, but no view. $$.

Hampton Inn. 4035 Arendell St.; (252) 240-2300 or (800) 467-9375. Morehead City's only waterfront hotel offers comfortable rooms, a complimentary continental breakfast with morning newspaper, and an inviting outdoor pool. It is adjacent to Bistro by the Sea, one of the town's more popular restaurants. $$.

Holiday Inn Express and Suites. Intersection of SR 24 and US 70; (252) 247-5001 or (800) 465-4329. Here you'll find reasonable rates, an outdoor pool, a sauna, an exercise room, a meeting room, laundry, and complimentary breakfast. $$.

The Lighthouse Inn. 2300 Bridges St.; (252) 247-3133. If you would prefer to avoid the national chains, try this small inn. Located near the Atlantic Beach Bridge and all area attractions, the Lighthouse Inn has five guest rooms with bath and two condo units that accommodate six. $$.

Quality Inn. 3100 Arendell St.; (252) 247-3434 or (800) 422-5404. The reliable comforts of this national chain are within close proximity to the Atlantic Beach Bridge. The economy of staying on the mainland and driving over the bridge to the beach is often an inviting alternative for overnight travelers. A complimentary continental breakfast and outdoor pool are available to guests. $$.

atlantic beach

The bridge to Atlantic Beach is in Morehead City at 24th and Arendell Streets. From the top of the high-rise bridge, the view that stretches ahead of you is of a densely developed beach resort town that meets the blue Atlantic.

At the bottom of the bridge, the road intersects with Fort Macon Road (SR 58). Ahead is Atlantic Beach Circle, a commercial and amusement area. The circle is the chosen destination of many day visitors to the beach because of lifeguard services and nearby beach food, especially hot dogs and beer.

Those who prefer less boardwalk and more natural ambience choose Fort Macon State Park as their destination, 1.5 miles east on Fort Macon Road.

Flanking the circle east and west are parallel streets of beach cottages with all the architectural flourish of eastern Carolina farmers' postharvest fishing retreats of the 1950s. Makeovers are adding some Caribbean color to these densely built blocks of clapboard rental cottages. Many permanent residences are now among the vacation rentals.

East of the circle toward Fort Macon State Park is a mix of condominium developments and small motels with fishing piers. One delightful development of vacation cottages is Sea Dreams, a string of three-story Caribbean-colored structures that seem to tumble over the dunes from Fort Macon Road to the beach. Sea Dreams is a head-turning happy sight by the ocean.

where to go

Fort Macon State Park. (252) 726-3775; www.ncparks.gov. Located on the east end of the island at Milepost 0 on SR 58, Fort Macon is a popular destination for the variety of activities available. The Civil War fort is an interesting site hiding in the dunes to protect Beaufort Inlet. From the fort walls, you can see the wreck site of Blackbeard's flagship, *Queen Anne's Revenge,* which lies in 20 feet of water just off the inlet. Rangers offer guided tours, too. The trailhead of a 1-mile nature walk from the fort leads to frequently good bird-watching. At the mouth of Beaufort Inlet, the rock jetty is a reliable destination for lucky surf fishing. A museum and bookstore are on-site. Open year-round with interpretive programs offered daily, there are picnicking facilities, a bathhouse (user fees are $4 per adult, $3 for ages five to twelve), and lifeguard services. Or take a nature walk on Coues Trail, which starts near the fort parking lots. The park is generally open during daylight hours. The swimming area is open in summer 10 a.m. to 5:45 p.m. The fort is open year-round daily except for Christmas Day 9 a.m. to 5:30 p.m.

North Carolina Aquarium. Roosevelt Drive at Milepost 7, SR 58; (252) 247-4003; www.ncaquariums.com. The aquarium is perfectly sited in the Theodore Roosevelt Natural Area. An interpreted trail through an ancient maritime forest begins at the aquarium parking lot. Another trail along a saltwater marsh begins inside the aquarium. The aquarium, in fact, takes guests on an aquatic journey through five galleries "from the mountains to the sea." You'll view creatures in aquatic ecosystems from the mountains, the Piedmont, the coastal plain, the tidal waters, and the open ocean. You can watch—and talk to—divers in the "Living Shipwreck" exhibit or meet an alligator face-to-face. It also has a snack bar and a gift shop. The aquarium also offers select programs and experiences throughout the area. Some programs require preregistration, so consult the aquarium's calendar. Contact the aquarium for a current schedule of events and to register for a kayaking trip, a surf-fishing workshop, a seafood cooking class, volunteer conservation opportunities, and any number of arts-and-crafts classes involving marine plant and animal life. Open daily 9 a.m. to 5 p.m. Admission for adults, $8; children ages six through seventeen, $6.

Roosevelt Natural Area. (252) 726-3775. At Milepost 7 on SR 58, this rare and undisturbed ancient maritime forest surrounds the North Carolina Aquarium, land preserved by the children of the twenty-sixth US president who inherited the part of the island that is now Pine Knoll Shores. There are two trails to explore here: The **Theodore Roosevelt Trail** is a thirty-minute walk among natural vegetation—especially the live oaks—and freshwater lakes (the trailhead is on the south side of the aquarium parking lot); The **Alice Hoffman Trail,** accessible from inside the aquarium, tours a salt marsh habitat with views of fiddler crabs and shorebirds. A reptile exhibit includes live animals that are at home in a salt marsh habitat and a maritime forest.

where to shop

Atlantic Station Shopping Center. West Fort Macon Road. With convenient park-and-walk shopping in Atlantic Beach, shops include Trillium, a bright and colorful stop for home accessories and women's sportswear (252-247-7210); and Boaters World (252-240-0055) with marine equipment and accessories from tools and outboards to hooks, line, and sinkers.

Capt. Stacy Fishing Center. 416 Atlantic Beach Causeway; (252) 247-7501 or (800) 533-9417; www.captstacy.com. Located right on the dock, this gift shop has more than you might expect at first glance. Jewelry, flags with nautical or beach themes, etched glass, crystal, and a variety of holiday decorations are offered. Of course, you'll find standard beach wares including t-shirts, beach bags, hats, sunglasses, and the like. The shop is open year-round, although winter hours are limited.

Kites Unlimited. 1010 West Fort Macon Rd.; (252) 247-7011. Located at Atlantic Station Shopping Center, this kite shop offers hundreds of styles of kites for fun on the beach and banners for beauty at home. You'll also find windsocks, windwheels, puzzles, and games for all ages.

where to eat

Crab's Claw Restaurant and Oyster Bar. 201 West Atlantic Blvd.; (252) 726-8222; www.crabsclaw.com. This restaurant on the beach is a popular lunch destination. Have a burger on the second-story deck, or try the salads and hot sauces, but the biggest treat may just be the steamed oysters. An oyster bar is open weekends on a seasonal basis. Open for lunch and dinner except Wed. $–$$.

Island Grille. 401 Money Island Dr.; (252) 240-0000. This cozy beach restaurant is located at the parking lot of Sportsman's Pier. There's no view, but the food is spectacular and the regulars are regular. Two-for-one specials are offered on Mon and Tues nights. One popular dish: filet stuffed with feta and served with garlic mashed potatoes. Choices always include a fish fillet (such as mahi mahi), and a shellfish and pasta dish. Make reservations if you want to be seated on Mon or Tues night, even in Jan. Open daily. $$–$$$.

Watermark. 1010 West Fort Macon Rd.; (252) 240-2811. Located in the Atlantic Station Shopping Center, this restaurant specializes in grilled steaks and seafood and is popular for its prime rib. No view to lure you, but the inside atmosphere is brightly tropical. Open daily. $$–$$$.

where to stay

Atlantis Lodge. 123 Salter Path Rd., Milepost 5 on SR 58; (252) 726-5168 or (800) 682-7057; www.atlantislodge.com. One of the oldest lodging properties on the Crystal Coast, this forty-two-room oceanfront lodge saw very little natural vegetation removed during its construction. Thus natural barriers, wildlife, and vegetation remain very much a priority. It's difficult to get a reservation here unless you've been a regular guest, but don't let that stop you from trying. The private pool is arguably the island's most invitingly cool place, the definition of "having it made in the shade." All rooms are efficiencies. $$–$$$.

Bogue Shores Suites. 1918 West Fort Macon Rd.; (800) 613-5043 or (252) 726-7071; www.bogueshores.com. Located on the sound across the street from the beach, this is an all-suite facility. Guests have access to fishing piers and a large pool. $$.

Sea Dreams. The Crystal Coast Tourism Authority (252-726-8148; www.sunnync.com) can offer details about this development of multistory beach houses of tropical pastel colors near the rolling sand dunes at Milepost 3 on East Fort Macon Road (SR 58). Some of these distinctive houses are available as vacation rentals.

Sheraton Atlantic Beach Oceanfront Hotel. 2717 West Fort Macon Rd. (Milepost 4.5 on SR 58); (252) 240-1155 or (800) 624-8875; www.sheratonatlanticbeach.com. A full-service oceanfront retreat, the Sheraton is great for families. There are ocean views from all guest rooms, an on-site restaurant, poolside and oceanfront food services, indoor pool, private pier, lifeguard services—everything for a comfortable family getaway by the ocean. Just park, check in, and vacation. $$$.

swansboro

Traveling west on either SR 24 inland or SR 58 down Emerald Isle will take you to Swansboro. The town began to develop in 1730, when the first permanent settlement was established on the former site of an Algonquian Indian village at the mouth of the White Oak River. In 1783 the colonial port town of Swansborough was incorporated in honor of Samuel Swann, former speaker of the North Carolina House of Commons.

The bustling port thrived, and shipbuilding became its major industry. The town's most famous shipbuilder was Captain Otway Burns, builder of the *Prometheus,* the first steamboat constructed in North Carolina. Captain Burns's earlier exploits as the commander of the privateer vessel *Snapdragon* had already brought much honor to the town. The port continued to prosper until the end of the Civil War.

The decline of the shipping industry initiated considerable growth of lumber and naval stores until the Great Depression. The townspeople then turned to another natural resource, the sea, and the development of the commercial fishing industry.

Swansboro has managed to retain the quaint charm and character of a picturesque colonial port. From the unique waterfront shops, boutiques, and dining, to boating, water sports, and fishing, this waterfront town on the White Oak River is well worth a visit. Shop along the river on Front Street and its adjoining side streets, take some time to walk along the White Oak River, enjoy lunch at one of the restaurants, and relax in Bicentennial Park.

where to shop

Phil Shivar and Sarah Lawrence Gallery of Art. 105 East Church St.; (910) 326-3600. Here you'll find limited-edition and original art by North Carolina resident Phil Shivar, who produces prints of lighthouses and local scenes. Co-owner and Naples, Florida, resident Sarah Lawrence displays her mixed-media impressionism. Ayers Antiques shares the same shop space and offers art glass, porcelain, and furniture. Open Mon through Sat year-round, Sun seasonally.

Russell's Olde Tyme Shoppe. 10 Front St.; (910) 326-3790. Stop at Russell's to browse the country crafts, jewelry, handcrafted clothing, pottery, furniture, baskets, and silk and dried flowers, along with kitchen and cooking utensils. Open daily.

Sunshine and Silks. 129 Front St.; (910) 326-5735. This quaint shop sells gifts and collectibles, including writing papers, tapestry throws, long-lasting candles, scented home sprays, beautiful Italian and American pottery, bell pulls, an extensive selection of Victorian greeting cards and holiday ornaments, and silk floral designs custom-made exclusively for Sunshine and Silks. Open daily.

Through the Looking Glass. 101 Church St.; (910) 326-3128 or (888) 367-8854. A broad selection of home and garden accessories, fragrances, jewelry, tableware, candles, wines, and children's gifts is sold here. Be sure to take a peek at the Christmas Wonderland department. Open daily, but call ahead in winter to verify.

where to eat

Capt. Charlie's Restaurant. SR 24 at 106 Front St.; (910) 326-4303. Specializing in fresh seafood, prime rib, and steaks, the restaurant offers fried seafood as well as stuffed flounder or broiled shrimp and scallops. Open evenings for dinner. $$–$$$.

Icehouse Waterfront Restaurant. 103 Moore St.; (910) 325-0501. Start with the tasty crab tostadas out on the porch if you can get a table there. If you like grouper, this is the place to try the grouper sandwich. $$.

White Oak River Bistro. 206 West Corbett St.; (910) 326-1696. Located near the bridge to Emerald Isle in an attractive white building with inviting porches, this bistro offers European cuisine—mostly Italian—for lunch and dinner. Service is in the brightly varnished dining room or on the porch overlooking a lawn that spreads under willow trees to the river. For lunch select from pastas and sauces or specialty Italian sandwiches. Dinner choices include pastas with veal, chicken, and seafood. Open year-round. Reservations are recommended. $$–$$$.

Yana's Ye Olde Drugstore Restaurant. 119 Front St.; (910) 326-5501. Yana's serves breakfast and lunch. If you're extra hungry, try the Bradburger, a hamburger with egg, cheese, bacon, lettuce, and tomato. Open daily. $–$$.

day trip 05

east

>>> **of pirates and pastimes:**
beaufort

beaufort

Travel US 70 east past Morehead City to Beaufort, the "crown jewel of the Crystal Coast." With homes dating to the 1700s, Beaufort has lots of charm and history. It used to be little more than a small commercial fishing village, but a couple of decades back, the town began a renewal program to heighten its appeal to visitors. Transient sailors were welcomed, the waterfront was restored, and today Beaufort is a wonderful walk-around small town with a rich maritime history. Begin on the town's shop-lined main thoroughfare, Front Street, and proceed past restored colonial homes on royally named back streets—Queen, Ann, Orange.

The third oldest town in North Carolina, Beaufort was named for Englishman Henry Somerset, the Duke of Beaufort. The town was surveyed in 1713, nearly twenty years before George Washington's birth, and was incorporated in 1722.

Blackbeard's ship, *Queen Anne's Revenge,* was found in 1996 at the mouth of Beaufort Inlet in 24 feet of water over which the locals had sailed and fished for years. Recent hurricanes shifted the sands, exposing pieces of the 289-year-old vessel. Following the loss of *Queen Anne's Revenge,* Blackbeard made his way to Bath, North Carolina's oldest town. There, in 1718, he received the king's pardon from North Carolina Governor Charles Eden. The pirate, however, was eventually tracked down and killed by volunteers from the Royal Navy.

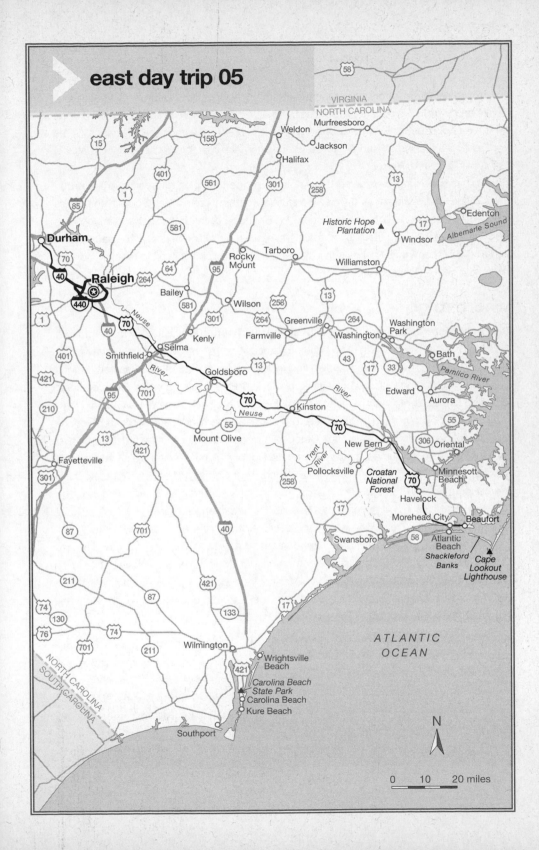

A number of operators offer sailing tours from the Beaufort waterfront to Shackleford Banks and Carrot Island for horse sightings (more than one hundred wild ponies roam freely on the island, let loose when a Spanish galleon ran aground here in the 17th century), as well as bird-watching, shelling, and self-guided tours along the Rachel Carson National Estuarine Research Reserve.

Sailors have long considered this tiny town a good jumping-off spot. Bermuda, 600 miles to the east, is almost as close as the state's western border. That proximity to the sea has served Beaufort well. Some leave here for Bermuda or the Bahamas, some stop here on their way up or down the Atlantic coast. Thus, what you'll find here is a true sailing town and all of the charm that it brings with it. If ever there was a place for you to drop anchor—or hoist your sails—Beaufort is it.

where to go

Beaufort Historic Site and Double Decker Bus Tour. 100 block of Turner St.; (252) 728-5225 or (800) 575-7483; www.beauforthistoricsite.org. Preservation efforts have kept Beaufort much as it was when the town was incorporated in 1723. At the Beaufort Historic Site, you can tour ten restored homes and public buildings of the 18th and 19th centuries, including the Carteret County Courthouse of 1796. The oldest home in Beaufort is Hammock House, built in 1709 and reputed to have been the headquarters of the notorious pirate Blackbeard. From April through October tour the historic district on a double-decker bus and listen to costumed guides wax poetic about the past, when Beaufort's visitors included pirates, sea captains, star-crossed lovers, and Confederate spies. Visit the old jail, the courthouse, and the apothecary shop, or join a tour of the Old Burying Ground. The Old Beaufort Museum gift shop offers a selection of books on local history, decoys by local carvers, fresh herbs, rugs woven by hand at the historic site, and other gifts. Staff offer guided tours of the historic site daily year-round at 10 a.m., 11:30 a.m., 1 p.m., and 3 p.m. Double-decker bus tours are offered Apr through Oct, Mon, Wed, Fri, and Sat at 11 a.m. and 1:30 p.m. The cost for each tour is $8 for adults and $4 for children. Tours of the Old Burying Ground are conducted Tues, Wed, and Thurs at 2:30 p.m. June through Sept. The cost is $8 for adults and $4 for children.

North Carolina Maritime Museum. 315 Front St.; (252) 728-7317; www.ncmaritime museum.org. The sea's influence on Beaufort—and on the entire Outer Banks region—is captured in the cozy, wood-paneled confines of the Maritime Museum, which contains centuries-old small boats, nautical tools, maps, and flags. At the museum's Watercraft Center, visitors can watch from a balcony as the museum's boatbuilder restores old sailing vessels. From the crafts of Native Americans to varnished Sun runabouts, boats tell a story of transportation, industry, life by the sea, and rescue from the sea. The newest additions to the collection are artifacts of Blackbeard's Queen Anne's Revenge. This shipwreck is one

environmental movement

Pennsylvania native Rachel Carson, the author of the 1962 book Silent Spring *that called attention to the dangers posed by pesticides, spent time conducting research in this area in the 1930s. Fascinated by the relationship between humans, animals, and their environments, Carson came to Beaufort's U.S. Fisheries Station to study shorebirds. Her observations were detailed in 1941's* Under the Wind *and 1955's* Edge of the Sea. *The "mother of the modern environmental movement" is honored through the small piece of land here.*

of the most significant marine archaeological finds in history. The museum's collection is extensive, ranging from martime fossils to exhibits that detail modern fishing technologies.

The museum offers a range of interpretive field programs that take visitors out to the marshes and natural reserves or for bike rides along the waterfront. Admission is free. Open Mon through Fri 9 a.m. to 5 p.m., Sat 10 a.m. to 5 p.m., and Sun 1 to 5 p.m. except New Year's, Thanksgiving, and the Christmas holidays.

Rachel Carson Estuarine Reserve. (252) 728-2170; www.nccoastalreserve.net. This complex of islands directly across from the Beaufort downtown waterfront is named for the author of *Silent Spring,* a book that forecast the devastation of the chemical DDT on the natural environment and stopped its use as an insecticide. A portion of this state reserve, composed of four islands, is an easy destination by rowboat or ferry service ($8 round-trip). It's a fast island getaway and a great place to rake clams and take home some steamers. The horses here are released domestic horses that have lived wild on the island since the 1920s, and about 200 species of birds make the reserve their home.

Shackleford Banks. (252) 728-2250; www.nps.gov/calo/ferry.htm. This island is visible from the third level of most any building in Beaufort or from the sandy beach of Fort Macon State Park. It is one of three barrier islands that compose the Cape Lookout National Seashore. Shackleford Banks is distinguished by its indigenous herds of wild horses that are traceable to the Spanish mustangs of the earliest New World explorers. These horses and their spring foals are a beautiful sight on the dunes of the island, which stretches 7 miles to the Cape Lookout lighthouse. Other than two park service docks and one toilet facility, there are no comforts on Shackleford Banks; if you go, take your own and bring back any trash. Take a bag for shells too, and prepare to enjoy a fabulous beach where you may be the only person in sight. Access is fastest from the Beaufort downtown waterfront, where several passenger ferry services operate year-round for $15 per adult and $8 per child round-trip.

Rand McNally Atlas picked Shackleford Banks as one of the "Best of the Road" destinations for its beaches and wild horses.

where to shop

With the transiting yachts at the dock, boating activity in Taylor's Creek, and the wild horses of the Rachel Carson Estuarine Reserve on the island that parallels Front Street, shopping along Beaufort's downtown waterfront is a pleasure. A few favorite retail stops along the four-block waterfront shopping area are:

Down East Gallery. 519 Front St.; (252) 728-4410 or (800) 868-2766. Here you'll find the beautifully detailed paintings and prints of artist Alan Cheek, whose favorite subject is the beauty of the Crystal Coast. Open daily, except Mon during winter.

The Jarrett Bay Boat House. 507 Front St.; (252) 728-6363. A broad selection of yacht-themed gifts is offered. Jarrett offers clothes, housewares, art furniture, and more. Open daily.

The Peddler. 222 Front St.; (252) 728-5361. You will enjoy the humor, color, and Down East saltiness of this gift shop's proprietors, as well as the selection of silver jewelry, sarongs, and coastal and tropical housewares. Open daily.

Tierra Fina. 119 Turner St.; (252) 504-2789 or (877) 504-2789. Featuring Spanish pottery and glassware, this shop offers a frequently changing variety of pottery and ceramics for home and garden. Open daily.

where to eat

Aqua Restaurant. 114 Middle Lane; (252) 728-7777. This tapas-style restaurant appropriately features seafood in an upscale atmosphere. You will want to make reservations here and be sure to take time to enjoy something from the wine list. Open for dinner Tues through Sat. $$.

Beaufort Grocery Company. 117 Queen St.; (252) 728-3899. Fabulous dishes with French and Greek influences come from a professional kitchen and inspired menus in a setting with brick walls, wood floors, and close tables, which can make it a noisy choice. Really great take-out lunches include specialty salads and breads. Pick one up and enjoy it outside in the Rachel Carson Reserve on the other side of Taylor's Creek from the downtown waterfront area. $$.

Clawson's 1905. 425 Front St.; (252) 728-2133; www.clawsonsrestaurant.com. The varied atmospheres of this restaurant include an espresso bar, a traditional bar, a dining room with private booths, and private dining in several locations. It's a great restaurant choice for a burger or the house specialty, a stuffed baked potato called a Dirigible. Entrees are varied, and seafood specials are announced each night. Lunch favorites typically include the seafood bisque in warm months and chili when it's cold. $$–$$$.

The Net House Steam Restaurant and Oyster Bar. 133 Turner St.; (252) 728-2002. Across the street from the Beaufort Historic Site, this restaurant specializes in local seafood. It's the restaurant of choice for a cool night in oyster season, and it's the only restaurant in the area where steamers include clams and crabs. $$–$$$.

The Sandbar at Town Creek Marina. 232 West Beaufort Rd.; (252) 504-7263. A perfect destination on an outdoor day when dining on the deck is essential. Away from the down-town hubbub, the Sandbar is distinctive among Beaufort restaurants for actually having a rather peaceful atmosphere. It's upstairs, with porches surrounding it on three sides. Views and breezes are constant. The lunch and dinner menus are food wise, may be a bit trendy, but reliably delicious and not overpriced. $$–$$$.

where to stay

Beaufort Inn. 101 Ann St.; (252) 728-2600 or (800) 726-0321; www.beaufort-inn.com. The AAA three-diamond Beaufort Inn has forty-four guest rooms, a dining room, an exercise room, and a large outdoor hot tub spa. Within walking distance of all attractions, its rooms have private balconies with rockers, and a complimentary breakfast is served in the dining room. $$–$$$.

Cousin Martha's Bed and Breakfast. 305 Turner St.; (877) 464-7487 or (252) 728-3917. Elmo is the chef here, not Martha, and everybody's treated like family. Rooms are decorated in island style, and the delightful upstairs porch is a great place to read a book or have a glass of wine. $$$.

Harborside Suites. 507 Front St.; (252) 728-5462; www.beaufortrlty.com/rentals/harbor side.html. Conveniently located over the street-level shops on Front St., Beaufort Realty rents efficiency and two- and three-bedroom suites at this property on the downtown waterfront of Beaufort. All units open to a private deck on top of the building with an upper deck that offers a fabulous view of Shackleford Banks, Beaufort Inlet, and the Cape Look-out Lighthouse. Distinguishing this property, other than its location and views, are the retro furnishings and tile work in each unit. But, come prepared: This property is BYOL—Bring Your Own Linens. However, if you forget, linens are provided for an extra per-bed fee. Units allow pets, but a non-refundable deposit applies. $$.

Inlet Inn. 601 Front St.; (252) 728-3600 or (800) 554-5466. Well-located, the inn offers some rooms with views to the Cape Lookout Lighthouse, Beaufort Inlet, and Shackleford Banks; others offer balconies, fireplaces, or window seats. All have cozy comforts on Beau-fort's downtown waterfront. $$.

Langdon House. 135 Craven St.; (252) 728-5499; www.langdonhouse.com. This bed-and-breakfast, the oldest in Beaufort, is a mere 265 years old. Hand-forged nails and hand-wrought timbers testify to the authentic charm of this old home. Owners Jimm and Lizzet Prest will help you wind down so that you can quickly adapt to the town's tranquillity. Rockers on their broad porches help, as does the absence of televisions in guest rooms. "We're out on the edge of the continent without all the day-to-day distractions," Jimm says. "It can be very refreshing, but it can also take some getting used to. I had a guest from New York tell me that he had to turn on his bathroom fan. It was too quiet for him. He couldn't get to sleep." Great breakfasts, genuine hospitality, and the delightful upper-floor porch turn guests into old friends. $$.

Pecan Tree Inn. 116 Queen St.; (252) 728-6733. This inn offers rooms or suites with Jacuzzis, Victorian architecture, English gardens, surrounding porches, and a half-block walk to the waterfront. $$–$$$.

day trip 06

east

farm living:
bailey, kenly, wilson, farmville, greenville

For this day trip, head east on US 64, taking the exit for US 264 east in the direction of Wilson, forty-five minutes from Raleigh. On the way, stop off in Bailey to visit the Country Doctor Museum, then detour on SR 581 south for a dot of a town known as Kenly. After crossing I-95, look for signs pointing the way to the Tobacco Farm Life Museum.

Hopefully you've timed your visit so that you will arrive in Wilson, north on US 301, for lunch at Dick's Hot Dogs, celebrating more than eighty years in business. Spend the afternoon in Wilson before kicking up the trail dust to make way for Farmville, where you can stretch your legs and learn a bit more about farm life.

Still east on US 264, head for Greenville, a college town that bills itself as the gateway to eastern North Carolina. If you have a long weekend, you could combine this day trip with Washington (East Day Trip 02) and New Bern (East Day Trip 01), making an extended loop back to Raleigh-Durham. If you do this make sure you see East Day Trip 03 to learn about "Barbecue Highway," which follows US 70, the main artery between New Bern and Raleigh.

bailey

Just thirty minutes east of the capital city is farm country. Bailey (population 670) was settled in about 1860, incorporated in 1907, and named for Joe Bailey, an early settler.

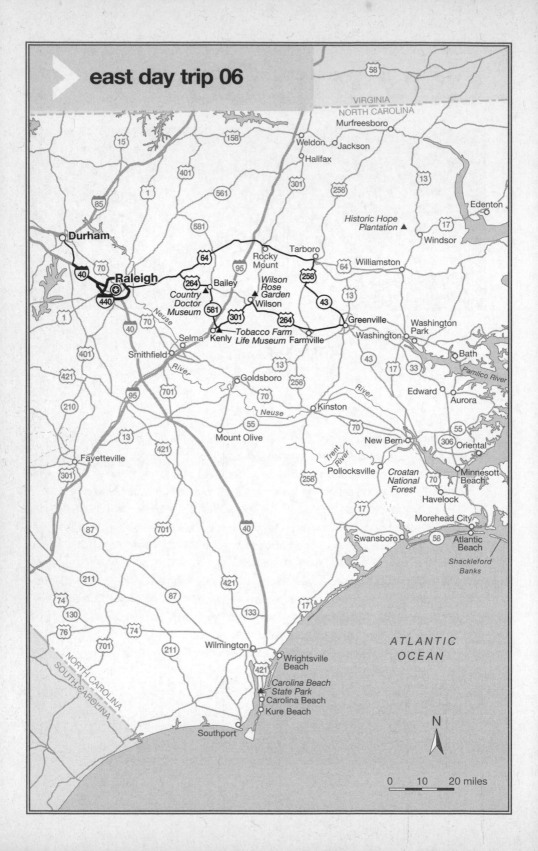

where to go

Country Doctor Museum. 6642 Peele Rd.; (252) 235-4165; www.countrydoctormuseum .org. This is the only medical museum in the nation dedicated to rural physicians who practiced medicine in North Carolina and the South during the 19th and early 20th centuries. A composite restoration of two doctors' offices includes the Dr. Howard Franklin Freeman Office, built in 1857, and the Dr. Cornelius Henry Brantley Office, ca. 1887, which illustrates the early doctor's office with instruments and equipment of the day. In three centuries-old buildings and two modern ones, the Country Doctor Museum collects and preserves the medical instruments and tools of pharmacy used by country doctors, and the diaries, papers, and medical books of these rural physicians. Docents lead tours through the facility. Admission is $5 for adults and $3 for ages eighteen and under. Open Tues through Sat 9 a.m. to 5 p.m.

where to shop

Finch Pottery and Nursery. 5714 Finch Nursery Lane; (252) 235-4664; www.danfinch .com. Browse through acclaimed potter Dan Finch's stoneware, porcelain, wood-fired, salt-glazed, and raku pottery selection. Along with pots, you'll also find handcrafted bluebird homes and blueberry plants at the nursery.

kenly

More than double the population of Bailey, Kenly is located in the heart of tobacco country. The town, settled in about 1875, was named for an executive of the Atlantic Coast Line Railroad.

where to go

Tobacco Farm Life Museum. 709 Church St. (US 301 north); (919) 284-3431; www .tobaccofarmlifemuseum.org. This exceptional museum bills itself as a "living time capsule, offering a window back in time through which visitors experience a way of life that has all but disappeared." That way of life was tobacco farming. Flue-cured tobacco became the first major cash-producing agricultural commodity for the region during the late 1800s. A 6,000-square-foot exhibit hall displays artifacts from all aspects of farm life, along with a hands-on children's exhibit. Household goods, musical instruments, clothing, and agricultural tools are displayed. A restored farmstead with main house, detached kitchen, and smokehouse depicts rural life as it was during the Great Depression. Open Mon through Sat 9:30 a.m. to 5 p.m., Sun 2 to 5 p.m. Adults, $6; children $4; seniors age sixty-five and over, $4; and children under two free.

where to eat

Country Pride Restaurant. 923 Johnston Pkwy.; (919) 284-5121. Down-home Southern cooking is a mainstay here. Its convenient location just off the highway makes it a popular stopping point for hungry travelers—and day-trippers! $.

wilson

The Tuscaroras were the first to settle in Wilson, but European settlers soon forced out the native tribe. The new settlers carved out family farms from the wilderness, and the town of Wilson, incorporated in 1849 as a farm market, could boast three grocery stores and two physicians a few years later.

During the Civil War, Wilson was strategically important to the Confederacy, although no battles were fought here. The Wilmington & Weldon Railroad, connecting Robert E. Lee's Army of Northern Virginia to its primary source of supplies at Wilmington, traveled through Wilson, which also served as the site of a military hospital.

Following the war, falling cotton prices prompted farmers in the region to adopt a new cash crop: tobacco. The first bright leaf tobacco was planted in the 1870s. From that time until the end of the last century, farmers, auctioneers, and buyers kept Wilson's tobacco warehouses humming.

where to go

Historic Walking Tour of Downtown Wilson. 124 East Nash St.; (800) 497-7398; www .wilson-nc.com. You can begin your tour here in the original Branch Banking & Trust, founded here in 1872 and now home of the Arts Council of Wilson and the Wilson Visitor Bureau. More than twenty-five buildings, churches, and homes are listed on the National Register of Historic Places. Enjoy the tree-lined streets of downtown Wilson on foot or by car.

Imagination Station. 224 East Nash St.; (252) 291-5113; www.imaginescience.org. Located in downtown Wilson, Imagination Station presents adventure for children and adults. You don't have to imagine this science center's more than 200 hands-on exhibits, with live science shows offered daily on topics from natural and physical sciences. Open Mon through Sat 9 a.m. to 5 p.m. Admission is $5 for adults, $4 for children four to seventeen.

Vollis Simpson's Whirligigs. 7219 Oscar Loop, Lucama; www.sci.mus.mn.us/sln/vollis. This extravagant collection of folk art is unique even among roadside attractions. 8 miles south of Wilson, Vollis Simpson has created large, sculptures in the form of windmills. To add to the effect, many pieces have reflective parts and clever devices to add sound. Drive by in the day to see the giant colorful creations, then again at night when the wind is kicking up. Some of Simpson's works have been exhibited in museums from Boston to Atlanta, as well as at the 1996 Olympics and have appeared in national magazines, including *Newsweek, People,* and *Time.* They are the subject of the Science Museum of Minnesota's Web site listed above.

Wilson Botanical Gardens. With its history deeply rooted in the agricultural industry, Wilson's leadership has worked hard to maintain economic stability as its tobacco warehouses closed over the past decade. They've done that through the development of a thriving cultural center. Among those cultural assets are three botanical gardens. All are generally open during daylight hours.

Wilson Rose Garden. 1800 Herring Ave.; (252) 399-2261; www.wilsonrosegarden .com. More than 1,200 rose plants consisting of 180 varieties include old garden roses, English roses (David Austin roses), hybrid teas, floribundas, grandifloras, climbing roses, miniatures, and shrub roses. Art statuary is incorporated into the garden, the centerpiece of the collection being a 10-foot-tall Georgia marble fountain sculpture by internationally known sculptor Horace Farlowe. The garden is open to the public daily from dawn until dark. Admission is free.

Wilson Botanical Gardens. 1806 Goldsboro St.; (252) 237-0111. Since 1997, the garden designed as a home demonstration facility, has been maintained in part by the Wilson County Master Gardeners and is located on the grounds of the Wilson County Agricultural building. It exhibits a collection of trees, grasses, bird and butterfly plants as well as a perennial gardens.

Library Rose Garden. 249 West Nash St. The Library Rose Garden features twenty-four varieties of Hybrid Tea Roses. Many of the varieties are champion "All American Rose Selections" or have received other significant awards.

where to shop

With more than thirty antiques shops, Wilson claims to be one of the largest antiques markets in the eastern United States. Most are open Mon through Sat 10 a.m. to 5 p.m. Here's a short list to get that antiquing started.

Antique Warehouse & Restorations. 320 East Barnes St.; (252) 243-7727.

Boone's Antiques. 2014 US 301 South; (252) 237-1508; www.boonesantiques.com.

Boykin Antiques & Appraisals, Inc. 2013 US 301 South; (252) 237-1700.

Fulford Antique Warehouse (formerly Antique Warehouse & Restorations). 320 East Barnes St.; (252) 243-7727. Among the treasures to be found here are grandfather clocks, millwork and heart pine flooring.

Marcia Stancil Antiques & Lamps. 2020 US 301 South; (252) 399-2093. This shop specializes in 18th and 19th century American and English furniture, decorative arts, lamps, and shades.

Tomorrow's Heirlooms Today. 5430 Wiggins Mill Rd.; (252) 239-1477.

where to eat

Bill's Barbecue and Chicken Restaurant. 3007 Downing St.; (252) 237-4372. A favorite among the locals, Bill's serves barbecue, chicken, and seafood. Open daily from 9 a.m. to 9 p.m. $–$$.

Dick's Hot Dog Stand. 1500 West Nash St.; (252) 243-6313. Founded in 1921 by Socrates "Dick" Gliarmis, a native of Samos, Greece, Dick's Hot Dog Stand is still going strong. Dick is long gone, but his son Lee ("Socrates") carries on the tradition. Ever optimistic about his business's continuing longevity, in 2001 he published a brochure, Dick's Hot Dog Stand: The First 80 Years, which thanks customers for their patronage. "We served Dick's Hot Dogs through the roaring '20s and both world wars and never missed a beat. Even through the Great Depression, we found the support to continue without ever having to close our doors." Actress Ava Gardner, who hailed from just down the road in Smithfield, dined here. Make sure to order your dog with chili, which Gliarmis makes from a secret family recipe. Open Tues through Thurs and Sun 10 a.m. to 8:30 p.m., Sat 7:30 a.m. to 3:30 p.m. Closed Mon. $–$$.

where to stay

Whitehead Inn. 600 West Nash St.; (800) 258-2058. Located in the gracious setting of downtown Wilson's historic district, quiet Victorian charm abounds in an atmosphere of modern-day conveniences. Whitehead is a complex of four buildings, all historic homes that together provide fourteen lovely overnight accommodations, ten of which are in the B&B inn. Guests have their choice of three king suites, two queen guest rooms, four double guest rooms, and one twin guest room. A full country breakfast is included. $$$.

farmville

Settled in about 1850 and known as New Town before it was incorporated in 1872, Farmville is a pretty, small town with a central main street lined with shops. As you may surmise, the town was named for the fact that it was in the center of rich farming land. For over 20 years it has been the site of the Dogwood Festival each April.

where to go

The May Museum and Park. 213 South Main St.; (252) 753-5814; www.farmville-nc .com. The museum, located in the Farmville Historic District, chronicles the cultural and commercial heritage of Farmville and western Pitt County from colonial times to the present. The museum is housed in an 1870s-era home and interprets the area's history through both permanent exhibits and special programs that are offered periodically throughout the year. The museum is home to an extensive collection of 19th and early 20th century quilts, one of the oldest collections in the state, which are displayed on a rotating basis. Open 9 a.m. to 5 p.m. Mon through Sat or by appointment. Free.

greenville

Founded in the mid-1700s, Greenville was originally known as Martinsborough in honor of Josiah Martin, who served from 1771 to 1775 as the last royal governor of North Carolina. The county seat of Pitt County changed its name in 1786 to honor Revolutionary War hero Nathanael Greene.

Home to East Carolina University (ECU), established in 1908, the city is the cultural, commercial, educational, and medical hub for Pitt County's 134,000 residents. Be sure to drive or walk through the College View Historical District, placed on the National Register of Historic Places in 1992, on the north side of Fifth Street.

Greenville presents national-quality performing arts, including Sun in the Park during the summer and Freeboot Fridays, a series of outdoor "Alive at Five"–style Friday night concerts preceding ECU Pirates home football games.

where to go

Greenville Museum of Art. 208 South Evans St.; (252) 758-1946. One of the state's oldest museums, founded in 1939, the Greenville Museum of Art presents changing exhibits from its permanent collection of 19th- and 20th-century American art, as well as traveling regional and national exhibits. The museum also owns one of the largest public collections of North Carolina Jugtown pottery. Open Tues through Fri 10 a.m. to 4:30 p.m., Sat and Sun 1 to 4 p.m. Admission is free.

Ledonia Wright African-American Cultural Center. Bloxton House on ECU campus; (252) 328-6495; www.ecu.edu/lwcc. The cultural center houses East Carolina University's 150-piece art collection, made by the Kuba of Zaire and works by ECU students. Open Mon through Thurs 8 a.m. to 8 p.m., Fri to 5 p.m.

River Park North and the Science and Nature Center. 1000 Mumford Rd.; (252) 329-4561. This environmental park and science center features outdoor recreational activities, including fishing and pedal boats. It also includes a small natural history museum with exhibits on North American wildlife.

Wellington B. Gray Gallery. East Carolina University School of Art, Fifth Street in the Jenkins Fine Art Center; (252) 328-6336; www.ecu.edu/graygallery. Located on the ECU campus, the gallery features exhibits of nationally and internationally known contemporary artists in fine arts, crafts, graphics, video, and installation art, as well as student and faculty exhibitions. Open Mon through Sat 10 a.m. to 5 p.m., Thurs to 8 p.m.

where to shop

Artisans. 150 Plaza Dr.; (252) 353-8008. More than sixty shops sell decorative accessories and fine gifts. Open Mon through Sat 10 a.m. to 6 p.m. and Sun 1 to 5 p.m.

City Art Gallery. 511 Red Banks Rd.; (252) 353-7000; www.city-art-gallery.com. This fine arts gallery features works of established local, regional, and national artists and craftspeople. It's open Mon through Sat 10 a.m. to 5 p.m.

New River Pottery. 3750 Sterling Point Dr., Winterville (6 miles south of Greenville's city center); (252) 756-1776. Offering selections of flowers, glassware, pottery, and linens, New River is open Mon through Sat 9 a.m. to 9 p.m., Sun 11 a.m. to 6 p.m.

where to eat

B's Barbecue. Corner of SR 43 and B's Barbecue Rd. Don't be put off by the appearance. It's been said that "B's Barbecue is . . . a joint so exclusive, elusive, and way cool that it doesn't even have a phone or published address." It's a small, unassuming place that has what is known as some of the best barbecue in the state. $–$$.

southeast

>>>

day trip 01

southeast

fun in the sun:
wilmington, wrightsville beach,
carolina beach, kure beach

This day trip, a straight shot from Raleigh-Durham on I-40 east, mixes history, Hollywood, beaches, amusements, and great food. The area offers riverboat tours, plantation visits, and beaches.

The core of this trip is Wilmington, which has the charm of Charleston, South Carolina, but without the crowds. Visitors can begin with a carriage ride, then visit the many historic homes downtown, dine by the Cape Fear River, and browse the eclectic shops.

Only fifteen minutes away from downtown is Wrightsville Beach. Located on an island, the small town still retains much of its turn-of-the-19th-century charm. A little farther is Carolina Beach, which offers several interesting nature excursions, including guided kayak ecotours of the coastal marshlands. Carolina Beach State Park is home to the endangered Venus flytrap.

Down the road at Kure Beach is historic Fort Fisher, a Civil War earthen fortress that was lost to Union troops. A few minutes from the historic site is a renovated 200,000-gallon ocean aquarium. From here you could head back to Wilmington or take the ferry to charming Southport (see Southeast Day Trip 02) before looping back to Raleigh.

wilmington

Although the town of Brunswick was founded on the west bank of the Cape Fear River in 1726, a new settlement farther upriver began to take root in 1729. The new settlement,

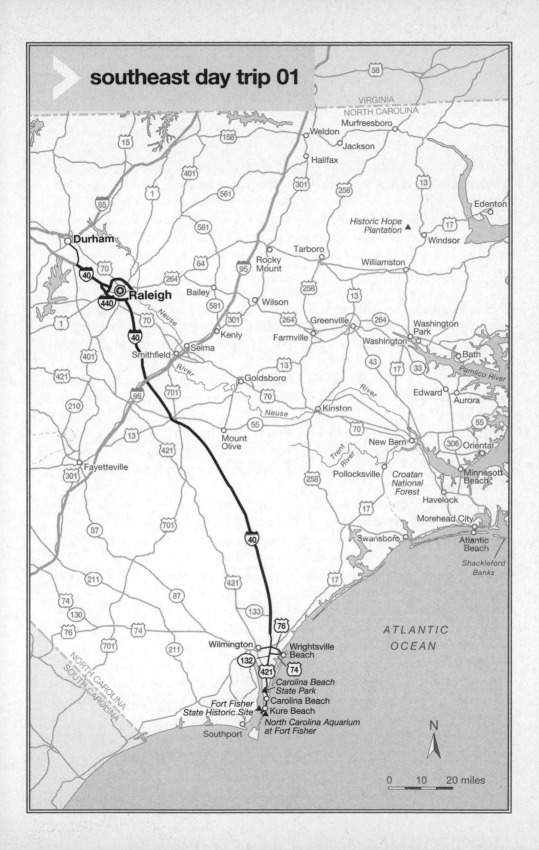

southeast day trip 01

a trading post, was referred to as Dram Tree and later called New Liverpool, New Carthage, New Town, and Newton. When colonial Governor Gabriel Johnston took office, he incorporated the City of Wilmington in 1740, naming it after Spencer Compton, Earl of Wilmington.

British forces captured the city in 1781. General Cornwallis occupied the Burgwin-Wright House, which you can visit on this day trip, but he withdrew to Yorktown later that year only to watch his army collapse. Following the Revolutionary War, Wilmington flourished. Estates and plantations were established on the outskirts, and fine homes were built downtown. Although nearly 30 miles from the Atlantic Ocean along the Cape Fear River, Wilmington flourished as a major port and shipbuilding center. The city became the site of the world's largest cotton exchange.

To get cotton and other exports to the port, the world's longest rail line, the Wilmington & Weldon Railroad, was completed in 1840 and helped to make Wilmington the largest city in the state that year. With its railroad and access to the Atlantic, Wilmington became the Confederacy's most important port. Nearby Fort Fisher was built in 1861 to protect the port city.

At the turn of the 20th century, the Wilmington & Weldon and several other railroads merged to become the Atlantic Coast Line Railroad. The company headquarters were established in Wilmington, but by 1910 the city had lost its claim as the state's largest as inland cities grew fat on the tobacco and textile industries. During World War I, shipbuilding and cotton exports thrived in Wilmington, but the Great Depression brought production in both industries to a halt. World War II saw a resurgence in shipbuilding, and the port city sent 243 ships to sea.

In 1960 the Atlantic Coast Line moved its headquarters, along with 1,000 employees and their families, to Jacksonville, Florida, representing the largest single move of employees ever staged by a southeastern industry. The move dealt a severe blow to Wilmington's economy. City leaders, however, undertook a major initiative to bring new industry to the area, and by 1966 Wilmington, showing signs of recovery, was designated an "All American City" by the National Civic League.

During the 1970s, downtown developers began a strong revitalization effort while preservationists sought protection for the historic downtown homes and buildings. Their combined efforts resulted in a reborn downtown that still attracts visitors.

In the 1980s a major film studio came to Wilmington. Often referred to as "Hollywood East" or "Wilmywood," Wilmington has consistently ranked among the nation's top locations for film production. Several stars call Wilmington home and was the locale for television hits *One Tree Hill* and *Dawson's Creek*.

A carriage tour is the best way to get an overview of the city's history. The historic district is compact enough that you can walk to the many buildings and sites open to visitors.

where to go

Cape Fear Coast Convention and Visitors Bureau. 24 North Third St.; (877) 406-2356; www.capefearcoast.com. Look for the tall red brick building with the clock. The CVB also operates a kiosk on the river at the foot of Market Street.

Battleship *North Carolina*. US 17; (910) 251-5797; www.battleshipnc.com. Moored across the river from downtown Wilmington, this 1941 vessel played a part in every major naval offensive in the Pacific during World War II. On her decks and below the guest begins to get an idea of what life was like upon the great battleship. It's both a museum and memorial to those who served and giving a glimpse of some of the stories of its occupants through audiovisual displays and memorabilia. Open daily from 8 a.m. to 8 p.m. mid-May through mid-Sept, to 5 p.m. the rest of the year. Admission: adults, $12; seniors and active military duty, $10; children ages six to eleven, $6; five and under, free.

Cape Fear Museum of History & Science. 814 Market St.; (910) 341-4350; www.cape fearmuseum.com. Established in 1898 as a Confederate museum, this is the state's oldest history museum. Explore regional history in the exhibition Cape Fear Stories, featuring a model of 1860 Wilmington and a diorama of the historic battle of Fort Fisher and through the Maritime Pavilion. Discover regional ecology in the Michael Jordan Discovery Gallery. (The basketball star was born nearby.) Open Tues through Sat 9 a.m. to 5 p.m., Sun 1 to 5 p.m. Also open Mon from Memorial Day through Labor Day. Admission: Adults, $6; children ages three through seventeen, $3; and seniors, $4.

The Children's Museum. 116 Orange St.; (910) 254-3534; www.playwilmington.org. The Children's Museum has hands-on exhibits and play areas for kids. Open Mon through Sat 9 a.m. to 6 p.m., and Sun 1 to 5 p.m. On Monday no field trips are allowed and Friday 9 to 10 a.m. are for toddlers and their parents only. Admission is $8 per person.

EUE/Screen Gems Studio Tour. 1223 North 23rd St.; (910) 343-3500; www.screen gemsstudios.com. A tour of this 50-acre lot takes about an hour and visits the set of the CW show *One Tree Hill*. Also included on the tour are bits of history from the more than 350 productions that have come from here. Tours are offered Sat at noon and 2 p.m. and on Sun at noon and 2 p.m. May to Sept. Tickets are $12 for adults and $5 for children five to twelve.

Ghost Walk of Old Wilmington. For location and reservations (required) call (910) 794-1866 or visit www.hauntedwilmington.com. Explore Wilmington's haunted alleyways and cemeteries. Under the shadows of moss-draped live oaks, discover acts of murder, mayhem, and betrayal. Offered Apr 1 through Oct 31, 6:30 and 8:30 p.m. nightly; Nov and Mar, nightly at 6:30 p.m.; and Dec through Feb, Thurs through Sat at 6:30 p.m. Admission is $12 for adults, $10 for seniors and children, under seven free.

Historic Downtown Wilmington. Protected as North Carolina's largest historic district, within these 230 blocks are beautiful homes dating from the late 1700s that are open for touring, and more than 200 specialty shops. In the core downtown are twenty-nine restaurants within five blocks, plus twenty-six inns and bed-and-breakfasts. **Wilmington Adventure Walking Tours** at the foot of Market and Water streets, (910) 763-1785, offers tours at 10 a.m. daily. **Springbrook Farms Inc.** is at Water and Market streets, (910) 251-8889; www.horsedrawntours.com. Owners John and Janet Pucci offer six separate carriage and horse-drawn-trolley tours through historic downtown Wilmington. Costumed drivers narrate the journey through past and present downtown. It's a great way to get acquainted with the rich history of this port city. Adults, $12; children under twelve, $5. Carriage tours are offered year-round, but call ahead for schedules in Jan and Feb.

Airlie Gardens. 300 Airlie Rd.; (910) 798-7700; www.airliegardens.org. Designed in the early 1900s, Airlie Gardens encompasses sixty-seven acres of post-Victorian European-style gardens, with ten acres of freshwater lakes. Offered is a 1-mile walking tour amid 100,000 azaleas, camellias, statuary, a butterfly garden, and the historic Airlie Oak that is believed to be nearly 500 years old. Also significant is the Minnie Evans Sculpture Garden that includes the Bottle Chapel, metal sculptures, mosaics, and ceramic sculptures. Open Tues through Sun 9 a.m. to 5 p.m. Admission is $5 for adults, $3 for ages six to twelve.

Bellamy Mansion. 503 Market St.; (910) 251-3700; www.bellamymansion museum.org. Built as the city residence of prominent planter and doctor John D. Bellamy, this home is one of the state's most spectacular examples of antebellum architecture. Wrapped by stalwart Corinthian columns, the restored twenty-two-room home features white marble mantels, ornate cornice moldings, and elaborate brass chandeliers. Open Tues through Sat 10 a.m. to 5 p.m., Sun 1 to 5 p.m. Admission is $10 for adults, $4 for children ages five to twelve.

Burgwin-Wright House. 224 Market St.; (910) 762-0570; www.burginwright house.com. Using an old jail as its foundation, the Burgwin-Wright House was built in 1770 by John Burgwin, planter, merchant, and treasurer of the colony of Carolina. In 1781 Lord Cornwallis occupied "the most considerable house in town" shortly before his defeat and surrender at Yorktown, Virginia. Purchased by Joshua Grainger Wright in 1799 for 3,500 Spanish milled dollars, the home was occupied as a residence until 1937, when the National Society of the Colonial Dames of America bought it. Beautifully restored, the Burgwin-Wright House is the oldest museum house in southeastern North Carolina. See fine details of Georgian-style architecture. A formal or parterre garden, a terraced garden, and an orchard grace the house. Open Tues through Sat 10 a.m. to 4 p.m. Guided tours are available. Admission is $10 for adults and $5 for children.

Latimer House. 126 South Third St.; (910) 762-0492; www.hslcf.org. Prosperous local businessman Zebulon Latimer chose the popular Victorian Italianate–style for his new home in 1852. Designed to be symmetrical, the fourteen-room home displays more than 600 historical objects, including furniture, jewelry, ephemera, tableware, tools, and more. Open Mon through Fri 10 a.m. to 4 p.m., Sat and Sun noon to 5 p.m. Admission is $10 for adults and $5 for children.

Thalian Hall. 102 North Third and 310 Chestnut St.; (800) 523-2820; www .thalianhall.org. Built in 1855 for combined government and theater use and restored in 1909, this classic 19th-century opera house hosted such famous performers as Buffalo Bill Cody, Lillian Russell, John Philip Sousa, and Oscar Wilde. Today, Thalian Hall hosts a variety of performing arts. Call for event listings.

Henrietta III **Riverboat.** Board at Dock and Water Streets; (800) 676-0162; www.cfrboats .com. Captain Carl Marshburn narrates the history of the Cape Fear River as North Carolina's largest riverboat makes its way downstream and back. Narrated sightseeing tours, some with lunch, are offered several times daily from Apr through Oct. Dinner cruises are offered through Dec and range from $30 to $49. The sightseeing tour with lunch costs $25, without lunch $15 for adults and $5 for children age two to twelve.

Jungle Rapids Family Fun Park. 5320 Oleander Dr.; (910) 791-0666; www.junglerapids .com. Cool off in the one million-gallon wave pool or lazy river. This waterpark and entertainment facility features water slides, go-kart tracks, jungle golf, laser tag, more than one hundred arcade games, kids' indoor playground, cafe, and pizzeria. Open year-round; waterpark open seasonally. Admission for adults: $29.99, children under 48 inches: $19.99.

Louise Wells Cameron Art Museum. 3201 South Seventeenth St.; (910) 395-5999; www.cameronartmuseum.com. Formerly St. John's Museum, the new 42,000-square-foot museum highlights two centuries of such North Carolina artists as Minnie Evans, Claude Howell, Mary Cassatt, Jugtown potters, and more. Its permanent exhibits are displayed on a rotating basis. Open Tues through Fri 11 a.m. to 2 p.m. and 11 a.m. to 5 p.m. Sat and Sun. Admission is $8 for adults, $5 for children ages five to eighteen, and free for children under age five.

Poplar Grove Plantation. 10200 US 17 North; (910) 686-9518; www.poplargrove.com. Poplar Grove was the homestead of a successful farming family. The home, outbuildings, and crafts are typical of an 1800s-era working community. The 628-acre plantation produced peas, corn, and beans and held some sixty-four slaves. Open Mon through Sat 9 a.m. to 5 p.m., Sun noon to 5 p.m. Closed Easter Sunday, Thanksgiving Day, and Christmas week through Jan. Admission, which includes home tour, is $10 for adults, $9 for seniors, and $5 for ages six to fifteen.

River Taxi. (800) 676-0162; www.cfrboats.com. Travels between the foot of Market Street and the battleship *North Carolina* during June, July, and Aug. The taxi can be boarded at either Market Street or the battleship. Roundtrip tickets are $4 per person.

Tregembo Animal Park. 5811 Carolina Beach Rd.; (910) 392-3604. This attraction was first opened in 1952 by the Tregembo family. They sold it but bought it back in 2005. The zoo provides a shady respite from the heat on the beach. Visitors can stroll down shady walkways to see African animals, including lions, tigers, and even a giraffe. In all, visitors can see seventy-five species of animals throughout the park. Additions to a three-acre area promise a new alligator pond and even more animals. The zoo is open daily 10 a.m. to 5 p.m. and is closed Dec through Feb. Admission is $10 for adults, $6 for seniors and children ages two to eleven.

Wilmington Railroad Museum. 501 Nutt St.; (910) 763-2634; www.wrrm.org. Displays include artifacts and memorabilia from the Wilmington & Weldon Railroad, which ran on 161 miles of track, making it the longest rail line in the world in 1840. For more than a century, railroading was Wilmington's chief industry. Explore extensive displays of model trains,

azalea festival

Wilmington's North Carolina Azalea Festival, (910) 794-4650; www.ncazalea festival.org, is more than a scheme to pay homage to one of the state's most prolific plants; it is one of the state's biggest and best celebrations. Twice listed as a top-twenty event by the Southeast Tourism Society, the coastal city has held the festival since 1958, and now it attracts more than 300,000 people. Appropriately, it's held in early April over several days and features big-time pop and country music stars. Past performers have included the Goo Goo Dolls, Hootie and the Blowfish, Michael McDonald, Montgomery Gentry, Travis Tritt, and Sara Evans. Future years promise big names too.

Travelers in the Wilmington area during the festival really can't escape it, not that they would want to. There are activities for practically every taste and interest, beginning with the arrival and coronation of the Azalea Queen at the opening on Wed. A full-fledged circus has come to town in recent years. Area churches offer gospel concerts. A coin show, a horse show, an air show, and even a comedy show make for one of the most eclectic festivals in the state.

Don't forget that this is an opportunity for Wilmington to highlight its gardens and the azalea. Airlie Gardens, Greenfield Lake Gardens, Orton Plantation Gardens, and as many as eight others associated with historic sites and public buildings are included in the events. Discount tickets good for the entire festival are offered for all gardens on the tour. "Azalea Belles" from the Cape Fear Garden Club are dressed in colorful antebellum hoop skirts and act as hostesses on the guided tours. Speakers and plant sales complete the event.

photographs, and artifacts, ranging from a 150-ton locomotive to a conductor's four-ounce timepiece. A steam locomotive (be sure to clang the working bell) and caboose may be boarded, and there's a hands-on children's corner. Open Mon through Sat 10 a.m. to 5 p.m. and Sun 1 to 5 p.m. Mar 15 through Oct 14; Mon through Sat 10 a.m. to 4 p.m. Oct 15 through Mar 14. Adults, $8; seniors/military, $7; children ages two to twelve, $4.

Wilmington Trolley Company. Duck and Water Streets; (910) 763-4483; www.wilming tontrolley.com. This 8-mile narrated sightseeing tour lasts forty-five minutes. Tours are conducted 10 a.m. to 5 p.m. daily from Apr through Oct and cost $11 for adults and $5 for children.

where to shop

Historic Downtown Wilmington. You'll find several shopping areas all within walking distance of one another: Wilmington City Market, Jacobi Warehouse, and the Coast Line Center, as well as Chandler's Wharf, an original ship's chandler that provided supplies for seagoing vessels, and the Cotton Exchange, once home to the largest cotton exporting company in the world, comprising eight buildings that date from the 19th century.

Lumina Station. 1900 Eastwood Rd.; (910) 256-0900; www.luminastation.com. For several decades near the turn of the 20th century, Lumina was the social center of this region. People came to dance to the sounds of such greats as Cab Calloway, Benny Goodman, Guy Lombardo, and "Satchmo." Today's Lumina Station remains true to the original landmark's style and spirit. Fine dining and shopping are to be found in the twenty-seven shops.

where to eat

Circa 1922. 8 North Front St.; (910) 762-1922. Located in the waterfront district, Circa 1922 offers a wide selection of tapas as well as great wine selections. $$–$$$.

Eddie Romanelli's. 5400 Oleander Dr.; (910) 799-7000. Voted best restaurant by *Encore* magazine, Eddie Romanelli's serves regional dishes with an Italian flair. Try the crab dip for starters, and follow it with a homemade 12-inch pizza. Open daily. $$–$$$.

Elijah's Restaurant. 2 Ann St.; (910) 343-1448; www.elijahs.com. Located on the picturesque Cape Fear River where the big ships run, Elijah's offers a great selection of fish and steaks. Open for lunch and dinner. The main dining room closes from 3 to 5 p.m., but the oyster bar is open all day. $$–$$$.

Paddy's Hollow Restaurant & Pub. 10 Walnut St.; (910) 762-4354. Located in the lower level of the Cotton Exchange, Paddy's Hollow has a great casual atmosphere. Paddy's does burgers as well as they do steaks. $$–$$$.

The Pilot House. 2 Water St.; (910) 343-0200. Providing Southern cuisine overlooking the Cape Fear River, the Pilot House offers indoor and outdoor dining in a quaint 1865 home moved here during the 1970s. River views can be enjoyed from the covered "uptown porch." Entrees include pasta, beef, lamb, pork, and seafood. Open daily for lunch and dinner. $$–$$$.

where to stay

Graystone Inn. 100 South Third St.; (910) 763-2000; www.graystoneinn.com. Luxurious rooms await you in this AAA four-diamond property. Originally "The Bridgers Mansion," the Graystone Inn was built in 1905–06 by Elizabeth Haywood Bridgers, widow of Preston L. Bridgers, a local merchant and son of Robert Rufus Bridgers, who was past president of the Atlantic Coast Line Railway, founder of the Wilmington & Weldon Railroad, and two-time representative to the Confederate Congress. A historic landmark and one of the most elegant structures in Wilmington, the inn has been completely remodeled and returned to its original "turn of the century grandeur." The Graystone Inn was chosen by American Historic Inns Inc. as one of the "Top 10 Most Romantic Inns in the U.S." $$$.

Stemmerman's Inn. 130 South Front St.; (910) 763-7776; www.stemmermans.com. Located downtown, Stemmerman's has a Victorian storefront style. Inside remodeled suites and rooms are contemporary with exposed bricks and beams. $–$$.

The Verandas. 202 Nun St.; (910) 251-2212; www.verandas.com. This elegant, 8,500-square-foot Victorian Italianate mansion in the historic district is only two blocks from the Cape Fear River and the Riverwalk. Originally built in 1853 by Benjamin Beery, the structure suffered extensive fire and water damage in 1992. Boarded up and decaying, the mansion was restored to provide a comfortable weekend retreat for tourists. All eight guest rooms are large corner rooms. Guests may choose from a selection of king, queen, or twin beds. Luxurious private baths have marble floors and oversize oval tubs. $$$.

Wilmington Hilton. 301 North Water St.; (800) 445-8667; www.wilmingtonhilton.com. Located on the downtown waterfront, the Hilton has 274 guest rooms, with half overlooking the river. The Hilton's Poolside and Cabana Bar, adorned with ceiling fans and palm trees, is a great place for a sunset cocktail, and on Friday evenings in the summer, the pool deck is the scene of the Sunset Celebration, a popular live-music party. $$$.

The Wilmingtonian. 101 South Second St.; (910) 343-1800 or (800) 525-0909; www .thewilmingtonian.com. Located in historic downtown Wilmington, surrounded by beautifully restored 19th-century homes and tree-lined neighborhoods, the meticulously renovated Wilmingtonian offers forty luxury suites. It provides the privacy of an intimate inn but has diverse services and accommodations. Extensive gardens and ponds with courtyards and balconies surround the buildings, dating from 1841 to 1994. The famed de Rosset House, built in 1841, provides sweeping views of the Cape Fear River. Its six luxurious suites are historically decorated yet equipped with modern conveniences, such as gas log fireplaces, large whirlpool tubs, and separate showers. The signature suite, the Cupola, offers views of the city and breathtaking sunsets. Amenities for all suites include kitchen or wet bar, refrigerator, coffeemaker, microwave, toaster, and DVD player. $$$.

wrightsville beach

Settled in 1889 and incorporated in 1899, the summer resort of Wrightsville Beach is a small island community that still retains its village charm. A variety of accommodations and restaurants can be found at Wrightsville. Downtown Wilmington is only a fifteen-minute drive.

where to go

Johnnie Mercers Pier. 23 East Salisbury St.; (910) 256-2743. With access at the town's main beach access, Johnnie Mercer's pier is the center of all the action in Wrightsville Beach and it has been since the 1930s. The only exception was about five years after the original pier was destroyed by a double punch in 1996 by hurricanes Fran and Bertha. The old wood pier was rebuilt—this time in concrete—and reopened in 2001. In addition to fishing, and fishing supplies you can grab lunch, ice cream, or play in the game room.

Wrightsville Beach Museum of History. 303 West Salisbury St. (910) 256-2569; www .wbmuseum.org. The beach cottage museum houses various exhibits on Wrightsville Beach history, and depicts the lifestyle at Wrightsville Beach ca. 1900. One of the oldest cottages on the island, the house was built by the Tidewater Power Company in 1907 as part of a plan to encourage residential development. Open Tues through Fri 10 a.m. to 4 p.m., Sat noon to 5 p.m., and Sun 1 to 5 p.m. Admission free.

where to eat

Bluewater, an American Grill. 4 Marina St.; (910) 256-8500. Overlooking the Intercoastal Waterway, the two-story Bluewater provides panoramas and great food. Try the hot crab dip for an appetizer. For entrees, the coconut shrimp plate and the seafood lasagna, or my favorite, the lump crab cakes are excellent choices. Sit indoors, on a waterside patio downstairs, or on an intimate covered terrace upstairs. The restaurant offers live entertainment on Sunday afternoons during the summer. Open daily for lunch and dinner year-round. $$.

The Bridge Tender. 1414 Airlie Rd.; (910) 256-4519. Overlooking the Intercoastal Waterway, the Bridge Tender has enjoyed a reputation for its prime rib and seafood since opening in 1976. Open Mon through Fri 11:30 a.m. to 2 p.m. for lunch, nightly for dinner from 5 p.m. $$–$$$.

The Oceanic. 703 South Lumina Ave.; (910) 256-5551. This oceanfront restaurant offers indoor and outdoor seating. Go for a basket of fresh fish and chips on the old Crystal pier that serves as the patio, but make sure you begin with the hot crab dip for two, a favorite among the regulars. The appetizer is made from local crabmeat broiled with fresh cream, cheese, a secret blend of seasonings, and garlic bread for dipping. Entrees include seafood, chicken, and beef dishes. Leave room for the key lime pie. $$–$$$.

Vito's Pizzeria. 8 North Lumina Ave.; (910) 256-5858. Vito's is a refreshing change of pace should you overdose on seafood during your visit. The specialties are pizza, pasta, and subs. Open daily for dinner and for lunch during the summer. $–$$.

where to stay

Blockade Runner Beach Resort. 275 Waynick Blvd.; (800) 541-1161; http://blockade-runner.com. Built in the 1970s, this 150-room beachfront property has been thoroughly renovated over the years. Beautifully landscaped with tropical plants, the hotel's grass lawn and gardens serve as a buffer between the beach and the hotel. Truly a paradise for young and old, kids' programs are offered during summer months. $$–$$$.

Holiday Inn Resort Wrightsville Beach. 1706 North Lumina Ave.; (877) 330-5050; www.wrightsville.sunspreeresorts.com. This beachfront hotel offers such resort amenities as indoor and outdoor pools, two oceanfront whirlpools, a poolside bar and grill, and guest rooms that face either the ocean or the marsh. On-site Kidspree Vacation Club is a complimentary supervised children's program and activity room, and there's a beach playground for kids. $$$.

carolina beach

The site of an engagement between Union and Confederate forces following the fall of Fort Fisher on January 15, 1865, this community was once known as Sugar Loaf.

Carolina Beach was incorporated in 1925 and became known throughout the state for its boardwalk. The boardwalk fell into demise over the years, but Carolina Beach has slowly recovered. Storefronts that were boarded up a little more than a decade ago, have reopened as colorful new restaurants, ice cream parlors, and retail establishments. Hotels are being renovated and the boardwalk is once again the center of life on this spot of land known as Pleasure Island. Carolina Beach State Park is home to a variety of natural areas that make it one of the most biologically diverse parks in North Carolina. This area is part of a small region of the world where the Venus flytrap grows naturally.

where to go

Carolina Beach State Park. 1010 State Park Rd.; (910) 458-8206; www.ncparks.gov. This state park offers fishing, camping, and miles of hiking trails that traverse a variety of distinct habitats, including the Venus flytrap trail, a half-mile loop through pocosin, longleaf pine and turkey oak, and savanna communities. Learn more about the Venus flytrap and other indigenous species at the park's visitor center 9 a.m. to 5 p.m. The park and visitors center are open daily.

Kayak Carolina. 103 Winner Ave.; (910) 458-9111; www.kayakcarolina.com. Join Angela and John Pagenstecher for a two-hour guided eco-tour of the coastal marshlands on extremely stable and comfortable touring kayaks, great for the uninitiated, plus day trips and skill-building for experienced kayakers. Kids Kayak Camp is offered during the summer. Rates for four-hour tours: $35 for adults, $17.50 for children eleven and under.

where to eat

Havana's Fresh Island Seafood. 1 North Lake Park Blvd.; (910) 458-2822. The pretty Caribbean-inspired decor matches the well-done Caribbean-inspired dishes. $$–$$$.

The Ocean Grill. 1211 South Lake Park Blvd.; (910) 458-2000. Burgers and sandwiches at lunch give way to steaks and seafood for dinner, which is as enjoyable in the dining room as it is on the oceanfront patio. Enjoy shrimp and grits, cornmeal pancakes, or a breakfast burrito during Sun brunch. Stick around Thurs through Sun evenings for live music at the Tiki Bar located on the old town pier beyond the patio. Winter hours are limited. $$.

kure beach

Named for the Kure family, who first came here in 1867, Kure Beach today is a small, family-oriented beach located at the southern extreme of US 421 but still on Pleasure Island. Kure Beach features large, uncrowded beaches, good seafood, and historic Fort Fisher, where you can tour the museum or take a hike around the Civil War earthworks.

Less than 2 miles away is the North Carolina Aquarium, where you can view live marine life and participate in special aquatic programs. In thirty minutes you can be in downtown Wilmington or take the ferry to Southport. (See Southeast Day Trip 02.)

where to go

Fort Fisher State Historic Site. 1610 Fort Fisher Blvd.; (910) 458-5538; www.fortfisher .nchistoricsites.org. Billed as "the last major stronghold of the Confederacy," the historic site includes interpretive exhibits and audiovisual presentations depicting two major battles fought here. Union forces overran the earthen fort and, in subsequent days, Wilmington. Today the site includes a gun battery with examples of cannons used in the Civil War, and a trail with markers and monuments. A museum traces the fort's history, the life of the soldiers who called it home, and technology used in interactive and audiovisual displays. Open Apr through Sept, Mon through Sat 9 a.m. to 5 p.m., Sun 1 to 5 p.m.; Nov through Mar, Tues through Sat 10 a.m. to 4 p.m. Free.

North Carolina Aquarium at Fort Fisher. 900 Loggerhead Rd.; (910) 458-8257; www
.ncaquariums.com. Here day-trippers get more than a glimpse of the waters of the Cape
Fear. Six galleries lead guests from nearby swamps to the ocean. The aquarium, one of
three in the state, features a centerpiece of a 200,000-gallon ocean aquarium that includes
a two-story multilevel viewing of large sharks, groupers, barracudas, and loggerhead turtles
swimming around re-created Cape Fear rock ledges. A touch pool, a variety of live demon-
strations by staff, and other programs provide a day full of fun. Open daily 9 a.m. to 5 p.m.
except for Thanksgiving, Christmas, and New Year's Day. Admission is $8 for adults, $7 for
seniors and active military, and $6 for children ages six to seventeen.

day trip 02

southeast

>>> **island hopping:**
southport, bald head island

Follow I-40 east from Raleigh for the 158-mile drive to Southport. Yes, it will take you a bit more than two hours to make the trip, even pushing along at 70 miles per hour on I-40, but the end of the line (in Wilmington, pick up US 17 south and follow it to either SR 87 or SR 133 south) is in one of the most charming seaside villages in the state.

Situated amid graceful live oaks, Southport garnered praise from Rand McNally as one of the best places to retire. For visitors Southport oozes coastal charm and boasts a rich maritime history. While walking the historic downtown, listen for the "Seneca Drums," mysterious, low-pitched offshore booms that locals attribute to chunks of the continental shelf dropping off cliffs in the Atlantic Ocean. Truth is, no one knows what causes the low rumbles.

A short ferry trip from Southport takes you to Bald Head Island. Once a preferred destination of pirates such as Blackbeard and Stede Bonnet, the island is now a refuge for those who truly enjoy getting away from it all.

To preserve Bald Head Island's unspoiled beaches and maritime forests, gasoline engines are prohibited. Hop on a bike, slide into an electric golf cart, or shuffle your peds to explore this resort.

If you opt to travel SR 133 south from Wilmington, you may want to take time to visit Brunswick Town and Fort Anderson State Historic Site (910-371-6613). Brunswick Town, a colonial site dating from 1726 to 1776, served as a Cape Fear river port that was the major export of naval stores and the location of the Stamp Act Rebellion. Fort Anderson,

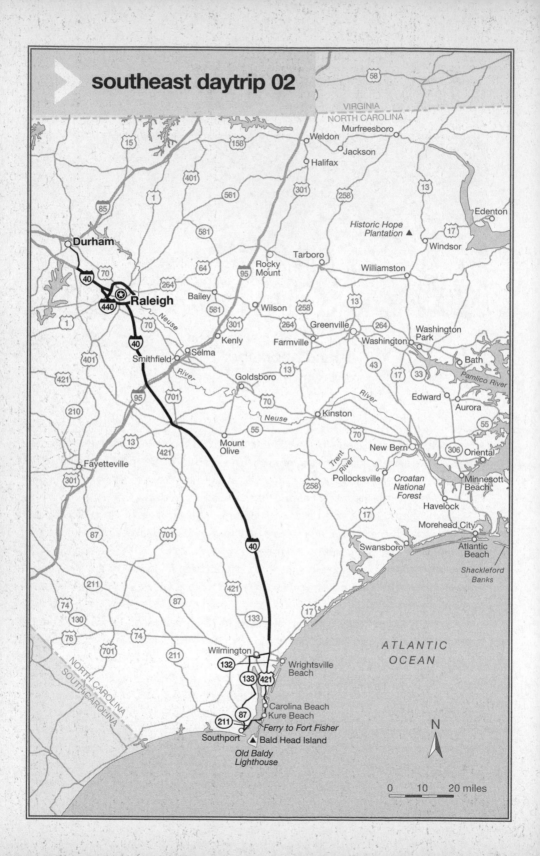

southeast daytrip 02

a Confederate fortification, was part of the Cape Fear defense system until the Civil War engagement of February 1865. Admission is free.

On your return trip, consider traveling by ferry from Southport to Fort Fisher, then driving to Wilmington. (See Southeast Day Trip 01.)

southport

Founded in 1792 as the town of Smithville, after North Carolina's colonial governor Benjamin Smith, Southport became the town's adopted name in 1887, when town fathers sought to attract a state port to the region. Although the port was later located up the Cape Fear River in Wilmington, the river still plays a major part in Southport's economy. Much as they did some 200 years ago, river pilots still race to meet transoceanic vessels and skillfully guide them up river. These large vessels tower over Southport's waterfront as they pass within 100 feet of Waterfront Park.

Southport is located at the mouth of the Cape Fear River, the Intracoastal Waterway, and the Atlantic Ocean. Filmmakers have used Southport as the backdrop for the films *Summer Catch* and *I Know What You Did Last Summer,* and for the TV series *Dawson's Creek.*

The town's protected harbor makes for popular water activities, such as boating, sailing, and fishing. The town was built in a live oak forest; the wide-crowned evergreen trees were cultivated as shade trees here and in other coastal regions of the southern United States. If you've ever been to Charleston, South Carolina, you have seen the live oak, but Southport's live oaks differ from their cousins in Charleston, where the branches are often covered with Spanish moss. In Southport the branches are covered with resurrection ferns, remarkable plants with fronds that curl up and appear dead in prolonged dry weather. They unfurl and spring back to life in wet weather.

Southport's old homes sit among the huge, sprawling oak trees that reach out over winding streets and sidewalks. Self-guided or guided tours of the town are the best ways to appreciate the character of this charming community. Don't miss the North Carolina Maritime Museum at Southport, with exhibits detailing the vast nautical history of the area.

where to go

Southport Visitor Center. 113 West Moore St.; (910) 457-7927; www.cityofsouthport .com. Begin the mile-long self-guided walking tour here. Devised by the Southport Historical Society, this relaxed walk takes you through charming Historic Southport. Pick up a free pamphlet with tour highlights numbered and explained. Grab a copy of *The Pelican Post,* a handy reference for the town. Your first stop, the Indian Trail Tree, is adjacent to the center. Cape Fear Indians bent the live oak sapling to point the way to tribal fishing grounds. That was 800 years ago. Today in the spring and the fall, you can see clusters of fishing boats on a line on either side of the tree. The Indian Trail Tree still points the way to the best spot to hook dinner. Open Mon through Sat 10 a.m. to 4 p.m.

Southport–Oak Island Area Chamber of Commerce Welcome Center. 4841 Long Beach Rd. Southeast; (800) 457-6964; www.southport-oakisland.com. Stop here for information on Oak Island, Bald Head Island, or Southport. Open Mon through Fri 8:30 a.m. to 5 p.m.

Adkins-Ruark House. 119 North Lord St. Built in 1890, the Adkins-Ruark House is where Robert Ruark spent many of his childhood summers in his grandfather's home. His book *The Old Man and the Boy* is an account of his boyhood years in Southport and is recommended reading for those making the trip here. The house is not open to the public.

Bald Head Island Ferry, Deep Point Marina. 1301 Ferry Rd.; (910) 457-5003. The ferry departs Southport for Bald Head Island daily every hour on the hour from 8 a.m. until 6 p.m. except at noon. The ferry returns on the half hour. Days and times vary by season; please call for information. The cost is $16 per person round-trip, $8 for children twelve and under. A guided historic tour of Bald Head Island, which includes a stop at the Smith Island Museum, lighthouse, and lunch, is $46 for adults and $41 for children twelve and under.

Franklin Square Art Gallery. 130 East West St.; (910) 457-5450; www.franklinsquare gallery.org. This association of local artisans showcases works in varying media, including painting and pottery, all displayed in a beautiful historic building. Open Mon through Sat 10 a.m. to 5 p.m. and during June, July, and Aug, Sun 1 to 4 p.m. Free.

North Carolina Maritime Museum at Southport. 116 North Howe St.; (910) 457-0003; www.ncmaritime.org. This collection of memorabilia illustrates the vast nautical history of Southport, the Lower Cape Fear, and southeastern North Carolina. The museum's twelve-station self-guided tour begins with a 2,000-year-old fragment of a canoe used by the Cape Fear Indians. In addition to an on-site research library, films and programs are offered year-round. Admission is free. Open Tues through Sat 9 a.m. to 5 p.m.

Progress Energy Visitors Center. 8520 River Rd.; (910) 457-6041. Hands-on and visual presentations of more than thirty energy-related exhibits cover the production of electricity, electrical safety, alternative energy sources, and energy conservation. Hours vary. Free.

where to eat

Dry Street Pub and Pizza. 101 East Brown St.; (910) 457-5994. Locals say this is the town's best-kept secret for lunch. Located in an old cottage just beneath the water tower, this cozy restaurant offers a range of freshly made sandwiches, salads, and pizza, with indoor and outdoor dining. Favorites include the cheddar bacon ale soup, the baked potato salad, and the chef salad with homemade chunky blue cheese vinaigrette dressing. $$.

Fishy, Fishy Café. 106 Yacht Basin Dr.; (910) 457-1881. The deck, the dining room, or the raw bar—you decide where to dine. Regardless of the selection, diners get a great view. The fun decor is reminiscent of Key West and the food goes a little farther. Not only can you enjoy fresh local catches or the taste of Key West, you can also get Maryland crab cakes and steaks. $$–$$$.

Mr. P's Bistro. 309 North Howe St.; (910) 457-0801. Mr. P's house specialty is Oysters Bienville. Chef Stephen Phipps adds a few touches of his own to this classic New Orleans recipe topping fresh oysters with a white sauce made from chopped shrimp, mushrooms, and sherry. He then sprinkles grated asiago cheese over the dish and bakes it until the cheese melts. $$$.

The Pharmacy Restaurant. 110 East Moore St.; (910) 457-5577. The house specialty, crab cakes, combines three all–lump-meat crab cakes seasoned with capers, white pepper, salt, and green onion. The crab cakes, each wrapped in phyllo dough, are served on a bed of baby greens. Chive oil, reduced balsamic vinegar, and a mustard dressing are drizzled on the plate to create bright green, dark brown, and gold streams of color. Little touches like these are what make dining at the Pharmacy so special, says owner Kelli Menna, noting that herbs are organically grown and hand-picked by the chef. Desserts are made each morning on the premises. Open daily 11 a.m. to 3 p.m. and Thurs through Sun 5 to 9 p.m. Reservations are required for dinner. $$$.

The Provision Company. 130 Yacht Basin Dr.; (910) 457-0654. If you enjoy sitting out by the water to have lunch, this is the place. The specialty is steamed shrimp. If you're really hungry, order the special, popular among the locals: crab cake, a half pound of shrimp, and cucumber salad. For lighter fare, you can get smaller portions of shrimp alone or the popular grouper salad. Also popular are the conch fritters, made with imported Bahamian conch. $$.

South Harbour Fish Market. 5001 O'Quinn Blvd.; (910) 454-7300. Located within the South Harbour Village Resort, the market offers family fare and waterfront dining. Calabash-style entrees and the sirloin burgers are a complement to the great coastal atmosphere on the waterway. $$.

where to stay

Brunswick Inn Bed and Breakfast. 301 East Bay St.; (910) 457-5278; www.brunswickinn.com. Those seeking a romantic getaway might knock on the door of the Brunswick Inn. The 7,000-square-foot, sixteen-room federal-style mansion overlooks the Cape Fear. Accommodations include spacious bedrooms with fireplaces and views of the waterway. $$$.

Lois Jane's Riverview Inn. 106 West Bay St.; (910) 457-6701; www.loisjanes.com. The rocking chair front porch of this turn-of-the-20th-century home affords views of the Cape Fear River. Inside, cozy rooms are appointed with period furniture. A full Southern-style breakfast is served at 8:30 a.m. and a wine and cheese reception is offered at 5 p.m. $$$.

Robert Ruark Inn. 119 North Lord St.; (910) 363-4169; www.robertruarkinn.com. Named for the mid-century newspaperman and best-selling author who lived in Southport as a boy, this inn is reflective of the Hemingway-like lifestyle Ruark lived. Four handsome, well-appointed rooms make up this extravagant inn. Breakfast is served daily from 8 to 10 a.m. in the Victorian dining room. $$$.

bald head island

With more than 10,000 of the island's 12,000 acres preserved and protected from development, Bald Head Island has 14 miles of pristine beaches. A meandering creek cuts through acres of salt marsh that border an expanse of maritime forest.

A world-class resort, Bald Head Island offers the vacationer a championship golf course, clubhouse facilities, croquet, a marina, tennis courts, swimming pools, restaurants, snack bars, a full-service grocery store, and hours of peaceful relaxation.

where to go

Bald Head Island Historic Tours. (910) 457-5003. Guided tours of the island include a visit to Smith Island Museum of History. Tour packages may include lunch or dinner, parking, and ferry tickets. Reservations are required. Off-island fare from Southport includes round-trip ferry passage and lunch: adults, $46; children twelve and under, $41. Tours depart at 10:30 a.m. Tues through Sat.

Old Baldy Lighthouse and Smith Island Museum. (910) 457-7481; www.oldbaldy.org. North Carolina's lighthouses are one of our state's greatest treasures. The oldest still standing is "Old Baldy," built in 1818. Retired in 1935 and recently renovated, visitors can now climb her steps to the top. The history of the lighthouse and area is told through exhibits at the small museum. Old Baldy is open to the public Tues through Sat 10 a.m. to 4 p.m., Sun 11 a.m. to 4 p.m.; closed Mon. Admission is $5 for adults and $3 for children ages three to twelve.

Shoals Club. (910) 457-7334. The Shoals Club on Bald Head Island will remind you of old-time beach pavilions. It serves as a place for families and friends to gather just off the beach, out of the hot, summer sun. The Shoals Club, with its oceanfront clubhouse, dining areas, lounge, fitness room, locker-room facilities, swimming pools, and direct beach access, is the perfect complement to the Bald Head Island Club. Many of the island's organized activities originate from here.

where to eat

Bald Head Island Club. (910) 457-7300. A private club for members and accompanied guests or for temporary members staying on the island. Open for lunch (lounge only) and dinner, except on Mon and Tues. Offers a prix fixe menu and dinner buffets during the summer months and holidays. $$$.

Eb & Flo's. (910) 457-7217. This open-air waterfront pavilion specializes in steam pots filled with crab legs, clams, mussels, shrimp, potatoes, and corn. This casual harborside restaurant provides an excellent vantage point for watching boats entering the marina. Open Thurs through Sun 11:30 a.m. to 10 p.m. $$.

The Pelicatessen. (910) 457-0266. Located near the Bald Head Island Club pool, the "Peli Deli," as you might call it after a few days here, offers deli-style sandwiches, hot dogs, a variety of snacks, and drinks. A phone on the ninth hole allows golfers to call in an order. Open seasonally. $$.

River Pilot Cafe. (910) 457-7390. Located in the harbor, River Pilot Cafe specializes in Southern cuisine, with the dinner menu offering appetizers such as crabmeat and artichoke dip, and entrees like island seafood Creole pasta or fresh catch grilled daily. Open daily for breakfast and lunch; Mon through Sat for dinner. The early-bird special offers 20 percent off dinner from 5:30 to 6:15 p.m. $$$.

where to stay

Bald Head Island Vacation Rentals. (800) 432-RENT; www.baldheadisland.com. Vacation rentals range from small forest cottages to large oceanfront homes. Included with the rental is temporary membership in the Bald Head Island Club, allowing access to its celebrated golf course, croquet greens, tennis courts, pool, dining room, and lounge. Also included are round-trip ferry passage and one or more electric carts. $$$.

Marsh Harbour Inn. (800) 680-8322; www.marshharbourinn.com. Located in Harbour Village, this New England–style inn's Cape Cod rockers, Shaker beds, and antique wood floors lend each room a simple appeal. All rooms offer television, DVD player, telephone, and private bath. Many of the inn's fifteen rooms have private decks overlooking Bald Head Creek or the Cape Fear River. Included with your stay: breakfast at the nearby River Pilot Cafe, afternoon hors d'oeuvres, use of an electric golf cart, and temporary membership in the Bald Head Island Club. $$$.

Theodosia's Bed and Breakfast. (800) 656-1812; www.theodosias.com. This ten-room bed-and-breakfast provides rooms with a view and a full breakfast. Golf carts and bikes are complimentary with each room, as is temporary Bald Head Island Club membership. Afternoon hors d'oeuvres are included. $$$.

Tiffany's Beach Rentals. (910) 457-0544; www.tiffanysrentals.com. Listings include a range of accommodations, from cottages to large homes. $$$.

south

day trip 01

south

>>> **out of the frying pan:**
benson, rose hill

A straight shot south on I-40 out of the Raleigh-Durham area takes travelers to the edge of the coastal plain, to the rural Piedmont town of Benson. Here, an active downtown with vibrant storefronts beckons. It's named for local entrepreneur Alfred Monroe Benson, who bought much of this land in 1874 and sold parcels to settlers who would develop farms. Benson is the site of one of the state's oldest agricultural celebrations—Mule Days. But the area's agricultural heritage of cotton and tobacco has given way to crops such as soy beans, sweet potatoes, corn, and even grapes. Traveling further south on I-40 will bring you to quaint, yet eclectic, Rose Hill.

benson

Located on fertile soil where the coastal plain meets the Piedmont, Benson is an expansive agricultural area. It's also located between the Neuse and Cape Fear river basins and is at the intersection of I-95 and I-40. The town's leaders have worked hard to preserve its agricultural heritage while diversifying its economic base.

where to go

Benson Mule Days. (919) 894-3825. More than 50,000 visitors invade this small town during the four Mule Days that include the fourth Saturday in September. It includes rodeos, a

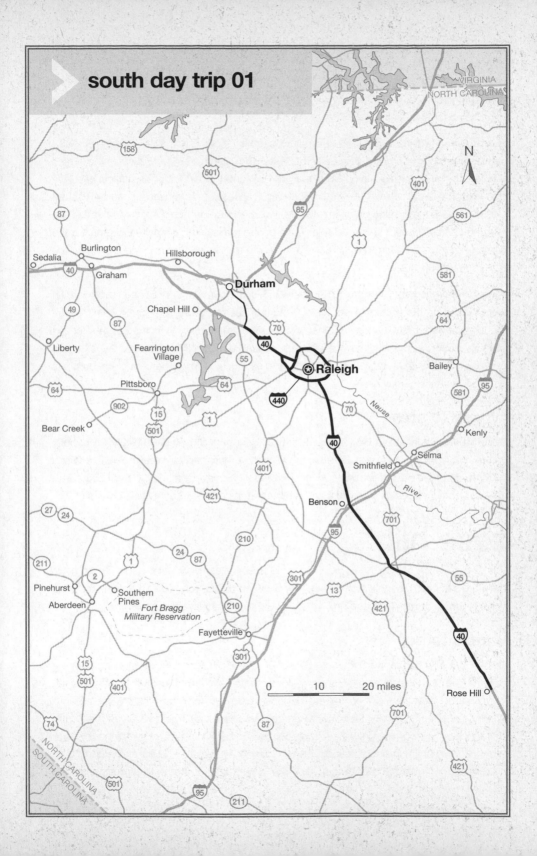

south day trip 01

mule pulling contest, parades, carnival rides, bluegrass shows, and more. Mule Days have been going on here since 1950.

Bentonville Battleground. 5466 Harper House Rd., Four Oaks; (919) 594-0789; www .nchistoricsites.org/bentonvi. The Battle of Bentonville, March 19–21, 1865, was the largest Civil War battle to take place on North Carolina soil and the last full-scale tactical offensive by the Confederate Army. The site is most easily accessible from Benson via I-40 south. Guests can walk the fields on which 80,000 Union and Confederate soldiers fought. Then tour the nearby Harper House, complete with period furnishings, a small museum, and the cemetery. Hours are Mon through Sat 9 a.m. to 5 p.m. Closed Sun and Mon, Oct through Mar. Admission is free.

Historic Downtown Benson. (919) 894-3553. Fifty-four acres in Benson's downtown were placed on the National Register of Historic Places in 1984. A leisurely walk through the town takes the day-tripper to Benson Museum of Local History, located at the Benson Municipal Building, formerly the local high school. Unlike many North Carolina towns there is no talk of downtown revitalization in Benson with as much as ninety percent of the buildings occupied on an ongoing basis.

where to stay

Preston Woodall House Bed & Breakfast. 201 East Hill St.; (919) 894-7025. A popular venue for weddings, this circa 1910 Queen Ann home has four rooms available in addition to three cottages on the property. All accommodations have remarkable furnishings with special attention to detail. Breakfast and afternoon teas are included. $$–$$$.

rose hill

With a population of less than 1,500, Rose Hill is about as quaint as it gets. The home of the state's largest winery, it's charming, too, with one unique roadside attraction. To get to Rose Hill from Benson just hop on I-40 and you'll be there within the hour.

where to go

Duplin Winery. 505 North Sycamore St.; (800) 774-9634; www.duplinwinery.com. In the early 1970s D.J. Fussell and his sons decided to start growing Muscadine grapes when they realized New York wineries were paying a premium for them. Today, their Duplin Winery has a tank capacity over one million gallons and is the largest winery in the South. Day-trippers can tour the vineyard and production facility, taste wine, have dinner here, or even take one of a number of periodic classes in wine appreciation. Store and winery hours are Mon through Wed and Sat 9 a.m. to 6 p.m. Thurs and Fri 9 a.m. to 9 p.m. Free tours are offered Mon through Sat, 9 a.m. to 4 p.m. Free tastings are offered Mon through Sat, 9 a.m. to 6 p.m.

World's Largest Frying Pan. 510 East Main St.; (910) 289-3159. It has to be a really special event when they pull out the World's Largest Frying Pan. Actually used for local fundraisers, the pan has become a symbol of the poultry industry that still thrives in the area today. At a weight of two tons and 15 feet in diameter, it can hold 365 chickens along with 200 gallons of cooking oil. At other times the pan is on display at the town square.

where to stay

The Duplin Inn. 506 North Norwood St., Wallace; (910) 285-4379. This inn located minutes from the winery is a small, charming facility located in the center of Wallace. Suites have full-sized kitchens. The inn is small with eleven rooms, but the spacious suites have full-sized kitchens. $.

Graham House Inn. 406 South Main St.; (800) 767-9397; www.grahamhouseinn.com. Located in the heart of historic Kenansville and built in 1855, this inn is listed on the National Register of Historic Places. Its four guest rooms provide a nice respite on the expansive wooded property. $.

day trip 02

south

>>> **a patriotic jaunt:**
fayetteville, fort bragg

With Fort Bragg and Pope Air Force Base nearby, Fayetteville has had to bear the brunt of being called a military town full of mind-numbing neon, tattoo parlors, and pawnshops. True, you may have to look beyond some of the less attractive development that goes hand in hand with the transient trainees arriving each week at one of the nation's largest military installations. But when you do get past the crass commercialism, Fayetteville has much to offer the day-tripper.

The town contains four designated historic districts: the downtown Historic District, Haymount Historic District, Liberty Point National Register District, and Market House Square National Register District. And nearly worth the trip alone is the city's Airborne and Special Operations Museum, the only museum of its kind in the country.

Moreover, Fayetteville's military presence contributes to the city's cultural diversity. Restaurants serving ethnic cuisine, particularly Asian food, are more abundant here than in any other place in the state. It's not unusual to see signs, even city-maintained signs, with Asian script.

Of course, any day trip to Fayetteville should include a tour of Fort Bragg. Visitors may pass freely (albeit through security checkpoints) through the military installation. The Fort Bragg Welcome Center (910-396-5401) is at Randolph and Knox Streets.

A trip through the base will no doubt leave you with a true appreciation for the sacrifices made by our nation's military, and in that regard, Fayetteville and Fort Bragg present a patriotic day trip within an easy drive from Raleigh-Durham along I-40 south to I-95 south.

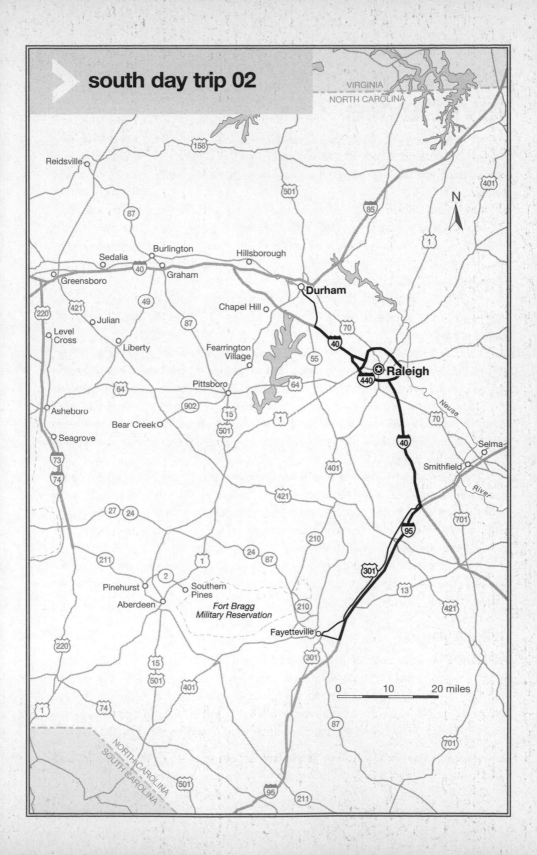

south day trip 02

fayetteville

Dozens of American cities and counties have been named after the Revolutionary War hero Marquis de Lafayette, but Fayetteville was the first and, reportedly, the only one he actually visited. The Frenchman arrived here by horse-drawn carriage in 1825 and was welcomed by the residents.

The original settlers of the Fayetteville area were from the Highlands of Scotland. They arrived in 1739 via the Cape Fear River and established two early settlements, Campbellton and Cross Creek. At Liberty Point, in the center of what would become downtown Fayetteville, patriots pledged local support for the Revolutionary War, while nearby, Scottish heroine Flora MacDonald rallied for the Loyalist cause.

After the Revolution, with no permanent state capital, the state's legislature periodically met here. It's not unusual to hear a Fayettevillian bitterly claim that Raleigh stole Fayetteville's capital status.

In 1783 Campbellton and Cross Creek merged and were named Fayetteville. In 1789 in a State House that the city built on aspirations of remaining the state capital, North Carolina representatives meeting in Fayetteville ratified the U.S. Constitution; they also chartered the University of North Carolina, America's oldest state university. The Great Fire of 1831 destroyed more than 600 buildings, including the State House, but Reconstruction resulted in many of the city's present-day landmark structures. Fayetteville's buildings are some of the oldest in the state.

The area grew as a center of government and commerce because of its location as an inland port and the hub of the early "plank roads" system, key to overland travel from the 1840s to 1850s. During the Civil War, the city found itself in the path of General Sherman's Union troops, who wreaked destruction and burned the North Carolina Arsenal, which had been a munitions center for the Confederacy.

An interesting tidbit about Fayetteville: At the old Cape Fear Fairgrounds, eighteen-year-old George Herman Ruth, the youngest player on the Baltimore Orioles, hit his first professional home run on March 7, 1914.

where to go

Fayetteville Area Convention and Visitors Bureau. 245 Person St.; (910) 483-5311 or (800) 255-8217; www.visitfayettevillenc.com. Stop here for maps and a visitor's guide Mon through Fri 8 a.m. to 5 p.m. In addition, the bureau operates an office within the Fayetteville Area Transportation and Local History Museum 10 a.m. to 4 p.m. Tues through Sat. Another satellite office is located in the customer service area of Cross Creek Mall.

Airborne and Special Operations Museum. 100 Bragg Blvd.; (910) 483-3003, (866) 547-0649; www.asomf.org. Part of the U.S. Army Museum System, this museum is the only one of its kind in the nation. It explores the sixty-year history of airborne and special operations units through dramatic, life-size, imaginative exhibits, a theater, and interactive displays such as a twenty-four-seat simulator that nearly replicates what troopers experience when parachuting or flying at treetop level over rough terrain. Located on six acres in downtown Fayetteville, the museum is open Tues through Sat (and on federal holiday Mondays) 10 a.m. to 5 p.m., Sun noon to 5 p.m. Free.

Arts Center. 301 Hay St.; (910) 323-1776; www.theartscouncil.com. Built in 1910 as a U.S. post office, the Arts Center houses the galleries and offices of the Arts Council of Fayetteville/Cumberland County. The galleries feature rotating art exhibits. Open Mon through Thurs 8:30 a.m. to 5 p.m., Fri 8:30 a.m. to noon, and Sat noon to 4 p.m.

Atlantic Coast Line Railroad Station. 472 Hay St.; (910) 483-2658. Built in 1911, the station is a rare example of Dutch Colonial architecture. The outside passenger and freight platform and shelter date to World War I. The depot serves as an Amtrak passenger station and houses the Atlantic Coast Line Depot Railroad Historical Center. Open alternating Saturdays.

Cape Fear Botanical Garden. 536 North Eastern Blvd.; (910) 486-0221; www.capefearbg.org. The eighty-five-acre garden, at the confluence of the Cape Fear and Cross Creek Rivers, contains an old farmhouse and heritage garden, perennial gardens, wildflowers, majestic oaks in an old-growth forest, nature trails, and numerous species of native plants. Among the 2,000 specimens of ornamental plants are 200 varieties of camellia that keep the garden beautiful year-round. Open Mon through Sat 10 a.m. to 5 p.m., Sun noon to 5 p.m. Adults $6; children six to twelve $1.

Cool Spring Tavern. 119 Cool Spring St.; (910) 433-1612. Built in 1788 and having survived the Great Fire of 1831, Cool Spring Tavern is the oldest structure in the city. The tavern housed the delegates who ratified the U.S. Constitution for North Carolina and was built in an attempt to entice them to base the state capital here. With federal-style architecture, it has double porches, a gabled roof, and brick chimneys. The interior is not open to the public.

Fayetteville Area Transportation and Local History Museum. 325 Franklin St.; (800) 255-8217. Located in the train station of the Cape Fear and Yadkin Valley Railroad Company, this museum details the development of the unique plank road system that made this area important throughout the state. From Native American trails to steamboats and trains, guests are invited to explore early trade communities and how they did business.

Fayetteville Independent Light Infantry Armory and Museum. 210 Burgess St.; (910) 433-1612. Shown by appointment only, the museum houses two centuries of artifacts from the oldest Southern militia unit in continuous existence—serving North Carolina since 1793.

Fayetteville Museum of Art. 839 Stamper Rd.; (910) 485-5121; www.fayettevillemuseumart.org. The first structure in North Carolina designed and built as an art museum, it offers a variety of changing exhibits, educational programs, concerts, workshops, and a gift shop. Open Tues and Wed 9 a.m. to 5 p.m., Thurs 9 a.m. to 1 p.m., and Sat and Sun 1 p.m. to 4 p.m. Free.

Heritage Square. 225 Dick St.; (910) 483-6009. Owned and maintained by the Fayetteville Women's Club, Heritage Square has three structures listed on the National Register of Historic Places: the Sandford House, built in 1800 and once home to artist Elliott Daingerfield and to the first United States bank in the state; the Oval Ballroom, a freestanding single room built in 1818; and the Baker-Haigh-Nimocks House, constructed in 1804.

Kyle House. 234 Green St.; (910) 483-7405. A victim of the Great Fire of 1831, this house was rebuilt in 1855 in Greek Revival and Italianate style, with unusual, 18-inch-thick walls lined with brick to provide insulation and fireproofing. Merchant James Kyle built the house following the fire that burned more than 600 buildings in the area. Open by appointment.

Liberty Point. Bow and Person Streets; (910) 433-1612. Here, on June 20, 1775, fifty-five patriots signed a petition declaring independence from Great Britain. The building at this site is the oldest known commercial structure in Fayetteville, constructed between 1791 and 1800.

Market House. Hay, Gillespie, Person, and Green Streets; (910) 483-2073. The focal point of downtown Fayetteville, the Market House was built in 1832 on the site of the old State House, where, in 1789 North Carolina ratified the U.S. Constitution, chartered the University of North Carolina, and ceded the state's western lands to Tennessee. The State House was destroyed by fire in 1831. Architecturally unique in North Carolina, the Market House is one of the few structures in America to use this town hall–market scheme found in England.

Museum of the Cape Fear Historical Complex. 801 Arsenal Ave.; (910) 486-1330; http://museumofthecapefear.ncdcr.gov. Museum exhibits chronicle the history of southern North Carolina from Native Americans to the 20th century. The 1897 E. A. Poe House examines the lifestyle of upper middle-class families from 1897 to 1917. Arsenal Park reveals the history of a federal arsenal, commissioned in 1836 by the federal government and taken over by the Confederacy at the outset of the Civil War. General Sherman seized Fayetteville in 1865 and ordered the arsenal to be razed by fire. Open Tues through Sat 10 a.m. to 5 p.m. and Sun 1 to 5 p.m. Free.

St. John's Episcopal Church. 302 Green St.; (910) 483-7405. Reconstructed in 1833, after Fayetteville's Great Fire of 1831, the church has ten pyramidal spires and stained-glass windows made in Munich, Germany.

where to shop

Angels and Antiques. 1213 Hay St.; (910) 433-4454. The owners tell us that their store carries the nation's largest selection of angels that include everything from statues and figurines to jewelry, ornaments, flags and even wind chimes. Open Mon through Fri 10 a.m. to 5:30 p.m., Sat 10 a.m. to 5 p.m.

As you may expect, the Fayetteville area has its share of military surplus and collectables stores. Here are a few, but call ahead to confirm hours.

> **Ed Hicks Antiques, Guns & Military Collectibles.** 819 Hope Mills Rd.; (910) 425-7000.

> **Memory Lane Antiques & Collectibles.** 2838 Owen Dr.; (910) 433-4395.

> **Tarbridge Military Collectibles.** 960 Country Club Dr.; (910) 488-7205.

where to eat

Hilltop House Café. 1240 Fort Bragg Rd.; (910) 484-6699; www.hilltophouse.com. Located in Fayetteville's historic Haymount district, the Hilltop House Café serves traditional American cuisine, including steaks, seafood, and the proprietor's Greek specialties. Located in an early 20th-century home, Hilltop House Café is open daily for lunch, dinner, and Sunday brunch. $$.

Huske Hardware House. 405 Hay St.; (910) 437-9905. This restaurant/microbrewery is located in a renovated hardware store, spacious and artfully restored. Its location makes it a good choice for combining a visit with the Airborne and Special Operations Museum; appropriately, the microbrew offers its signature Airborne Ale. The lunch menu offers a variety of soups, salads, and "starters," as well as sandwiches and specialties, including items such as pesto chicken and Cajun shrimp. Dinners include a selection of pasta, seafood, and beef. $$–$$$.

The Mash House. 4150 Sycamore Dairy Rd.; (910) 867-9223. Adjacent to the Wingate Inn (see "where to stay"), the Mash House is known for its award-winning microbrewed beer—with nine varieties on tap at last count—served in a chilled pint glass with a pretzel on a straw. If you're indecisive about which microbrew to have, try the Mini-Mash (four 4-ounce glasses of beer) or the larger version (eight 4-ounce glasses). Begin your dinner with "the Wedge," which includes half a head of iceberg lettuce, fried sweet onions, tomatoes, and Gorgonzola dressing. Follow it with one of the delicious entrees, such as wood-fired oven-roasted filet mignon, served with fried sweet onions, asparagus, roasted potatoes, and béarnaise. Open daily. $$–$$$.

New Korea House. 4608 Yadkin Rd.; (910) 864-2772. Great Korean cuisine is served daily for lunch and dinner in this discreet location at Cross Creek Mall. $$.

Rude Awakening Coffee House. 227 Hay St.; (910) 223-7833; www.rudeawakening.net. In the historic downtown district, this coffee shop offers all varieties of coffees, including specialty cappuccinos, as well as breakfast, lunch, and desserts. Check out the courtyard at the back of this great little coffee shop. Open Mon through Sat. $.

where to stay

Hotel Prince Charles. 450 Hay St.; (910) 433-4444. Reminiscent of an Italian palazzo, this 1925 eight-story landmark has Palladian windows and doors, marble floors and staircases, and soaring columns and pilasters. Located in historic downtown Fayetteville, the hotel is listed with Historic Hotels of America, a private nonprofit National Trust. $$–$$$.

Wingate Inn. 4182 Sycamore Dairy Rd.; (910) 826-9200 or (800) 228-1000. The Wingate offers spacious, well-equipped rooms with a desk, coffeemaker (and coffee), refrigerator, safe, ironing board, and free high-speed Internet access. A complimentary continental breakfast features forty-one items. The inn has a fitness club and whirlpool, and is a good base camp for exploring the region. $$–$$$.

fort bragg

Named for General Braxton Bragg, a native of Warren County who served in the U.S. Army during the Seminole and Mexican Wars and in the Confederate Army during the Civil War, "Camp Bragg" was established by Congress in 1918 as an Army field artillery site. Five years later the camp was renamed Fort Bragg, and in 1934 the airborne tradition began with the first military parachute jump, which used artillery observation balloons as platforms.

In 1952, Fort Bragg became headquarters for the Army's Special Forces (Green Berets) when the Psychological Warfare Center, now the Special Operations Command, was established here.

With a total area of more than 138,000 acres—three times the size of the District of Columbia—Fort Bragg today is home of XVIII Airborne Corps and the 82nd Airborne Division, as well as of thousands of non-jumping troops. It is one of the largest military reservations in the United States; because of the number of troops it houses, it is considered to be the state's tenth largest city.

where to go

82nd Airborne Division War Memorial Museum. Ardennes and Gela Streets; (910) 432-3443. The museum chronicles the history of the 82nd Airborne Division from 1917 to the present through featured photographic exhibits, static displays, and more than 4,000 artifacts on display. Outdoor equipment displays and an hourly film provide additional insights into this historic unit. Open Tues through Sat and federal holidays 10 a.m. to 4:30 p.m. Free.

John F. Kennedy Hall of Heroes. Ardennes Street. Located across the street from the John F. Kennedy Special Warfare Museum, the JFK Hall of Heroes honors nineteen Special Forces, three Rangers, and ten Indian Scout Medal of Honor recipients.

John F. Kennedy Memorial Chapel. Ardennes Street; (910) 432-2127. Beautiful stained-glass windows are dedicated to Special Forces soldiers. There's also a monument given by John Wayne to the Special Forces for assistance during the filming of The Green Berets.

John F. Kennedy Special Warfare Museum. Ardennes Street, Building D-2502; (910) 432-4272. This museum provides a behind-the-scenes look at unconventional warfare, with an emphasis on Special Forces (Green Berets) and Special Operations from World War II until today. It houses a collection of weapons, military art, and cultural items from all over the world. Open Tues through Sun 11 a.m. to 4 p.m. Free.

Main Post Chapel. Half and C Streets.; (910) 396-8016. Established in 1932, the chapel features stained-glass windows that were handcrafted with 14,000 pieces of antique glass from around the world.

day trip 03

south

>>> **fore!:**
pinehurst, southern pines,
aberdeen

The "Golf Capital of the World" is a little more than an hour's drive from the Raleigh-Durham area. A straight shot down US 1 south, Pinehurst, Southern Pines, and Aberdeen provide duffers with action aplenty. The area has more than forty-three championship courses—720 holes. That translates to fewer than one hundred residents per golf hole, making it one of the highest-density golf areas in the country. There are, in fact, more than 165 miles of fairways, and more are scheduled to open soon. This area is geographically designated as the "Sandhills," for its sandy soil, and its golf courses have 2,900 bunkers and no shortage of sand to fill them.

In publications such as *Golf Digest,* the area consistently ranks high among the most popular golf destinations in the United States, but the region has much more to offer. There's also the Spa at Pinehurst, with more than forty services, such as workouts, body wraps, and massages to replenish body and soul.

Riding enthusiasts and bicyclists favor the rolling sand hills. The region is home to five past Olympic equestrian champions, and Olympic bicycle teams have trained here. If you like to spin, you'll find plenty of quiet roads to roll on.

Speaking of quiet, one of the state's best-kept secrets is the Weymouth Center for the Arts and Humanities in Southern Pines. Weymouth's writers-in-residence program offers writers and composers stays of up to two weeks to pursue their work. Not ready to pen your great novel? Stop in to visit North Carolina's Literary Hall of Fame for inspiration.

Nearby, quaint Aberdeen, named for a seaport in Scotland, reflects the strong Scots heritage of this region.

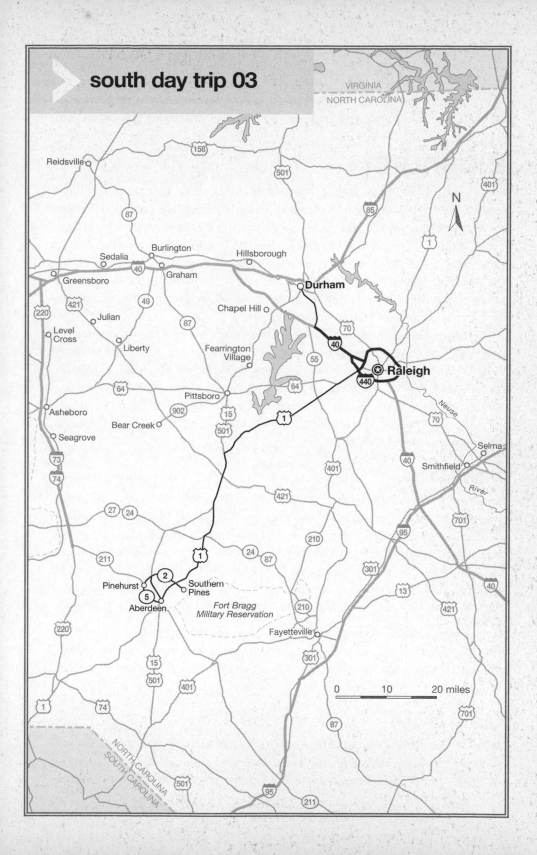

VIRGINIA
NORTH CAROLINA

N

Reidsville

Sedalia   Burlington   Hillsborough
Greensboro   Graham
Julian   Durham
Level
Cross   Liberty   Chapel Hill
    Fearrington
    Village
Asheboro   Pittsboro
Seagrove   Bear Creek

Raleigh

Neuse

Selma
Smithfield

River

Pinehurst   Southern
    Pines
Aberdeen   Fort Bragg
    Military Reservation
Fayetteville

NORTH CAROLINA
SOUTH CAROLINA

0   10   20 miles

Pinehurst, Southern Pines, and Aberdeen all are charming small towns. Each could pass for a storybook village, and you will enjoy strolling through these easily walkable towns.

pinehurst

Boston soda-fountain magnate James Walker Tufts, who wanted to build a southern winter retreat and a health-driven resort for recovery from the day's maladies, developed Pinehurst in 1895. Tufts purchased 5,000 acres of ravaged timberland in the Sandhills of North Carolina and built an inn and New England–style village he called Tuftstown. He later changed it to Pinehurst, after selecting the name from a runners-up list in a town-naming contest in the New England coastal area. Pinehurst officially opened on December 31, 1895, and has since hosted some of the most famous athletes, business leaders, philanthropists, government officials, and heroes from America and beyond.

Pinehurst's evolution as a revered golf venue is rooted in the 1898 development of its first golf course. However, it was the hiring of Donald J. Ross as golf professional in 1900 that undeniably altered the focus of Pinehurst Resort forever. His famed Number Two course has laid claim to and continues to serve as the site of some of the most honored amateur and professional golf events in the world, including the U.S. Open in 1999 and 2005. In 1996, Pinehurst was declared a National Historic Landmark, forever protecting its quaintness and ageless quality.

where to go

Sandhills Horticultural Gardens. 3395 Airport Rd.; (910) 695-3882; www.sandhillshorti culturalgardens.com. Ten major gardens, covering 27 acres, are featured here, including the Ebersol Holly Collection (the largest on the East Coast), a specialized conifer garden, the Sir Walter Raleigh Garden (a 1.5-acre formal English garden), Hillside Garden, Azalea Garden, and the Desmond Native Wetland Trail Garden. Horticulture students at Sandhills Community College, whose graduates have gone on to find notable horticultural jobs at such places as the White House, maintain the gardens. Open during daylight hours. Free.

Tufts Archives, Given Memorial Library. 150 Cherokee Rd.; (910) 295-3642; www.tufts archives.org. James Walker Tufts's dream of Pinehurst unfolds in the displays of letters, pictures, and news clippings dating from 1895. Open Mon through Fri 9:30 a.m. to 5 p.m. and Sat 9:30 a.m. to 12:30 p.m. Free.

where to golf

National Golf Club. One Royal Troon Dr.; (910) 295-4300 or (800) 471-4339; www .nationalgolfclub.com. This is a straightforward golf course; approach shots and short game are critical. Jack Nicklaus designed this course, which opened in 1989. Eighteen holes, par 72.

Pinehurst Resort and Country Club. 800 Carolina Vista Dr., Village of Pinehurst; (910) 235-8507 or (800) 487-4653; www.pinehurst.com. The resort's eight golf courses make it the world's largest golf resort. Pinehurst's Number Two course regularly ranks high in *Golf Digest*'s biennial ranking of America's one hundred greatest golf courses. Accordingly, in 2005, the U.S. Open Championship returned to Pinehurst, which had hosted the event in 1999. Seldom does the Open return to a golf course so quickly, but Pinehurst Number Two is an exceptional course and will host the men's and women's events again in 2014.

As many as four of North Carolina's top ten courses, as ranked by *Golf Digest* magazine, are in the Pinehurst and Southern Pines region. Descriptions of the best courses follow. Be forewarned, however, that these courses can cost as much as $225 per person for eighteen holes, and to play those holes properly you'll want to hire a caddie for an additional $50 or so plus tip per round of golf.

The region does feature less expensive golf courses. For more information, order the free Area Golf Course Guide from the Pinehurst, Southern Pines, Aberdeen Area Convention and Visitors Bureau, (910) 692-3330 or (800) 346-5362, or log on to www.homeofgolf .com.

Pinehurst Number Two, Pinehurst Resort and Country Club. Opened in 1901, and host of the U.S. Open in 1999 and 2005, this course was called "the fairest test of championship golf I have ever designed" by architect Donald Ross. Players have to drive the ball well and hit long irons well. Most of all, players must have a razor-sharp short game because of small greens (by modern standards) that fall off around the edge. Length: back, 7,252 yards (74.1 rating, 131 slope); middle, 6,309 yards (71.4 rating, 127 slope); forward, 5035 yards (74.2 rating, 135 slope). Eighteen holes, par 72/74.

Pinehurst Number Four, Pinehurst Resort and Country Club. Officially opened in April 2000 and dubbed Tom Fazio's "tribute to Pinehurst," Number Four was built with crowned greens similar to those found on Number Two and complemented by British-style pot bunkers and sand areas planted with native grasses. Although Number Four begins and ends where the old course did and shares some playing corridors, this is a completely new golf course.

Pinehurst Number Eight, Pinehurst Resort and Country Club. With an Audubon International Signature Sanctuary designation, Number Eight was the site of the 1997 and 1998 PGA Club Professional Championships. Solid, straightforward golf, free from theatrics like artificial earth moments and forced carries. The course was created by Tom Fazio to celebrate the 100th birthday of the resort in 1996. Length: championship, 7,092 yards (74.0 rating, 135 slope); back, 6,698 yards (71.7 rating, 125 slope); middle, 6,302 yards (69.8 rating, 121 slope); forward, 5,177 yards (68.9 rating, 112 slope). Eighteen holes, par 72.

where to shop

The Theatre Building. 80 Carolina Vista Dr.; (910) 235-8507. The village's boutique shops have storefront windows that invite browsing, but be sure to stop at this gem. It has been graced by such luminaries as Helen Hayes, Will Rogers, and Gloria Swanson. It now houses a group of stores, ranging from G. Monroe's, a clothing shop, to King's Gifts & Collectibles.

where to eat

Visitors to Pinehurst typically purchase packages that include modified American meal plans. Golf packages, for example, may include breakfast and lunch. See restaurant descriptions under "Where to Stay."

where to stay

Magnolia Inn. 65 Magnolia St.; (910) 295-6900 or (800) 526-5562. Old South hospitality can be found in this charming inn located in the center of the village of Pinehurst. Enjoy gourmet dinners ($$–$$$), but especially try the crab cakes. Served in the dining room, on the porch in the pub, or poolside. Golf packages are available. $$$.

Pinehurst Resort. 1 Carolina Vista Dr.; (910) 295-6811 or (800) 487-4653; www.pinehurst .com. Nestled among the pines, this four-diamond resort has played host to travelers since 1895. Pinehurst has eight signature golf courses.

At Pinehurst Resort, there are opportunities to improve your golf game at the Pinehurst Golf Academy, have "wicket fun" playing croquet at any of the resort's three full-size croquet courts, or play tennis.

A 31,000-square-foot, $12 million spa features twenty-eight private treatment rooms and eight salon stations. The spa also showcases a golf fitness studio. Also available from the resort are thirty-minute guided carriage tours of the village of Pinehurst for $15 per person.

Pinehurst Resort offers three inns (descriptions follow) as well as condominium and villa rentals. All accommodations in Pinehurst are priced in the $$$ category. For reservations call (800) 487-4653.

The Holly Inn. 2300 Cherokee Rd. Originally opened on December 31, 1895, was the village's first inn. The newly restored Holly Inn has eighty-five rooms with period furnishings. The inn offers two distinctive dining options in Pinehurst Resort's modified American meal plan. The 1895 Grille ($$$) is the resort's premier dining experience, featuring regional cuisine in an elegant Southern grill, with a buffet breakfast and innovative New American–style cuisine for dinner. The cozy Tavern ($$–$$$), with its century-old hand-carved imported Scottish bar, working fireplace, and outdoor patio, is open daily for lunch and dinner.

The Carolina. 1 Carolina Vista Dr. Built in 1901, this is one of America's Historic Hotels. This stately Victorian structure is the centerpiece of the resort, housing 210 guest rooms and twelve suites, all recently renovated. The hotel's Carolina Dining Room ($$$) serves breakfast, lunch, and dinner, and the Ryder Cup Lounge ($$) is for lighter meals and cocktails.

Manor Inn. 5 Community Dr. This forty-five-room inn has the intimate feel of a bed-and-breakfast and is a popular choice of golfing groups and families because of its value pricing and room configuration options.

golf not for you?

The rolling green hills, distinctive architecture, and first-class amenities of one of the nation's premier golf locales make an unmistakable statement about what is most important here in the Sandhills of North Carolina. Problem is, you took up golf and put it back down long ago. So what does the Pinehurst/Southern Pines area have to offer the non-golfer?

There is of course shopping and those first-class amenities, including some great restaurants. Antebellum and turn-of-the-twentieth-century homes make a driving tour a pleasure. In addition, the area offers a selection of activities with a European flair.

For 2,500 years, the "Game of Kings" has reigned in Asia and Europe. They've played polo in Pinehurst for eighty years. Polo traces its tradition through the Middle East to India and more recently to England and the United States. Now, weekends throughout the year, the sport lives on at the **Pinehurst Harness Track** *(800-433-8768) on SR 5. There you can also catch horse shows and a glimpse of training sessions, which in the past have included Olympic equestrian champions.*

Does your croquet stroke need some work? The **Pinehurst Resort** *has a croquet pro on staff to help with just that. But here, croquet is more than just a backyard cookout activity. Throughout the year, some of the best mallet-wielding players from around the state, sometimes the world, come out to compete. You thought the U.S. Open was intense!*

European tradition is alive and well in Southern Pines too. Thanksgiving Day here is marked not only by football games but also smart red jackets and riders upon their steeds. The **fox-hunting season** *begins with the blessing of the foxes by an Anglican priest. No actual foxes are harmed during the event.*

For the budget-minded, the Southern Pines and Pinehurst region offers a variety of chain hotels. For more information, contact the **Pinehurst, Southern Pines, Aberdeen Area Convention and Visitors Bureau,** 10677 SR 15–501, Southern Pines 28388. Call (910) 692-3330 or (800) 346-5362, or visit www.homeofgolf.com.

southern pines

Incorporated in 1887, Southern Pines was known earlier as Vineland, but the U.S. Postal Service refused to accept the name on the basis that the North Carolina town would be confused with a New Jersey town by the same name. In search of a new name, the popular winter resort chose to identify itself with its geographic location along the edge of the long-leaf pine belt.

Downtown Southern Pines is divided by train tracks, mostly hidden by magnolia and pine trees. They divide Broad Street, where you'll find most of the tourist activity—on both sides of the tracks. To get to Southern Pines from Pinehurst take SR 2, also known as Midland Road.

where to go

Historic Shaw House Properties. Morganton Road and Broad Street; (910) 692-2051; www.moorehistory.com. Operated by Moore County Historical Society, these three historic houses (including the Shaw, Garner, and Bryant Houses, built 1770–1820) are furnished with plain-style furniture, depicting life in the early Sandhills. Also included are the Britt Sanders and Joel McLendon Cabins (ca. 1760–1790). Open Tues through Fri 1 to 4 p.m. Free.

Taxidermy Hall of Fame of North Carolina Creation Museum. 156 Northwest Broad St.; (910) 692-3471. On exhibit is every kind of North Carolina wildlife (within the law), state and national taxidermy ribbon winners, and "the oldest rock on earth." The museum is located in the Christian Book Store on Broad Street.

Weymouth Center. 555 East Connecticut Ave.; (910) 692-6261; www.weymouthcenter .org. This 1920s Georgian mansion, situated on twenty-four acres with extensive gardens, offers arts and humanities activities. The former home of author James Boyd, it's listed on the National Register of Historic Places. Open Mon through Fri 10 a.m. to 2 p.m. Admission is $5.

The Weymouth Center is home to the **North Carolina Literary Hall of Fame.** (910) 692-6261. At this shrine of the most distinguished Tarheel men and women of letters, you'll find displays, photographs, and lists of works for such notable writers as Thomas Wolfe, O. Henry (William S. Porter), Paul Green, and James Boyd. Open Mon through Fri 10 a.m. to 2 p.m.

Weymouth Woods Sandhills Nature Preserve. 1024 North Fort Bragg Rd.; (910) 692-2167; www.ncparks.gov. Named for Weymouth, England, the 898-acre nature preserve of longleaf pine forest is home to the endangered red-cockaded woodpecker, a permanent resident of the Sandhills. Tour the nature center museum, dedicated to the study of this unique ecosystem; hike the more than 4.5 miles of year-round trails. Guided tours and programs are presented. Hours are Nov through Mar daily 9 a.m. to 6 p.m. and Apr through Oct 9 a.m. to 7 p.m.

where to shop

Campbell House Galleries. 482 East Connecticut Ave.; (910) 692-4356, www.arts council-moore.org/campbell.html. This historic home of the Arts Council of Moore County provides three spacious exhibit areas that display the work of a featured artist each month. Most artwork is offered for sale. Open Mon through Fri 9 a.m. to 5 p.m. and the third Sat and Sun of each month, 2 to 4 p.m.

where to eat

Chef Warren's. 215 Northeast Broad St.; (910) 692-5240. This cozy French bistro presents you with mouthwatering menus that feature nightly specials and seasonal dishes. Open for dinner Mon through Sat. $$$.

Ice Cream Parlor. 176 Northwest Broad St.; (910) 692-7273. A popular spot with the lunch crowd, the Ice Cream Parlor specializes in old-fashioned hand-pattied burgers served Southern-style with mustard, chili, slaw, and onions. It also serves homemade chicken salad, cakes, and, of course, ice cream. Open daily. $.

Restaurant 195. 195 Bell Ave.; (910) 692-7110. Specializing in all-natural cuisine, this restaurant features a grilled portabello mushroom sandwich that ranks as the favorite menu item. Other popular items include the grilled Angus beef burger with Maytag blue cheese, and the linguine with grilled shrimp, broccoli, and garlic. Open for lunch and dinner Wed through Fri, lunch only on Tues. Closed Sun and Mon. $$.

Sweet Basil. 134 Northwest Broad St.; (910) 693-1487. Sweet Basil is popular for its soups, salads, and sandwiches, particularly the grilled eggplant sandwich with sweet roasted peppers and arugula on focaccia. Another favorite is tuna and fusilli salad with capers, served with la vache bread. Open Mon through Fri 11 a.m. to 3 p.m., Sat 11:30 a.m. to 3 p.m. $$.

where to stay

Jefferson Inn. 150 West New Hampshire Ave.; (910) 692-9911. Established in 1902, the Jefferson Inn is a noted landmark located in the historic district of Southern Pines. The inn has fifteen luxurious rooms and extravagant suites. Experience fine cuisine in the dining room of One Fifty West or slightly more casual dining at the Tavern and Courtyard. $$.

Knollwood House. 1495 West Connecticut Ave.; (910) 692-9390; www.bbonline.com/nc/knollwood. Five acres of longleaf pines, dogwoods, magnolias, holly trees, and flowering shrubs surround visitors at this English manor house, appointed with 18th-century antiques and the comforts of home. From the back terrace, it's 100 feet to the fifteenth fairway of championship golfing. Enjoy swimming, tennis, and golf. Full breakfast. Knollwood House has five guest rooms and suites with private baths. $$$.

aberdeen

Early settlers in this area were predominantly Scottish, and their heritage is still prevalent. Originally known as Blue's Crossing, Aberdeen was renamed in 1887 for the seaport city in Scotland. US 1 will get you to Aberdeen in about ten minutes from Southern Pines.

where to go

Malcolm Blue Farm. Bethesda Road; (910) 944-7558. Built around 1825, this antebellum farm has been recognized by the National Register of Historic Places for its authenticity and uniqueness. Structurally the site contains the farmhouse and barns, the old gristmill, and a wooden water tower, and stands as a significant preservation of rural history in Moore County. Annual events at the Malcolm Blue Farm include the Historic Crafts and Farm Skills Festival the last weekend of Sept and the Christmas Open House on the second Sun of Dec. Open Wed through Sat 1 to 4 p.m. Free.

where to stay

Inn at Bryant House. 214 North Poplar St.; (910) 944-3300; (800) 453-4019; www.innat bryanthouse.com. A Historic Registry property that has been completely restored to its original 1913 splendor, the inn is located one block east of US 1 in the historic district of downtown Aberdeen, six minutes from Pinehurst. It offers ten guest rooms (all with private baths), a spacious parlor, living and dining areas, and shaded porches and outside areas, as well as a full breakfast. $$.

west

day trip 01

west

>>> **the southern part of heaven:**
chapel hill

I-40 West takes you to the town that locals call the "southern part of heaven." Although Wolfpack and Blue Devil fans may beg to differ, a day trip to this destination gives you the chance to visit a truly great rival, the University of North Carolina, and the town it inspired.

chapel hill

Chapel Hill was named after the New Hope Chapel, which stood on a hill at the crossing of two primary roads in the late 1700s. Town lots were auctioned in 1793 when construction began on the university. In 1795 residents occupied permanent homes.

Authorized by the North Carolina Constitution in 1776, the University of North Carolina at Chapel Hill was chartered in 1789, delayed by the Revolutionary War. The cornerstone for Old East, the first state university building in the United States, was laid in 1793. The University of North Carolina at Chapel Hill was the first state university to open its doors when the first student, Hinton James, arrived in the winter of 1795 after walking the 170 miles from Wilmington.

As part of the sixteen-campus University of North Carolina system, today UNC-CH is ranked among the great institutions of higher education in the nation. The campus covers 740 acres and provides education to more than 24,000 undergraduate, graduate, and professional students.

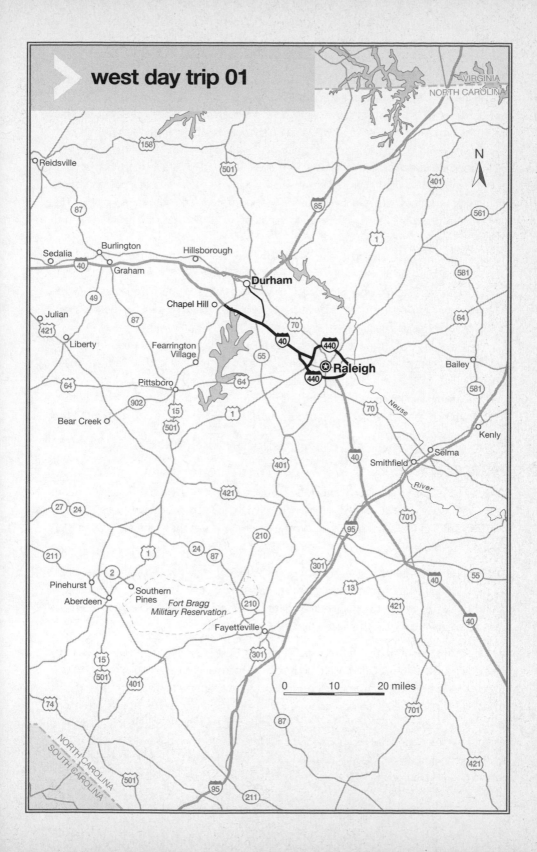

west day trip 01

In the early years, Chapel Hill grew along with the university. In 1818 there were twenty-two buildings in Chapel Hill, including eighteen residences, inns, and stores. By 1836 Chapel Hill had one physician, but no lawyer and no schools except for the university. The town was incorporated in 1851.

Today the idyllic college town has a population of about 49,000. Its main thoroughfare is Franklin Street (named after Benjamin Franklin), which borders the campus and offers shops and boutiques, restaurants and cafes, movie theaters, and houses of worship. The town has historic districts, museums, performing and visual arts activities, a library, parks, malls, and many recreational facilities.

In 1997, *Sports Illustrated* called Chapel Hill "the best college town in America." The city woos visitors with its down-home charm on Franklin Street, where you can sit at the soda fountain at Sutton's Drug Store, and wows them with such attractions as the Morehead Planetarium, where you can gaze at some 8,900 fixed stars on the Star Theater's vast dome, a true celestial treat.

Visit the university, browse the shops, and have lunch or dinner at one of the many "institutions" that are now Chapel Hill landmarks, such as the Spanky's or Carolina Coffee Shop.

You might want to consider bringing bikes along. Chapel Hill and neighboring Carrboro are extremely bike-friendly towns with dedicated bike paths between and in each of the two towns and good signage.

where to go

Chapel Hill/Orange County Visitors Bureau. 501 West Franklin St., Suite 104; (888) 968-2060; www.visitchapelhill.org. The visitor bureau, located downtown, has free parking at the rear of the building. Pick up brochures or ask questions of the staff. Open Mon through Fri from 8:30 a.m. to 5 p.m. and Sat 10 a.m. to 2 p.m.

UNC Visitors' Center. 250 East Franklin St.; (919) 962-1630; www.unc.edu/visitors. Chartered in 1789, the nation's first state university covers more than 700 acres. Start your tour at the visitors' center, in the lobby of the Morehead Planetarium, where you can pick up a map for a self-guided tour Open Mon through Fri from 9 a.m. to 5 p.m.

Ackland Art Museum. South Columbia Street (off East Franklin Street on the University Campus); (919) 966-5736; www.ackland.org. The permanent collection of over 15,000 objects includes the art from around the world and throughout the ages. The museum holds the most significant collection of Asian art in the state and one of the largest collections of works on paper in the Southeast. Long known for its strength in European painting and sculpture, the Ackland has recently added additional emphasis to the building of its collection of contemporary art. Open Wed through Sat 10 a.m. to 5 p.m. and Sun 1 to 5 p.m. It is also open the second Fri of the month until 9 p.m. Admission is free.

Carolina Basketball Museum. 450 Skipper Bowles Dr.; (919) 843-9921; www.tarheel blue.com. Adjacent to the Dean Dome in the Ernie Williamson Athletic Center is the Carolina Basketball Museum with artifacts and highlight tapes of some of the greatest moments in the university's storied basketball program. Championship trophies, audio-visual displays and exhibits are found throughout the facility.. Open Tues through Fri 10 a.m. to 4 p.m. and Sat 9 a.m. to 1 p.m.

Chapel Hill Museum. 523 East Franklin St.; (919) 967-1400; www.chapelhillmuseum.org. The museum is a never-ending pursuit to identify and define the special nature of the history and heritage of Chapel Hill and its environs. Self-guided tours are available. Free. Open Wed through Sat 10 a.m. to 4 p.m., Sun 1 to 4 p.m.

Charles Kuralt Learning Center. UNC School of Journalism; (919) 962-1204; www.kuralt .jomc.unc.edu. The Kuralt Center is on the second floor of Carroll Hall on the UNC campus. Much of Kuralt's TV works, including the famous CBS News "On the Road" episodes, have been digitized so visitors can watch the programs using touch-screen technology. The contents of Kuralt's three-room office suite on West 57th Street in midtown Manhattan have also been re-created here. Open Tues and Thurs 2 to 4 p.m. and by appointment.

Governors Club Golf Course. 10100 Governors Dr.; (800) 925-0085; www.governors club.com. Nonmembers may play on this private golf course while guests at club cottages. The twenty-seven-hole championship course was designed by Jack Nicklaus and awarded a MetroBravo! for Best Private Golf Course from *MetroMagazine*.

He's Not Here. 112½ West Franklin St.; (919) 942-7939. One of the oldest and best-known nightspots in Chapel Hill, featuring classic rock and blues, He's Not Here is known for big (thirty-three-ounce) Carolina Blue cups of beer. Cover charge is $2 to $3 for live entertainment only.

Horace Williams House. 610 East Rosemary St.; (919) 942-7818; www.chapelhillpreser vation.com. As the only historic house in Chapel Hill open to the public, the facility features changing art exhibits in its octagon wing and throughout the house, and hosts chamber music concerts on a regular basis. A self-guided tour takes you to a number of Chapel Hill's historic homes, as well as the oldest church in town. Open Tues through Fri 10 a.m. to 4 p.m.; Sun 1 to 4 p.m.; closed on major holidays and the first two weeks in Aug.

Jordan Lake Educational State Forest. 2832 Big Woods Rd.; (919) 542-1154 or (800) 468-6242; www.ncparks.gov. Jordan Lake Educational State Forest is the newest of North Carolina's educational state forests. A variety of wildlife can be found here, including birds of prey, deer, songbirds, flying squirrels, and beavers. The three-quarter-mile Talking Tree Trail features—you guessed it—"talking trees," each with a recorded message about its history and surroundings.

tar heel born and bred

*Carolina. It's not just about basketball. Well, a lot of it is. With coaching legends Dean Smith and Roy Williams at the helm of "your team," it's hard not making basketball the center of an alumni's life. But there is more to life and to Chapel Hill. The bar scene changes ever so slightly. Trolls Bar is gone but **He's Not Here** is still here. On campus, the bell remains a good place to meet and a sip from the well, **Old Well,** still brings good luck. The stone wall, still a great place for lunch. A stroll down **Franklin Street** renews the soul. A Saturday afternoon among the pines watching football in a place commonly called the best place on the planet to do so can sometimes be frustrating.*

I didn't truly understand what a special place my alma mater was until I was long gone. In journalism school a great professor treated me to a writing lesson from a man who had had one from Ernest Hemingway. I crossed paths with the likes of Michael Jordan and walked the same halls as Charles Kuralt, Andy Griffith and soccer great Mia Hamm (the women's soccer team is even more storied than men's basketball with 20 NCAA championships since 1982). At twenty-one, I didn't understand that I was in the presence of greatness.

Perhaps anyone could substitute words and names above to describe their old school. But to miss all this sky-blue town has to offer would be unfortunate. You can't get the same writing lesson that Philip Meyer gave me, but you can grab a big blue bucket of beer at that bar off Franklin Street and you can get breakfast anytime at Breadman's. Your spirit can be renewed and your heart can be twenty-one again. What's best is you just might understand what it means to be Tar Heel born.

Morehead Planetarium and Science Center. 250 East Franklin St.; (919) 549-6863 (info line) or (919) 962-1236 (office); www.moreheadplanetarium.org. The first planetarium in the South and at one time a training center for NASA astronauts, Morehead Planetarium has been teaching space sciences education since 1950. The planetarium features public shows in the Star Theater, digital theater, educational exhibits, the Rotunda Portrait Gallery, Infinity gift shop, and a sundial rose garden. Self-guided tours are offered. Star Theater admission is $6 for children, senior citizens, and students; $7.25 for adults. Digital theater presentations are free. Building hours are Tues through Thurs 10 a.m. to 3:30 p.m., Fri and Sat 10 a.m. to 3:30 p.m. and 6:30 to 9 p.m., and Sun 1 to 4:30 p.m.

North Carolina Botanical Garden. 100 Old Mason Farm Rd.; (919) 962-0522; www.ncbg .unc.edu. The largest natural botanical garden in the Southeast, the North Carolina Botanical

Garden consists of 600 acres of preserved land, including nature trails, carnivorous plant collections, and aquatic and herb gardens. Collections of North Carolina and Southeastern plants are arranged by habitat in simulated natural settings. Walk from the beach to the mountains, botanically speaking, in just a few minutes. Be sure to visit North Carolina playwright Paul Green's restored cabin, moved here from a site nearby. Group guided tours by advance arrangement and self-guided tours for individuals are available. The facility also presents revolving exhibits of paintings, quilts, and other media, plus sculpture in various sections of the botanical collection. Open year-round, Mon through Fri 8 a.m. to 5 p.m.; Sat, 9 a.m. to 6 p.m.; and to 6 p.m. during daylight savings time and Sun 1 to 6 p.m. Free.

North Carolina Collection Gallery. UNC–CH Louis Round Wilson Library, South Road; (919) 962-1172; www.lib.unc.edu/ncc/gallery.html. The gallery presents exhibits on the history of North Carolina and UNC. The world's largest collection of resource materials related to Sir Walter Raleigh is here, including a document signed by Queen Elizabeth I in 1570. Be sure to visit the North Carolina Collection, a treasure trove of historical material relating to the state, and the Southern Manuscripts Department, which includes the Charles Kuralt Collection (the latter is closed on Sun, so visit this one Sat if it's high on your list). Standing guided group tours are conducted every Wed at 2 p.m. Open Mon through Fri 9 a.m. to 5 p.m., Sat 9 a.m. to 1 p.m., Sun 1 to 5 p.m. Free.

University Lake. 130 University Lake Rd.; (919) 942-8007. This 213-acre lake was created in 1932 as a source of drinking water for the university and the communities of Chapel Hill and Carrboro, as well as an outdoor recreation facility. The lake has fishing, picnic, and sunbathing areas; rowboats, canoes, motorboats, and paddleboats are available for rent.

where to shop

Carr Mill Mall. 200 North Greensboro St., Carrboro; (919) 942-8669. Carr Mill Mall is a beautifully-restored textile mill, built in 1899 and listed on the National Register of Historic Places. It houses many specialty stores, restaurants, a chocolate shop, boutiques, and galleries

Chapel Hill Downtown, University Square, The Courtyard. 133 West Franklin St. East and West Franklin Streets and East and West Rosemary Streets offer mostly family-owned and independent shops and restaurants. University Square at 133 and 143 West Franklin Street contains a selection of specialty stores on the concourse level of two midrise office buildings. The Courtyard at 431 West Franklin Street has a small arcade of shops and offices.

Glen Lennox. SR 54 East. On the northeast corner of Fordham Boulevard (US 15-501) and Raleigh Road (SR 54), this was Chapel Hill's first shopping center. Built in 1950, it offers a selection of small shops and service businesses.

where to eat

Breadmen's Restaurant. 324 West Rosemary St.; (919) 967-7110. This is the place to get breakfast anytime—day or night. Breakfast is served all day, including their specialty omelets. It's also a good place to get a big burger, sandwiches, fresh salads and home-made soups, and desserts. Open daily 7 a.m. to 9 p.m. $–$$.

Carolina Brewery. 460 West Franklin St.; (919) 942-1800. Chapel Hill's first microbrewery and restaurant serves contemporary American cuisine and handcrafted ales and lagers. Many dishes, including desserts, are made with beer. Live blues acts perform every Thursday. Open daily. $$.

Carolina Coffee Shop. 138 East Franklin St.; (919) 942-6875. A Chapel Hill landmark established in 1922, this dim pub has wooden church-pew booths where you can order a cup of coffee or a brew as well as a meal. $$.

Carolina Crossroads. 211 Pittsboro St.; (919) 918-2777. Located on the UNC campus in the historic Carolina Inn, this Mobil and AAA four-star restaurant serves elegant American cuisine that melds world-class cooking with North Carolina seasonal specialties. It also has an award-winning wine list. British tea service daily at 3 p.m. Patio dining is available. Open daily for breakfast, 6:30 to 11 a.m.; for lunch, 11 a.m. to 2 p.m.; for dinner, 5:30 to 10 p.m. $$–$$$.

Crook's Corner. 610 West Franklin St.; (919) 929-7643. Fine, seasonal Southern dining and fresh seafood specialties are served inside and on a patio. The menu changes daily at this home of shrimp and grits and vegetarian jambalaya. Open daily 5:30 to 10 p.m., Sun brunch from 10:30 a.m. to 2 p.m. $$–$$$.

Il Palio Ristorante. The Siena Hotel, 1505 East Franklin St.; (919) 918-2545. Enjoy classic Italian cuisine in North Carolina's only AAA four-diamond Italian restaurant. The chef prepares memorable Tuscan cuisine with an emphasis on flavorful infused oils and healthy alternatives, paired with fine Italian wines. Open for breakfast Mon through Fri 6:30 to 10 a.m., Sat and Sun 7 to 10 a.m.; for lunch daily 11:30 a.m. to 2 p.m.; and for dinner nightly 5:30 to 10 p.m. $$$.

Mama Dip's Kitchen. 408 West Rosemary St.; (919) 942-5837. "Put a little South in your mouth!" Cookbook author Mama Dip has been preparing down-home Southern food since she was nine. Her restaurant offers an abundance of traditional American food, especially vegetables, and the most popular menu item: fried chicken that can't be beat. Open Mon through Sat 8 a.m. to 10 p.m., Sun 8 a.m. to 9 p.m. $$.

Spanky's Restaurant & Bar. 101 East Franklin St.; (919) 967-2678. Spanky's is a Chapel Hill tradition, and traditional American favorites reign here. They include a variety of burgers, its famed brown-sugar baby back ribs, and salads that make for a great meal anytime. Spanky's is open for lunch and dinner seven days a week. $$.

Top of the Hill Restaurant and Brewery. 100 East Franklin St.; (919) 929-8676. Overlooking downtown Chapel Hill from a large third-floor outdoor patio, Top of the Hill offers casual, upscale dining. The restaurant has won twenty "Best of Triangle" awards, including Best Restaurant in Chapel Hill, Best Microbrew, and Best Outdoor Deck. There's live music Thurs evenings. Open daily 11 a.m. to 2 a.m. $$–$$$.

Weaver Street Market and Cafe. 101 East Weaver St., Carrboro; (919) 929-0010. Just a short hike or bike from downtown Chapel Hill, this co-op and organic-foods grocery store features a great salad bar, baked goods, sushi, and outdoor seating. The cafe is open Mon through Fri 7:30 a.m. to 9 p.m. $–$$.

where to stay

Best Western University Inn. 1310 Raleigh Rd.; (919) 932-3000 or (800) 528-1234; www .bestwestern.com/universityinnchapelhill. This eighty-four-room property is convenient to the UNC campus and Friday Center. Amenities include a free continental breakfast and an outdoor swimming pool. $$.

The Carolina Inn. 211 Pittsboro St.; (919) 933-2001 or (800) 962-8519; www.carolinainn .com. A historic AAA four-diamond 184-room hotel with a Mobil four-star restaurant, the Carolina offers gracious Southern hospitality and elegance. Located on the campus of UNC, one block from charming downtown shops and restaurants, the inn has many amenities, including a fitness center, on-command video, room service, nightly turndown service, antiques, and a self-guided history tour. The Carolina Inn is listed on the National Register of Historic Places. $$$.

Days Inn. 1312 North Fordham Blvd.; (919) 929-3090; www.daysinn.com. Close to UNC and conveniently located near restaurants and shopping, Days Inn's suites feature Jacuzzis, king- and queen-size beds, in-room microwave ovens and fridges, and a complimentary continental breakfast. $$.

Hampton Inn Chapel Hill. 1740 North Fordham Blvd.; (919) 968-3000 or (800) 426-7866; www.hampton-inn.com. Hampton Inn offers a complimentary continental breakfast, an outdoor swimming pool, free local phone calls, free use of a health facility near the hotel, and the convenience of the UNC campus. $$.

Holiday Inn Chapel Hill. 1301 North Fordham Blvd.; (919) 929-2171 or (888) 452-5765; www.holidayinnchapelhill.com. On-site amenities include the Timeout Sports bar, a fitness center, an outdoor swimming pool, and room service. The hotel provides a free shuttle to downtown. $$.

The Inn at Bingham School. 6720 Mebane Oaks Rd.; (919) 563-5583 or (800) 566-5583; www.chapel-hill-inn.com. Situated west of Chapel Hill on ten beautiful country acres, this award-winning historic inn (ca. 1790, 1801, and 1835) offers five rooms with private baths, fireplaces, suite with whirlpool, full breakfast, wine and cheese, and free local calls. It was completely renovated in 2005. $$–$$$.

Rock Quarry Farm Bed & Breakfast. 1700 SR 54 West; (919) 929-1408. This simple country three-room B&B is just west of UNC. The property includes a vast expanse of lush, flowering shrubs and green lawns, dating back to the late 1800's. Now fully refurbished, the inn includes all modern amenities, organic breakfast in the morning, and local wine and cheese in the evening. $$–$$$.

The Siena Hotel. 1505 East Franklin St.; (919) 929-4000 or (800) 223-7379; www.siena hotel.com. This elegant AAA four-diamond boutique hotel offers exceptional service amid fine antique furnishings. Classic Italian cuisine is served in Il Palio, the state's only AAA four-diamond Italian restaurant. Rates include a full buffet breakfast, nightly turndown service, local phone calls, and daily newspaper. On-site services: restaurant, lounge, fitness center, business center, room service, and airport shuttle. $$$.

day trip 02

west

>>> **courthouse to devil's tramping ground:**
pittsboro, bear creek, siler city

Chatham County and its county seat, Pittsboro, were named for the first Earl of Chatham, William Pitt (1708–1778). The good earl reportedly was a staunch defender of American independence, as were the fiercely independent residents of the newly formed Chatham County. Their Court of Pleas and Quarter Sessions abandoned the customary extolling of the king and his titles in 1773, long before the first shot rang out in New England.

pittsboro

Located in the heart of North Carolina, Pittsboro offers beautiful rolling landscape, quaint antiques stores, pottery shops, and more than fifty art studios and galleries.

To get to Pittsboro from Raleigh-Durham take US 64 West. Pittsboro is a great day trip to combine with Chapel Hill (see West Day Trip 01). Should you pair the two, plan to stop at Fearrington Village while traveling between Chapel Hill and Pittsboro on US 15-501. Tucked away on farmland dating to the 1700s, Fearrington Village is the anchor to a bustling center of shops and services that serve the 1,500 residents of this special community.

where to go

Chatham County Courthouse and Historical Museum. Historic Traffic Circle at the intersection of US 15-501 and US 64; (800) 316-3829; www.chathamhistory.org. Built in 1881 and designed by a local lawyer after the roof blew off an earlier building during a trial,

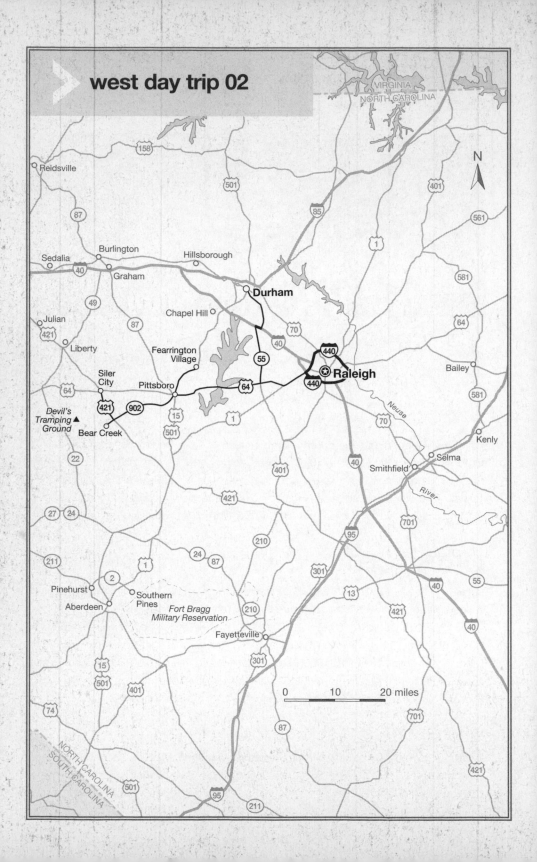

this is the fourth courthouse built in the county since 1771. Listed on the National Register of Historic Places, it was extensively renovated in 1959 and again in the late 1980s. In March 2010, during the fourth revision of this book, fire devastated the building and damaged the museum and its contents. Call to check on the resolution to the disaster and the public display of museum artifacts.

Fearrington Gardens. 2000 Fearrington Village Center; (919) 542-1239 or (800) 316-3829; www.fearrington.com. Formal and informal gardens weave through the facilities at Fearrington Village, a complete home and retreat style community located on an historic farm. The more than fifty beds of annuals, perennials, and shrubs provide interest throughout the year. Stroll through on your own at any time. Be sure to see the Belted Galloways—the black-and-white "Oreo" cows—a rare breed of Scottish beef cattle. Fearrington's Galloways have escaped the butcher, as their role here is strictly to add to the bucolic setting. Fearrington Village is open daily year-round.

Hall-London House. 206 Hillsboro St.; (919) 542-2400. Henry Armand London was a lawyer, state senator, and founder-editor of the *Chatham Record,* a local newspaper that has been in continuous publication since 1878. The Winnie Davis chapter of the United Daughters of the Confederacy was founded here in 1898 by London's wife, Bettie Louise Jackson, and others. The home has been converted to offices and is open during normal business hours.

Manly Law Office. Masonic St., US 15-501; (919) 542-3603. Charles Manly was governor of North Carolina from 1849 to 1850. A native of Chatham County, Manly had his law office built on Hillsboro Street (US 15-501), calling it Fort Snug. Moved and restored by the Chatham County Historical Association in 1971, the building may be visited by appointment.

Pittsboro Historic District. Listed on the National Register of Historic Places, the district stretches beyond the original four-block center of the town to include Chatham Mills, the Patrick St. Lawrence House, the Pittsboro Community House, the County Courthouse, and other homes and buildings erected between the 1780s and 1949.

Visitors may request a Pittsboro Historic District brochure (and a complete visitor information packet) from Chatham County Tourism (www.visitchathamcounty.com).

Pittsboro Presbyterian Church. 95 East Road; (919) 542-4702. The pews in Pittsboro's second brick structure (built in 1850) are believed to be the originals. The church bell, imported from London, was offered to and refused by the Confederate government during the Civil War. Open during church services and by arrangement.

where to shop

Cooper Mays Pottery. 4222 US 15-501 North; (919) 542-1518; www.coopermays.com. Creating hand-thrown pottery, dinnerware, and one-of-a-kind art pottery for more than twenty-five years, the Cooper Mays studio and gallery are located on the banks of the Haw River. Seven cabins and kiln houses built on ten acres contain the production and retail gallery.

Fearrington Farmers' Market. 2000 Fearrington Village Center; (800) 316-3829 or (919) 542-2121; www.fearrington.com. Stop here for baked goods, eggs, cut flowers, orchids, honey, jams, jellies, soaps, plants of all kinds, poultry, and other meats. Look for the market in the back of the Fearrington Village Center parking lot across from the pond. Open Tues 4 p.m. to dusk Apr through Thanksgiving, rain or shine.

Pittsboro Antique Walk. (919) 542-5722; www.pittsboroshops.com. Visit twelve great antiques shops covering more than 25,000 square feet of antiques. Visitors will find a variety of antiques with other types of shops and small restaurants mixed in.

Stone-Crow Pottery. 4269 US 15-501 North; (919) 542-4708; www.stone-crowpottery .com. Stone-Crow has been producing high-fire stoneware and porcelain since 1976. The gallery is a restored 120-year-old log cabin sitting high above a waterfall on the Haw River.

where to eat

Fearrington House Country Inn and Restaurant. 2000 Fearrington Village Center; (919) 542-2121; www.fearringtonhouse.com. The Fearrington House is one of only a handful of AAA five-diamond award winners and Mobil five-star recipients in the nation. Enjoy gourmet dining Tues through Sat 6 to 9 p.m., Sun to 8 p.m. $$$.

The General Store Cafe. 39 West St.; (919) 542-2432. The cafe fare consists of home-made soups and innovatively prepared sandwiches and salads in a cozy, laid-back setting. For vegans, there's the tofu eggless salad sandwich. Enjoy local artwork on display through-out the place. Open Mon through Sat. $$.

The Old Granary. 200 Fearrington Village Center; (919) 542-5505. Considerably less for-mal than the Inn's Restaurant, the Old Granary is part country store, part deli. You can also check out the espresso bar and grab something sweet to eat. $.

S & T's Soda Shoppe. 85 Hillsboro St.; (919) 545-0007. Enjoy good food and reminisce about the past in this nostalgic soda shop. Restored woodwork, a marble counter with bar stools, and several pieces from the past make this place a great stop in between shopping. Open Mon through Sat 11 a.m. to 7:30 p.m. $$.

Virlie's Grill. 58 Hillsboro St.; (919) 542-0376. Located in the former Scoreboard restau-rant, Virlie's serves homemade soups, salads, and sandwiches. Breakfast features tradi-tional southern fare as well as breakfast burritos. Lunch and dinner feature light dishes as well as pasta dishes. $.

where to stay

Fearrington House Country Inn and Restaurant. 2000 Fearrington Village Center; (919) 542-2121; www.fearringtonhouse.com. A member of the prestigious Relais & Chateaux organization, Fearrington House is also a recipient of AAA's five-diamond award and Exxon Mobil's five stars; it's the only establishment in North Carolina to receive both designations. Rates include gourmet breakfast and afternoon tea. $$$.

Rosemary Bed and Breakfast. 76 West St.; (919) 542-5515 or (888) 643-2017; www .rosemary-bb.com. This 1912 colonial revival home in the heart of Pittsboro offers five guest rooms with private baths, telephones, cable TV, ceiling fans, fireplaces, two-person whirl-pools, and a full gourmet breakfast. $$–$$$.

bear creek

One worthwhile side trip is to Bear Creek, located about 20 miles west of Pittsboro on SR 902. It's an unincorporated community named for a nearby creek. Not to be confused with the town of the same name in western North Carolina, it's got a lot going for it to be such a secluded area.

where to go

Devil's Tramping Ground. SR 1100. This site takes its name from a local legend attached to a circular path said to have been worn down by the devil's pacing as he plotted new forms of mischief.

On January 22, 1898, James I. Morris visited the area, when the Tramping Ground was in an undisturbed condition, and published a good description of it in *The Messenger,* a Siler City weekly newspaper. "On Saturday we visited that noted place known as the 'Devil's Tramping Ground.' This is the most peculiar spot of earth that we remember ever having seen. It is about 1¼ miles from the X Roads and just a fourth of a mile from the old militia muster ground, known as Rock Spring . . . The Tramping Ground is, we found to be on measurement, a perfect circle of 36 feet in diameter and resembles a large wheel or circus ring. The path is about 12 inches wide and as smooth and even as if rolled with some heavy iron instrument—nothing growing on this path whatever. It looks as slick as an otter slide. Crossing at right angles are two other paths similar to the outside one; making the whole thing look like a great big wheel. No vegetation whatever grows in these paths. But the strangest thing of it all is that inside of these angles grows the only wire grass that grows perhaps in 400 miles of this spot, and no other vegetation has ever, in the memory of those now living, grown on it, and there are persons nearly if not quite 90 years old living who remember seeing and hearing of it when they were little children, and so far as we can learn this phenomenon or freak or whatever you may call it existed before the knowledge of even their parents."

Follow SR 902 West to Harpers Crossroads and turn right on State Road 1106, then immediately turn left on State Road 1100. Go 1.7 miles until arriving at a gravel parking area on the left. The Tramping Ground is down a small path about 150 feet.

Southern Supreme. 1699 Hoyt Scott Rd.; (336) 581-3141; www.southernsupreme.com. While you're in Bear Creek, stop by for a tour and samples at the state's largest nutty fruit-cake factory. In addition to the often re-gifted traditional holiday treat, Southern Supreme also offers nuts, candy, jellies, and other great edible gift items.

siler city

Take US 421 from Bear Creek or US 64 west, then turn onto US 421, from Pittsboro to reach the town of Siler City, still in Chatham County. Few more than 8,500 people call Siler City home, nestled among the woodlands and green farmland. While it is losing some of its faming economic base the town is basing a revitalization effort on burgeoning interest in the arts.

where to go

The Arts Incubator. 223 North Chatham Ave.; (919) 663-1335; www.ncartsincubator.org. Located near Historic Downtown Siler City are five buildings that make up one of the state's most innovative art projects. The incubator hosts up to thirteen artists who work in various media, including fiber, ceramics, glass, and even in the production of musical instruments. A performance stage is located amongst the buildings in a manicured courtyard.

Celebrity Dairy. 144 Celebrity Dairy Way; (919) 742-5176 or (877) 742-5167; www.celebrity dairy.com. Part of a growing number of agritourism sites in the area, Celebrity Dairy is a working goat farm. It includes a Greek revival where guest can stay overnight, but visitors can also tour the barns during several events throughout the year. Celebrity Dairy hosts dinners on the third Sunday afternoon of each month. Dinner menus change with the seasons and always include award-winning Celebrity Dairy goat cheese.

day trip 03

west

>>> **living history:**
hillsborough

hillsborough

Heading south on I-85 or west on I-40 takes you to Hillsborough, a flourishing small town that remains much as it has been since the 18th century. True to its heritage, Hillsborough is a refreshing stopover for the traveler interested in Southern and national history.

As a capital of colonial and revolutionary North Carolina, Hillsborough was the scene of many important and dramatic events, including the War of the Regulation (1768–1771), the Third Provincial Congress (1775), and the raising of the royal standard by General Cornwallis (1781).

As the seat of Orange County, Hillsborough remained an important center of politics. It was the final residence of William Hooper, a signer of the Declaration of Independence, and the birthplace of Thomas Hart Benton, who was instrumental in the expansion of the United States during the first half of the 19th century. Prominent statesmen and jurists lived here, including William A. Graham, Thomas Ruffin (Senior and Junior), Frederick Nash, James Hogg, Francis Nash, and Alfred Moore.

In 1754 William Churton, surveyor and agent for John Carteret, Earl Granville, laid out Hillsborough as a town near where the Great Indian Trading Path crossed the Eno River. A pleasing mixture of modern convenience and rural charm, Hillsborough features shaded avenues that are a virtual record of the passing of two centuries, a combination of colonial, antebellum, Victorian, and modern styles of architecture.

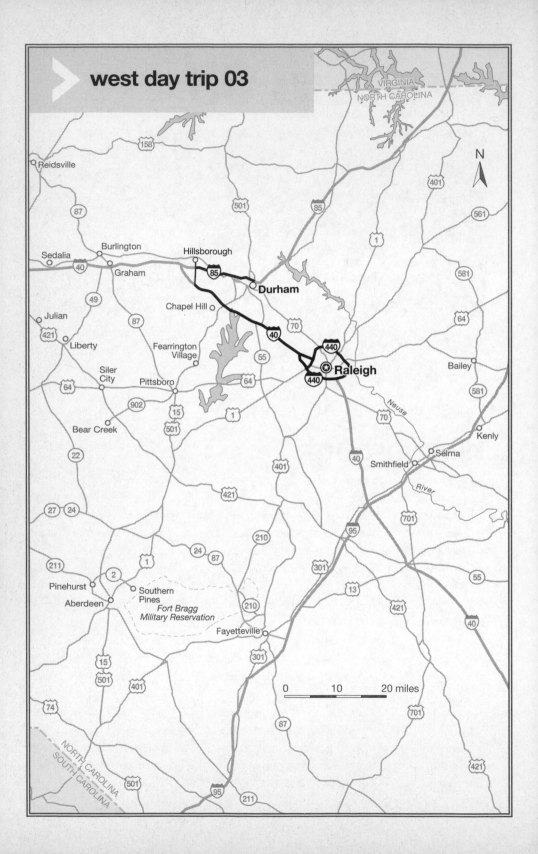

A living community rather than a reconstructed one, Hillsborough nevertheless has many lovingly restored buildings, both public and private, and the Town Hall is located in a former residence, complete with outbuildings.

Today you'll find more than one hundred sites listed on the National Register of Historic Places, some antedating the Revolutionary War. Gardens, flowering shrubs and trees, and a beautiful historical bed-and-breakfast add to the attractiveness of this small town. Antiques shops offer regional treasures, and the downtown area preserves a village atmosphere.

where to go

Alexander Dickson House. The Orange County Visitors Center and Office of the Alliance for Historic Hillsborough are both located at 150 East King St.; (919) 732-7741; www .historichillsborough.org. This late 18th-century Quaker-plan house was moved from its original site nearby and has been restored as the Orange County Visitors Center. An adjacent garden displays traditional 18th- and 19th-century plants used for cooking, medicine, and dyeing cloth. The site also includes an office used by Confederate General Joseph E. Johnston in April 1865. Open Mon through Sat 10 a.m. to 4 p.m., and Sun noon to 4 p.m.; closed on major holidays.

Ayr Mount. 376 Saint Mary's Rd.; (919) 732-6886. One of North Carolina's finest Federal-era plantation homes (ca. 1815), Ayr Mount has been carefully restored and exquisitely furnished with period antiques and fine art. Included are many original family pieces of William Kirkland, who built the original 500-acre home for his wife and their fourteen children. The home was occupied by four generations of the family until 1971. Guided tours are offered from mid-Mar to mid-Dec, Wed through Sat at 10 a.m., Thurs through Sun at 2 p.m., and other times by appointment. The house tour is $10 per person, and there's a free 1-mile self-guided tour called "Poet's Walk" around the site. The grounds are open daily 9 a.m. to 6 p.m.

The Burwell School. 319 North Churton St.; (919) 732-7451. Site of the Rev. and Mrs. Burwell's School for Young Ladies from 1837 to 1857, it includes a two-story frame house (circa 1821), brick music building (circa 1840), brick necessary house (circa 1840), and formal gardens. A half-hour guided tour focuses on the family, slaves, and students in antebellum Hillsborough. Open Wed through Sat 11 a.m. to 4 p.m., Sun 1 to 4 p.m. Free. Closed mid-Dec to mid-Jan and on major holidays.

Colonial Guides of Hillsborough. (919) 732-7741. Experienced guides dressed in colonial wear will fill you in on the facts, fantasy, and folklore of Hillsborough. The tour stops inside the Norwood Law Office, the Orange County Historical Museum, the Burwell School Historic Site, and the Hughes Academy while weaving through the streets of Hillsborough; groups pass the Old Orange County Courthouse, historic churches, cemeteries, colonial and antebellum homes, and more. Walking tours are scheduled periodically on Saturdays, departing from the Alexander Dickson House at 150 East King St. Tours are $5 per person.

Montrose Gardens. 320 Saint Mary's Rd.; (919) 732-7787. These nationally known gardens were first planted in the 19th century by Governor and Mrs. William Alexander Graham. In addition to a large garden, specimen trees, a rock garden, a woodland garden, and sunny perennial borders, several 19th-century buildings and architectural points of interest remain. Guided tours are $10 per person, available by appointment on Tues and Thurs at 10 a.m., and Sat at 10 a.m. and 2 p.m.

Occaneechi Indian Village. Foot of South Cameron Street; (919) 304-3723. This Indian village was reconstructed with a palisade, huts, a cooking site, and a sweat lodge, just as it existed in the general area in the late 17th century when native tribes in south-central Virginia and western North Carolina used it along a trading path. The Occaneechi–Saponi Spring Cultural Festival is held here each year, along with various Occaneechi Living Village Days. Don your archaeological duds to poke around the old mill sites and dams along the Eno River, where Native American relics are still found. This was once an important trading route that connected native towns for thousands of years before Europeans arrived. Self-guided tours are available. Open daily during daylight hours.

Old Orange County Courthouse. 201 North Churton at East King St.; (919) 732-7741. Designed and built by John Berry in 1844–45, the courthouse is an outstanding example of Greek Revival architecture, with details of woodwork and stair brackets from Asher Benjamin's pattern book. It's still the working county courthouse. An English clock (ca. 1769), a gift to the town of Hillsborough, is in the courthouse cupola.

Orange County Historical Museum. 201 North Churton St.; (919) 732-2201. Museum exhibits illustrate the first hundred years of Orange County's history and include the collection of silversmith William Huntington, colonial weights and measures (the only complete set in the United States), and portraits of notable colonial figures. A second-floor gallery features a different local artist each month. It's located on the site of North Carolina's 1788 constitutional convention. Open Tues through Sat 11 a.m. to 4 p.m., Sun 1 to 4 p.m. Free.

where to shop

Hillsborough Farmers' Market. Hampton Pointe Shopping Center, SR 86 at I-85, Exit 165; (919) 732-8315. The finest and freshest locally grown produce, prepared foods, flowers, and crafts can be found here every Sat from 8 a.m. to noon Apr through Nov, Sat 10 a.m. to noon Dec through Mar, plus every Wed from 4 to 7 p.m. from June through Labor Day.

Hillsborough Gallery of Arts. 121 North Churton St.; (919) 732-5001. Eighteen local artists exhibit paintings, sculpture, mouth-blown glass, fused glass, hand-turned wood, pottery, fiber art, jewelry, collage, and enamels. Hours are Mon through Sat 11 a.m. to 6 p.m. and Sun 1 to 4 p.m.

The Shops at Daniel Boone. South Churton Street; (919) 732-2361. Look for the Daniel Boone Statue near I-85 to find more than thirty antiques shops and a working blacksmith shop.

where to eat

Occoneechee Farm Steak House. 378 South Churton St.; (919) 732-6939. Specializing in steak and seafood, Occoneechee Farm is open seven days a week for breakfast, lunch, and dinner. $$–$$$.

Saratoga Grill. 108 South Churton St.; (919) 732-2214. This charming second-story restaurant in the heart of Hillsborough specializes in grilled seafood. Open for lunch Tues through Sat 11:30 a.m. to 3 p.m., dinner Tues through Thurs 5 to 9 p.m., and Fri and Sat to 10 p.m. $$.

Sonny's Sandwiches. 145 Mayo St.; (919) 644-7222. For a quick lunch or a light dinner, stop in at Sonny's. It's hard to beat the burgers here and the teriyaki chicken sandwich hits the spot, too. $.

Tupelo's Restaurant. 101 North Churton St.; (919) 643-7722. A diverse seasonal menu fuses Southern, Creole, Southwestern, and other regional flavors and includes creative specialty entrees, daily fresh seafood, and sandwiches. Open for lunch and dinner Mon through Sat. $$.

Village Diner. 600 West King St.; (919) 732-7032. There's a real hometown feel to this cafe, which serves great country cooking and is a great stop for breakfast. Save room for banana pudding. $–$$.

where to stay

Holiday Inn Express. 202 Cardinal Dr.; (919) 644-7997 or (800) 465-4329; www.hiexpress.com. Amenities include a complimentary continental breakfast, outdoor swimming pool, and fitness center. Kids up to age seventeen stay for free. $$.

The Inn at Teardrop. 175 West King St.; (919) 732-1120. This simple B&B with six rooms and a small garden was built in 1769 and enlarged in 1880. The house is beautifully furnished and decorated with antiques. Breakfast includes homemade muffins, a variety of egg dishes, and gourmet coffees. $$.

Microtel Inn and Suites. 120 Old Dogwood St.; (919) 245-3102 or (888) 771-7171; www.microtelinn.com. Nicely furnished rooms have chiropractor-approved mattresses. It's located near the Antique mall and Shops at Daniel Boone. $$.

day trip 04

west

>>> **gateway to the west:**
burlington, graham, reidsville

Centrally located on I-85 and I-40 between the Blue Ridge Mountains and the Atlantic seashore, Burlington and Graham can be reached from Raleigh by car, bus, train, or plane (or, if you were really ambitious, by boat or canoe). Two trains daily, operated by Amtrak, chug between Raleigh and Burlington and beyond. (800-USA-RAIL; www.amtrak.com.)

As a side trip, travel north on SR 87 to Reidsville, where you'll visit Chinqua-Penn Plantation, a twenty-seven-room mansion that was the home of Jeff and Betsy Penn. Penn's father and uncle started the Penn Tobacco Company, which they sold to the American Tobacco Company in 1911. Jeff subsequently purchased several hundred acres of land in Rockingham County and called the new tract "Corn Jug Farm," which later became Chinqua-Penn Plantation, named for the chinquapin, a dwarf chestnut tree.

burlington

In 1851 the North Carolina Railroad built its repair shops here and dubbed the community—what else?—Company Shops. Citizens wanting a real name submitted a list of suggestions in 1887. Katherine Scales, daughter of the governor, suggested Burlington.

Burlington's attractions include a Revolutionary War battleground, museums of local history, special events like hot air ballooning, and an abundance of outlet shopping. Relax at a park with a restored carousel or at a working historical farm. The performing arts are presented at local outdoor dramas and theaters. If you decide to spend the night, rest your

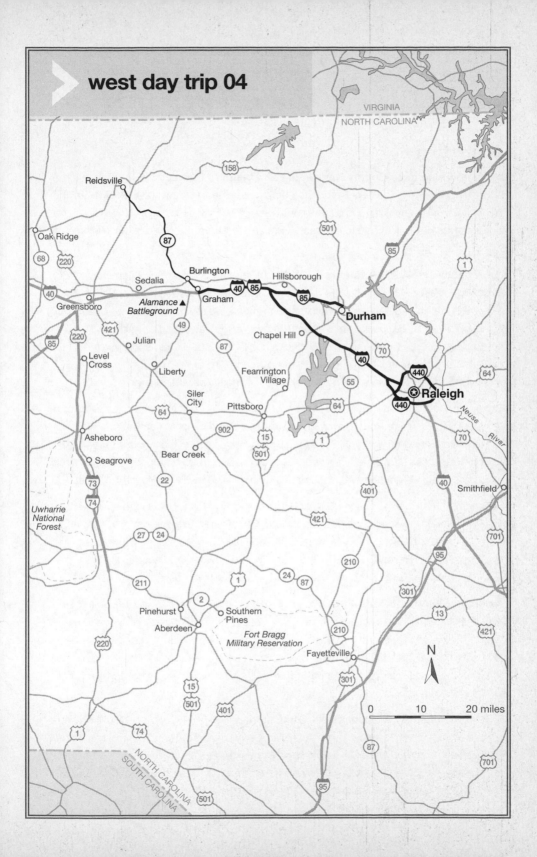

head in a pre–Civil War cabin, an upscale bed-and-breakfast, or one of Burlington's many hotels or motels.

where to go

Burlington/Alamance County Convention and Visitor's Bureau. 610 South Lexington St.; (800) 637-3804; www.burlington-area-nc.org. Located in downtown Burlington, the county's visitor bureau is a good place to begin your visit. Pick up brochures and maps and ask questions of the friendly staff. In fact, you can start from the office to visit downtown Burlington attractions.

ACE Speedway/NASCAR Racing. 3401 Altamahaw–Race Track Rd., Altamahaw; (336) 585-1200 (office) or (336) 584-6354 (race nights); www.acespeedway.com. 7 miles north of Burlington, this NASCAR-sanctioned speedway hosts weekly races in season. See stock car racing on a four-tenths-of-a-mile asphalt track every Friday night from April to September. Racing divisions include late-model stock, modifieds, super stock, and mini stock. Pits open at 4:30 p.m.; grandstands open at 6 p.m.; race begins at 7:50 p.m. Admission is $12 for adults, $6 for ages thirteen to sixteen and free for ages twelve and under.

Alamance Battleground. 5803 South SR 62; (336) 227-4785; www.nchistoricsites.org/alamance. This is where Royal Governor William Tryon led the North Carolina militia against the Regulators on May 16, 1771. Located on the grounds is the Allen House, a log dwelling characteristic of those lived in by frontier settlers. Constructed around 1780, the Allen House has been restored and refurbished with its original furnishings. Hours vary. Free.

Ballooning. The Hospice League Balloon Festival and Airshow is held in the spring, annually. For private balloon trips, the following pilots are commercially rated by the FAA: Aerial Impressions, Ken Draughn, 2834 McKinney St.; (336) 227-5414; Balloon Promotions of NC Inc., Chip Groome/Beverly Ray, 4265 Shepherd Dr.; (336) 584-7473 (features a balloon that will fly five people); Paisley Hot Air Balloons, 1104 East Willowbrook Dr.; (336) 227-0218.

Cedarock Historical Farm. 4242 Cedarock Park Rd.; (336) 570-6759; www.alamance-nc.com. Part of the county's parks and recreation department, Cedarock Historical Farm is located on the original site of the Garrett farm dating back to 1830. Buildings have been restored to closely mirror their original use. Livestock on the farm include sheep, goats, dairy and beef cattle, and a team of draft mules. It's typically open during daylight hours. Admission is free.

Dentzel Menagerie Carousel. South Church Street (SR 70); (336) 222-5030. The centerpiece of the seventy-six-acre Burlington City Park is a restored 1910 Dentzel Menagerie Carousel with forty-six hand-carved animals. Worldwide only fourteen Dentzel Menagerie Carousels remain intact. Dentzel carvers were renowned for their realism, apparent in the animals' facial expressions and muscle definition. The horses have real horsehair tails, and all the animals have shiny, round glass eyes. No two animals are alike. Hours vary by season, so call ahead. Admission is 75 cents. A train, boats, and other amusement rides are also available.

Glencoe Mill Village. River Road; (336) 228-6644; www.presnc.org. Travel back in time to when a cotton mill was the center of a community. The Glencoe Mill Village consists of a cotton mill complex and associated worker housing community built on a 105-acre site along the Haw River between 1880 and 1882. Two sons of Edwin M. Holt, arguably the most influential textile pioneer in the 19th-century South, developed the mill. Glencoe remains one of the best-preserved mill villages in North Carolina, providing a picture of the social and commercial organization of a late 19th-century water-powered Southern cotton mill village. The village, currently undergoing restoration, welcomes drive-by visitation.

Paramount Theater. 128 East Front St.; (336) 222-5001. This renovated theater in Historic Downtown Burlington has an art deco motif. The theater is home to such groups as the Gallery Players, the Alamance Children's Theater, and its own Paramount Acting Company. Hours and admission vary with events.

where to shop

Burlington Outlet Village. 2389 Corporation Pkwy.; (336) 227-2872; www.bmocoutlet .com. Quality name brands, selection, and value can be found here at more than seventy-five outlet and designer stores.

where to eat

B. Christopher's. 2461 South Church St.; (336) 222-1177. Because this restaurant fronts an office complex, it's easy to overlook B. Christopher's as just another law office or staffing company. Inside you'll find great food, including Chicken Savannah, herb-marinated chicken breasts served with mashed potatoes and a cucumber relish, along with tenderloin medallions and the restaurant's most requested entree, shrimp and grits. Open Mon through Sat 5 to 10 p.m. $$–$$$.

Blue Ribbon Diner. 2465 South Church St.; (336) 570-1120; www.bestfoodintown.com. Designed to resemble a 1950s diner, the Blue Ribbon serves a daily blue-plate special, hamburgers, cheeseburgers, and grilled chicken platters or baskets. Be sure to save room for an old-fashioned milk shake or dessert. "Haw River Mud" is an oversize, fresh-baked brownie topped with Breyers vanilla ice cream, Hershey's chocolate syrup, whipped cream, and a cherry; the peach cobbler sundae is topped off with vanilla ice cream. Open daily for lunch and dinner. $$.

Hursey's Pig-Pickin' Bar-B-Q. 1834 South Church St. and 1234 South Main St., Graham; (336) 226-1695; www.hurseysbarbq.com. Recognized by *USA Today* as serving some of the best barbecue in the country, Hursey's barbecue was described by reporter Jerry Shriver as "hickory-smoked shoulder meat laced with just the right amount of vinegar and a little sweetener." Seafood and chicken are also available. Open Mon through Sat 11 a.m. to 9 p.m. $–$$.

where to stay

Burke Manor Inn Bed and Breakfast. 303 Burke St., Gibsonville; (336) 449-6266 or (888) 287-5311; www.burkemanor.com. Although it's 20 miles from Greensboro, this upscale, elegant retreat decorated in period furniture is worth the drive. The inn has an on-site restaurant and an outdoor pool. $$–$$$.

Comfort Inn. 2701 Kirkpatrick Rd.; (336) 584-4447. The Comfort Inn offers a complimentary continental breakfast, free local calls, fitness center, spa, sauna, and outdoor pool. It's conveniently located at I-85 and I-40. $$.

Courtyard by Marriott. 3141 Wilson Dr.; (800) 321-2211. The Marriott has a lounge with fireplace, an outdoor pool, an exercise room and Jacuzzi, and a restaurant with a full breakfast buffet. Appetizers are also served nightly in the lobby. While it's made for business travelers it's a good choice for a couple of nights. $$.

Quality Inn and Suites. 2444 Maple Ave.; (336) 229-5203. Formerly the LaQuinta, this facility has an outdoor pool, fitness center, business center, restaurant, lounge, and Jacuzzi suites. It's located near many of the area's major attractions. $$.

graham

Formerly part of Orange County, Alamance County was formed in 1849; Graham was designated the new county seat. In the act providing for the town, Graham was first named Gallatin, then Montgomery, Berry, and finally Graham, after William A. Graham, who was governor from 1845 to 1849. An equal distance from the coastal region in the east and the Blue Ridge Mountains in the west, Graham is the second largest city in Alamance County. From Burlington, retrace your steps on SR 87 to reach Graham.

where to go

Alamance County Arts Council/Captain James and Emma Holt White House. 213 South Main St.; (336) 226-4495; www.artsalamance.com. Through adaptive restoration, the Alamance County Arts Council has turned the 1871 Queen Anne–style mansion of Captain James and Emma Holt White into an art gallery and a home for the Arts Council office. The gallery's changing exhibits showcase artists of local, regional, and national acclaim, and the sales gallery carries handmade gifts and crafts by North Carolina artisans. The house offers formal reception rooms and a garden. Open Mon through Sat 9 a.m. to 5 p.m. Free.

Alamance County Courthouse. 1 Court Square; (336) 438-1002. The neoclassic Revival Alamance County Courthouse is a three-story stone building located on a hexagonal plot in the center of Graham's commercial district. Designed in 1925 by Harry Barton, a noted architect of the period, the structure replaced the original brick courthouse built in 1849. Sophisticated and richly detailed, the courthouse is the major landmark in Graham. Its scale, style, and materials blend well with the town's commercial buildings, many of which are contemporaries of the courthouse.

City of Graham Historical Museum. 135 West Elm St.; (336) 513-4773. The museum is the home for Graham Fire Department's Engine 1, a 1930 Seagraves fire truck. Other firefighting equipment is on display, along with local pottery, weapons, military artifacts, and other historical pieces that are related to the history of the citizens of Graham. Open Sun 2 to 5 p.m. and by appointment.

Graham Cinema. 119 North Main St.; (336) 226-1448. According to the owners, the Graham Cinema offers "one theater with one big screen, not a bunch of little bitty screens back in a corner somewhere." With rocking-chair seats, free refills on popcorn and drinks, and second-run movies, the Graham Cinema also features amusing synopses of current flicks. Admission is $3.

Sesquicentennial Park. Court Square; (336) 570-1444. Relax in this pleasant park, which was developed to commemorate Alamance County's 150th birthday, celebrated on April 24, 1999. The 2,500-square-foot park has a garden, an arbor for vines, park benches, brick walls, and a 10,600-pound bell that sat atop the original courthouse in Graham.

where to eat

Barrister's Cafe. 28 Northwest Court Square; (336) 221-1112. Located in the Paris Building on the Graham Courthouse Square, Barrister's Cafe offers wonderful sandwiches, soups, and salads. With choices such as the turkey bacon club, blackened chicken salad, and hot house chili, Barrister's is a great place for lunch or dinner. Open Mon through Thurs 11 a.m. to 9 p.m., Fri and Sat to 10 p.m. $$.

Carver's on Elm. 106 West Elm St.; (336) 229-0641. With daily specials of good home cooking, Carver's on Elm is a great restaurant for families. Selections range from prime rib to chicken tenders to oysters. Open Sun through Fri for lunch, Tues through Sat for dinner. $$.

reidsville

In May 1814, farmer Reuben Reid moved his family to a 700-acre farm on the ridge between Wolf Island and Little Troublesome Creeks in south Rockingham County. Reid became a successful farmer, operated a store and a public inn maintained in a private home, and served the county as a constable and justice of the peace. When the family secured a post office in 1829, sixteen-year-old David Reid was appointed its first postmaster. He later became a public servant in the form of a state senator (1835–42), a US congressman (1843–47), a governor of North Carolina (1850), and a US senator (1854).

The town was incorporated in 1873 by the North Carolina State Legislature. Tobacco was a mainstay of the local economy for many years, and the history of the city was tightly woven with that of American Tobacco Company, which was sold and moved from Reidsville in 1994.

where to go

Chinqua-Penn Plantation. 2138 Wentworth St.; (336) 349-4576; www.chinquapenn .com. The 1920s come alive at this remarkable, historic twenty-seven-room mansion surrounded by award-winning gardens. Stroll through twenty-two acres of historic landscape that was the home of Jeff and Betsy Penn. Chinqua-Penn reflects the Penns' lavish lifestyle of entertaining, traveling, and collecting art and furniture from around the world. Art and furniture in the home represent some thirty countries the Penns visited. Wines made from local grapes are available for tasting and purchase. House-tour hours are Sat 10 a.m. to 4 p.m. and Sun 1 to 4 p.m. The grounds are open until 5:30 p.m. during regular tour days. The wine-tasting room is open Mon through Sat noon to 5 p.m. and Sun 1 to 5 p.m. Admission is $20 for adults, $15 seniors, and $10 for children ages six to fifteen. Admission to the wine tasting room is an additional $5.

day trip 05

west

>>> **triad center:**
greensboro, julian, oak ridge

West out of Raleigh on I-40 just beyond Burlington is Guilford County, created by the North Carolina General Assembly in 1771. The county includes Greensboro, the state's third largest city and this guide's largest, and the small towns of Julian and Oak Ridge as well as High Point and Jamestown, which we'll travel to a little later. This is the central section of an eleven-county area known as the Triad.

Greensboro and the immediate area are bustling with business. The area's educational stature is eclipsed by Raleigh-Durham's, but there are eight colleges in the county. Sports, arts, and culture are also alive and well, with a host of activities from which to choose.

As you will discover, Guilford County's role in the Revolutionary War was significant. Perhaps what is just as significant is the role that residents of this area played in the 1960s civil rights movement and earlier, at the turn of the century, in the significant advancements in the education of black Americans. In this day trip, we'll travel to the Charlotte Hawkins Brown State Historic Site to learn how this granddaughter of slaves helped elevate black men and women to professional jobs in this area.

Then we're off on two quick side trips. We'll head north briefly on SR 68 to the town of Oak Ridge for a quick history lesson, and south on US 421 to the town of Julian for a lesson in speed.

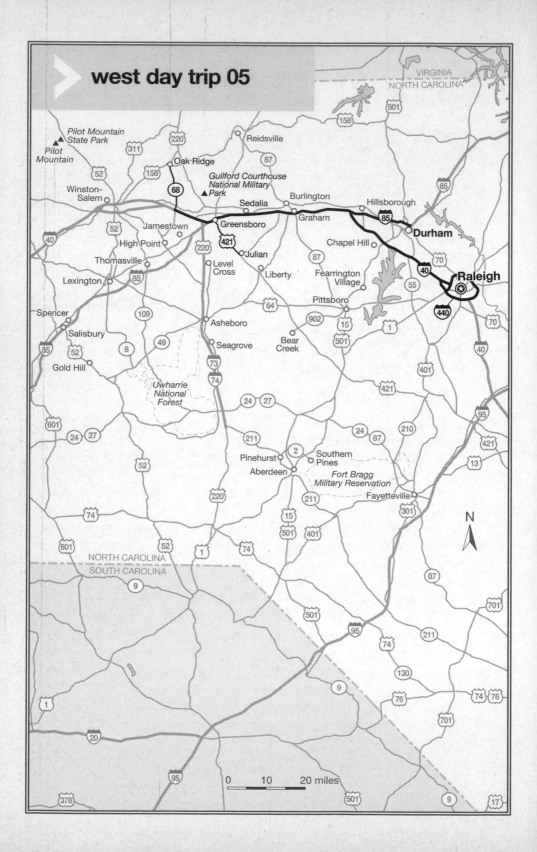

greensboro

Travel back in time as you head west on I-40/I-85 from Raleigh-Durham to Greensboro. This Triad city allows you to relive history from the Revolutionary War battle to the sit-ins that helped launch the national civil rights movement.

The Saura and Keyauwee Indians were the earliest inhabitants of the region. Germans, Quakers of Welsh and English descent, and Scotch-Irish from the northern colonies were the first European settlers in the Greensboro area. Permanent settlement began around 1740.

In 1767, a Presbyterian minister, David Caldwell, started a local school known as the Log College to educate young men for the ministry. One of his students was John Motley Morehead, governor of North Carolina from 1841 to 1845.

In 1774 a log courthouse and jail were built in a place called Guilford Courthouse, the site of a fierce battle on March 15, 1781. That day, American Major General Nathanael Greene deployed 4,400 rebels at the Battle of Guilford Courthouse to thwart the invasion of North Carolina by 1,900 redcoats under Lord Cornwallis. Cornwallis held the field after an intense fight, but he lost a quarter of his army, which hastened his defeat at Yorktown seven months later.

In 1807 the residents of the area voted to create a new, more centrally located seat of government. The following year elected officials mapped out a forty-two-acre tract of land, paid $98 to purchase it, and suggested that it be named Greensborough in honor of General Greene.

The railroad was a key factor in Greensboro's prosperity and industrial growth. John Motley Morehead campaigned for two decades to have Greensboro included as a stop on the North Carolina Railroad. Finally in 1856 a special east-west line of tracks was completed.

During the Civil War, Greensboro was both a storehouse and a railroad center for the Confederacy, a vital source of supplies and troops for Robert E. Lee's Army of Northern Virginia. Civilian refugees and wounded soldiers were transported and sheltered here. Greensboro became the seat of the Confederacy on April 11, 1865, when Confederate President Jefferson Davis arrived here after Lee's surrender at Appomattox to discuss the military situation of General Joseph E. Johnston and the weakened Army of the Tennessee.

A reluctant Davis was advised by Johnston that the Confederate position was untenable and that he should enter into surrender negotiations with Sherman. These negotiations led to Johnston's surrender to Sherman on April 26, 1865, at Bennett Place outside Durham. Later, all Confederate forces in North Carolina were mustered out and paroled in Greensboro.

William Sydney Porter was an eyewitness to the Union occupation of Greensboro. Years later, using his pen name, O. Henry, he recounted these experiences in some of his short stories. Porter's uncle ran a successful town drugstore in the 1890s. Lunsford Richardson, one of the store's investors, later developed a line of "Vick's Family Remedies." Vicks VapoRub was one of his successful creations.

Textiles were important in Greensboro as early as 1828, when Henry Humphreys built North Carolina's first steam-powered cotton mill. In 1895, Moses and Caesar Cone selected Greensboro for their Southern Finishing and Warehouse Co., forerunner of Cone Mills. By 1920 Blue Bell was a successful maker of bib overalls. In 1935, attracted by the city's railroad and airport, Burlington Industries moved its headquarters to Greensboro. Guilford Mills began operations in 1946.

Greensboro was again a military center during World War II, when railroads brought thousands of soldiers here for army training. In 1944, the training facility became the Overseas Replacement Depot (ORD) for the Army Air Corps in the eastern United States. Today, Greensboro is a vibrant Piedmont city with much to offer the visitor.

where to go

Greensboro Area Convention and Visitors Bureau. 2200 Pinecroft Rd., Suite 200; (800) 344-2282 or (336) 274-2282; www.greensboronc.org. Stop here for free guides, maps, and information on area attractions, accommodations, shopping, restaurants, golf, and a wide variety of activities and special events. Hours are Mon through Fri 8:30 a.m. to 5:30 p.m., Sat 9 a.m. to 4 p.m., and Sun 1 to 5 p.m.

Blandwood Mansion and Carriage House. 400 West McGee St.; (336) 272-5003; www .blandwood.org. This elegant 19th-century Italian villa was home to one-time North Carolina Governor John Motley Morehead. The 1844 addition by renowned architect Alexander Jackson Davis contributed to Blandwood's designation as a National Historic Landmark. Today it still displays many of its original furnishings and is operated as a museum by Preservation Greensboro Inc. and the Blandwood Guild. Open Tues through Sat 11 a.m. to 4 p.m., Sun 2 to 5 p.m. The last tour begins thirty minutes before closing. Closed the first week of Jan. Admission is $8 for adults, $7 for seniors, and $5 for children under age twelve.

The Broach Theatre. 520 South Elm St.; (336) 378-9300; www.broachtheatre.org. A professional theater company that offers a full season of adult and children's theater in the heart of the Old Greensborough Historic District. Originally built in 1927 as the Salvation Army, this intimate theater is within walking distance of five of Greensboro's finest restaurants. Adult season runs Feb through July and Sept through Dec. Children's theater runs Sept through June.

Carolina Theatre. 310 South Greene St.; (336) 333-2605; www.carolinatheatre.com. First opened in 1927, this restored vaudeville theater serves as one of Greensboro's principal performing arts centers, showcasing theater, dance, concerts, and films. The theater is listed on the National Register of Historic Places.

Celebration Station. 4315 Big Tree Way; (336) 316-0606; www.celebrationstation.com. Enjoy a great collection of attractions designed to entertain the whole family, with miniature golf, go-karts, bumper boats, arcade games, batting cages, and two theme restaurants. Birthday and group party packages are available. Call for hours.

Charlotte Hawkins Brown Memorial State Historic Site. 6136 Burlington Rd., Sedalia; (336) 449-4846; www.nchistoricsites.org/chb. 10 miles east of Greensboro off I-85 exit 135, this is North Carolina's first official historic site to honor an African American and a woman. The site is the former location of the Palmer Institute, a preparatory school for African Americans established by Brown in 1902. Open, Mon through Sat 9 a.m. to 5 p.m. Free.

The Greensboro Arboretum. Near Wendover Avenue at West Market Street and Starmount Drive; (336) 373-2199; www.greensborobeautiful.org. Twelve labeled plant collections, special garden displays, and distinctive features are contained within a seventeen-acre portion of Lindley Park. The natural beauty of this area is inviting, and the planted collections provide appeal throughout the year. Open daily, sunrise to sunset.

Greensboro Children's Museum. 220 North Church St.; (336) 574-2898; www.gc museum.com. Hands-on exhibits and activities are designed for one- to ten-year-olds. Fly in an airplane, dig for buried treasure, or wrap yourself in a gigantic bubble. Stroll through "Our Town," complete with a grocery store and bank, then take in the transportation, theater, and early childhood exhibit areas. Open Tues through Sat 9 a.m. to 5 p.m., Fri to 8 p.m., and Sun 1 to 5 p.m. Open on Mon in the summer. Admission is $6 for anyone over age one.

Greensboro Cultural Center at Festival Park. 200 North Davie St.; (336) 373-4678; www.greensboro-nc.gov. Browse through this architectural showplace housing twelve visual and performing arts organizations, four art galleries, rehearsal halls, a sculpture garden, a privately operated restaurant with outdoor cafe-style seating, and an outdoor amphitheater. Open Mon through Fri 8 a.m. to 10 p.m., Sat 9 a.m. to 6:30 p.m., and Sun 1 to 6:30 p.m. Free.

Greensboro Historical Museum. 130 Summit Ave.; (336) 373-2043; www.greensboro history.org. Discover American history through the stories of Piedmont people and events in twelve galleries and two restored houses. You'll learn about the 1960 Greensboro civil rights sit-ins, Guilford native Dolley Madison's lasting legacy as first lady, and the popular short stories written by O. Henry. See the city through 20th-century photography, imagine travel in a Model T, and marvel at furniture created by Piedmont craftsmen. You'll also have the chance to see a world-class collection of Civil War firearms, stroll through a historic cemetery, and check out the merchandise of an old-fashioned general store. Open Tues through Sat 10 a.m. to 5 p.m., Sun 2 to 5 p.m. Closed on City of Greensboro holidays except the Fourth of July. Free.

Guilford Courthouse National Military Park. 2332 New Garden Rd.; (336) 288-1776; www.nps.gov/guco. On more than 200 acres, twenty-eight monuments of soldiers, statesmen, and patriots of the American Revolution honor the site of the March 15, 1781 battle. Park activities include a self-guided auto tour (audiotape tour available) and colorful, informational on-site exhibits. In the visitor center, see a dramatic thirty-minute live-action film (shown on the hour), an animated battle map program, and information-packed museum exhibits featuring original Revolutionary War weaponry and artifacts. The park also provides paved walking trails and a bookstore. Open daily 8:30 a.m. to 5 p.m. Closed New Year's Day, Thanksgiving, and Christmas. Free.

The International Civil Rights Center and Museum. 134 South Elm St.; (336) 274-9199; www.sitinmovement.org. On a chilly, windy February day in 1960, four black students from North Carolina A&T University walked into a Greensboro five and dime, sat down, and began to write a new chapter in American history. Today that F.W. Woolworth's store has been converted into a center and museum dedicated to telling the story of the civil rights movement. Central among archival displays is the lunch counter where those students and their classmates would sit in peaceful protest over segregation that was a way of life in the 1960s South. Through one-hour guided tours, visitors begin to understand the history and the effects of segregation from 18th and 19th century slavery to the Jim Crow South. It documents, through three levels of exhibits, the efforts of those students and others who contributed to change a society. Open Tues through Sat 10 a.m. to 6 p.m. and Sun 1 to 5 p.m. Admission is $8 for adults, $6 for students, $4 for children ages six to twelve and $6 for seniors.

Mattye Reed African Heritage Center. 1601 East Market St.; (336) 334-7108. Located in the Dudley Building on the North Carolina A&T State University campus, the museum houses one of the best collections of African culture in the country. See more than 3,500 arts and crafts items from more than thirty African nations, New Guinea, and Haiti. Open Mon through Fri 10 a.m. to 5 p.m. Free.

Natural Science Center and Animal Discovery Zoological Park. 4301 Lawndale Dr.; (336) 288-3769; www.natsci.org. At this hands-on museum, zoo, and planetarium, roam through the Dinosaur Gallery and learn about gems and minerals. Visit snakes and amphibians in the Jaycee Herpetarium, explore Kids Alley, and interact with exciting traveling exhibits. The facility's newest exhibit includes a zoo with tigers, crocodiles, primates, a farm petting zoo, and many other animals. Find unusual gifts and educational toys for imaginative minds in the Thesaurus Shoppe. Open Mon through Sat 9 a.m. to 5 p.m., Sun 12:30 to 5 p.m. The Animal Park is open Mon through Sat 10 a.m. to 4 p.m. and Sun 12:30 to 4 p.m. Admission is $8 for adults, $7 for children ages two through thirteen and for seniors.

O. Henry Statues. Corner of North Elm and Bellemeade Streets; (336) 373-2043. This three-piece outdoor sculpture group honors Greensboro's best-known writer, William Sydney Porter (O. Henry). It features a bronze likeness of the author, a 7-by-14-foot open book of his renowned short stories, and a statue of his small dog, Lovey. An exhibit of the life and times of O. Henry may be seen at the Greensboro Historical Museum.

Old Greensborough and the Downtown Historic District. 122 North Elm St.; (336) 379-0060. This revitalized century-old commercial, residential, and industrial district features antiques, art, and other unique shops and restaurants. The Antique and Art Festival is held each April on South Elm Street, providing antiques appraisals, entertainment, and more than fifty invited vendors of antiques, art, and food. Be sure to pick up the free downtown shopping guide, available at most merchant locations, the Greensboro Area Convention and Visitors Bureau, Greensboro Historical Museum, and the Downtown Greensboro Incorporated office.

Tanger Family Bicentennial Garden and David Caldwell Historic Park. 1105 Hobbs Rd., just north of Friendly Avenue; (336) 373-2199; www.greensborobeautiful.org. This beautiful garden has flowering and deciduous trees, shrubs, and annual beds, and the Bog Garden, a marsh of ferns, bamboo, and other plants. The adjacent park is named in honor of Caldwell, who served as a local minister and educator and owned much of this land.

Tannenbaum Historic Park. 2200 New Garden Rd.; (336) 545-5315. Operated by the City of Greensboro's Parks and Recreation Department, this seven-and-a-half-acre park was the 18th-century farmstead of Joseph Hoskins, who served the Guilford County community as constable, tax collector, and sheriff. During the Revolutionary War Battle of Guilford Courthouse, Hoskins's land served as a staging area for British troops under Cornwallis's command. The Colonial Heritage Center offers a variety of exhibits depicting life in colonial Guilford County. Living history programs are scheduled throughout the year. The park also offers a museum store and picnic area. Open Fri through Sun 8:30 a.m. to 5 p.m. Free.

Triad Stage. 232 South Elm St.; (336) 272-0160; www.triadstage.org. Classic, contemporary, and new theatrical works, both drama and comedy, are presented in this 300-seat live performance theater with two spacious lobbies and many other amenities in the former Montgomery Ward store in Greensboro's downtown historic district. No performances in Aug and Sept.

Walkway of History. South Elm Street at February One Plaza. Sidewalk markers chronicle six chapters in local African-American history, ranging from the first fugitive slave on the Underground Railroad to the first black state Supreme Court justice. The walkway was unveiled on the thirty-fourth anniversary of the Woolworth civil rights sit-ins by the "Greensboro Four."

Weatherspoon Art Museum. Spring Garden and Tate Streets. (336) 334-5770. On the campus of UNC–Greensboro, this fine museum houses a nationally recognized collection, outstanding special exhibitions, and educational activities. With six galleries and a sculpture courtyard, the museum has a collection of more than 5,000 objects, including paintings, sculptures, drawings, prints and photographs, and objects in miscellaneous media. Highlights include the Dillard Collection of art on paper and the Cone Collection of prints and bronzes by Henri Matisse. Open Tues, Wed, and Fri 10 a.m. to 5 p.m., Thurs 5 to 9 p.m., and Sat and Sun 1 to 5 p.m. Free.

Wet 'n Wild Emerald Pointe Water Park. 3910 South Holden Rd., I-85 exit 121; (336) 852-9721 or (800) 555-5900; www.emeraldpointe.com. The largest water park in the Carolinas and one of the top twelve in the United States offers more than thirty-five rides and attractions. The park provides exciting summer fun. Thunder Bay, one of only four tsunami pools in the country, makes massive, perfect waves. Dr. Von Dark's Tunnel of Terror sends you down a 40-foot drop spinning 360 degrees in total darkness. Enclosed slides, drop slides, tube rides, and cable glides provide thrills for all ages and sizes. Two great children's areas and a drifting lazy river complete the fun for everyone. Tickets are $21.99 for those under 48 inches and $32.99 for those 48 inches or taller. Call for seasonal hours of operation.

where to shop

Four Seasons Town Centre. I-40 at High Point Road/Koury Boulevard; (336) 292-0171; www.shopfourseasons.com. The Centre's three levels include more than 200 specialty stores and eateries, as well as department stores Belk, Dillard's, and JCPenney. Stop by for a bite to eat in the food court, or enjoy free and regularly scheduled entertainment in the new performing arts amphitheater. Open Mon through Sat 10 a.m. to 9 p.m., Sun 12:30 to 7 p.m.

Friendly Center. Friendly Avenue near the Wendover Avenue Overpass; (336) 292-2789; www.friendlycenter.com. This shopping center, originally opened in 1957, is a telling example of how to manage a retail shopping establishment successfully. "The secret of our success is that we have not stood still," says Bill Hansen, the center's director of property management. Renovations began in 1992 and have continued since. Shops include an Ann Taylor Loft and Chico's. Also located here is a multiplex theater, the Grande. Other shops include Barnes & Noble Booksellers, Old Navy, Banana Republic, Eddie Bauer, Victoria's Secret, Gap, and anchors such as Belk, Macy's, and Sears. Friendly Center also boasts several restaurants, including Harpers and the ever-popular Jay's Deli. Open Mon through Sat 10 a.m. to 9 p.m. and Sun 1 to 6 p.m.

Greensboro Farmers' Curb Market. 501 Yanceyville St.; (336) 373-2402. The best in homegrown vegetables, fruits, and produce is only half the story: Fresh-cut herbs and flowers, baked goods, pottery, and crafts also are available. Linger, chat with the crowd as goods are unloaded, and shop the old-fashioned way. Open Jan through Apr, Sat 6 a.m. to noon; May through Dec, Wed 7 a.m. to 1 p.m., and Sat 6 a.m. to noon.

Piedmont Triad Farmers' Market. 2914 Sandy Ridge Rd.; (336) 605-9157; www.triad farmersmarket.com. Get to know some of the South's friendliest people while shopping for local Piedmont fruits, vegetables, flowers, baked goods, jams, honey, crafts, and more. Make sure you visit the garden center and Moose Cafe while you're there. Open daily 7 a.m. to 8 p.m.

Replacements, Ltd. Knox Road off I-85/40 exit 132 at Mt. Hope Church Road; (336) 697-3000 or (800) REPLACE; www.replacements.com. The world's largest retailer of old and new china, crystal, flatware, and collectibles that claims to have more than 13 million pieces of inventory in 300,000-plus patterns. During the free daily tours of the showrooms, museum, warehouse, and restoration facility, patrons can inquire about patterns and shop Replacements' 13,000-square-foot showroom for giftware, dinnerware, one-of-a-kind items, antiques, and collectibles. Open daily 9 a.m. to 7 p.m.; closed Christmas Day.

Shopping in Old Greensborough. For more information, call Downtown Greensboro Incorporated, (336) 379-0060. Browse more than a dozen antiques shops, including old-fashioned clothing stores, a grocery and seed store, and a haven of bookstores, to name a few of the downtown treasures. A free downtown shopping guide is available at most merchant locations, the Greensboro Area Convention and Visitors Bureau, Greensboro Historical Museum, and Downtown Greensboro Incorporated. The district is located in and around South Elm Street from the 100 block south through the 600 block. It also includes the 300 blocks of South Davie and South Greene Streets, as well as portions of East and West Washington Streets.

State Street Station. Between North Elm and Church Streets, just north of Wendover Avenue. (336) 275-8586. Stroll through a cordial, relaxed neighborhood of thirty-five unique shops, restaurants, and boutiques housed in elegantly refurbished 1920s vintage buildings.

where to eat

Anton's Restaurant. 1628 Battleground Ave.; (336) 273-1386; www.cellarantons.com. A family restaurant serving Greensboro since 1960, Anton's specializes in Italian, steaks, seafood, salads, and sandwiches. Dine underground in the cellar. Open Mon through Fri for lunch and dinner, Sat for dinner only. $$.

Barn Dinner Theatre. 120 Stage Coach Trail; (336) 292-2211 or (800) 668-1764; www .barndinner.com. Enjoy a popular Broadway-style play after sampling a traditional buffet at what is reportedly the oldest dinner theater in the country. Performances are Wed through Sun evenings year-round. Matinees are offered Sun through Tues. $$$.

Bert's Seafood Grille. 4608 West Market St.; (336) 297-4881; www.bertsseafoodgrille .com. Specializing in fresh, non-fried seafood, Bert's wine list has earned a Wine Spectator

Award of Excellence, and the seafood has been named best of the Triad. Open daily for dinner. $$.

Di Valletta Restaurant. Grandover Resort and Conference Center, 1000 Club Rd.; (336) 834-4877. As the most elegant dining room in the Triad, this AAA four-diamond restaurant overlooks the golf course and offers unique Mediterranean dishes to suit all tastes. Outdoor dining is available. Open daily for breakfast, lunch, and dinner. $$–$$$.

Europa Bar and Cafe. Greensboro Cultural Center at Festival Park, 200 North Davie St.; (336) 389-1010; www.europabarandcafe.com. At this informal but stylish cafe, you can enjoy a full menu or dine lightly on a variety of hors d'oeuvres or appetizers. Enjoy wines from around the world, reasonably priced by the bottle or glass. Outdoor dining is available. Open Mon through Sat for lunch and dinner, Sun for brunch and dinner. $–$$.

Gate City Chop House. 106 South Holden Rd.; (336) 294-9977; www.chophousesofnc .com. Known throughout North Carolina, this upscale steakhouse specializes in certified Angus beef, ocean-fresh seafood, veal, lamb, and pork entrees. You'll find Chop Houses in Winston-Salem, Wilmington, and Raleigh, but this is the original. $$$.

The Green Valley Grill. 622 Green Valley Rd.; (336) 854-2015. Adjacent to the O. Henry Hotel, enjoy internationally elegant dining with an Old World influence. Changing menus feature regional European recipes that may be from Provence one month and Tuscany the next. $$–$$$.

Liberty Oak. 100 West Washington St.; (336) 273-7057; www.libertyoakrestaurant.com. Rated four stars by Greensboro's *News & Record,* Liberty Oak offers casual elegance, a changing menu, extensive wines by the glass, and outdoor dining. Open Mon through Sat for lunch and dinner. $–$$.

Lucky 32. 1421 Westover Terrace; (336) 370-0707; www.lucky32.com. Changing menus every month or so offering regional American cuisine. Menus might feature recipes from the Pacific Northwest one month and from New Orleans the next. Open daily for lunch and dinner, Sun for brunch. $$–$$$.

Rearn Thai Restaurant. 5109 West Market St.; (336) 292-5901. As one of only a few Thai restaurants here, it provides a cultural and spicy twist on typical Asian cuisine and offers lunch specials. Open Mon through Sat for lunch and dinner. $–$$.

Red Oak Brew Pub. 714 Francis King St.; (336) 299-3649. North Carolina's largest microbrewery offers a twenty-minute tour of the Bavarian-built brewhouse and fermentation cellar. See how lagers are brewed according to the 1516 Bavarian Law of Purity. Taste samples of Red Oak, Battlefield Black, and other smooth beers. Red Oak raises its own free-range Angus beef and uses only fresh, all-natural ingredients in homemade specialties. Brewery tours are by reservation. Outdoor dining is available. Open daily. $$.

Ruth's Chris Steak House. 800 Green Valley Rd., Suite 100; (336) 574-1515; www.ruths chris.com. The nationally known chain, Ruth's Chris specializes in corn-fed aged Midwestern beef that is broiled at 1,800 degrees. Open daily. $$$.

Saigon Cuisine Restaurant. 4205 High Point Rd.; (336) 294-9286. This small, intimate restaurant serves Vietnamese cuisine. It is consistently listed as one of the Triad's top ten restaurants. Open Mon through Sat. $$–$$$.

223 South Elm. 223 South Elm St.; (336) 272-3331. Located in a facility that has changed hands a number of times in recent years, this establishment boasts "innovative Southern cuisine." It has an extensive wine list and dishes that range from rosemary barbecue shrimp and crab cakes to pork tenderloin brojole and grilled Angus rib eye. The Chef's Shin Dig is a daily changing item on the menu that promises "five courses of today's ingredients and unique ideas." The restaurant is open for lunch and dinner with reservations recommended for dinner. $$$.

Yum Yum Better Ice Cream Co. 1219 Spring Garden St.; (336) 272-8284. A Greensboro institution located near UNC–G, Yum Yum serves ice cream and hot dogs. Open Mon through Sat. $.

where to stay

Biltmore Greensboro Hotel. 111 West Washington St.; (336) 272-3474 or (800) 332-0303; www.biltmorehotelgreensboro.com. Accommodations at this unique European boutique hotel, conveniently located in historic downtown Greensboro, include a complimentary deluxe continental breakfast. $$$.

Grandover Resort and Conference Center. 1000 Club Rd.; (336) 294-1800 or (800) 472-6301; www.grandover.com. Located on 1,500 acres, this AAA four-diamond resort has 247 guest rooms in an eleven-story tower, men's and women's spa facilities, a four-court tennis complex, two racquetball courts, an indoor/outdoor swimming pool, five food and beverage outlets, and lush gardens, as well as the rolling terrain of the resort's top-rated golf courses. The resort has a spa with five treatment rooms and an 1,800-square-foot fitness center. $$$.

Greenwood Bed and Breakfast. 205 North Park Dr.; (336) 274-6350 or (800) 535-9363; www.greenwoodbb.com. A culinary escape where great conversation is standard fare, this turn-of-the-20th-century "chalet on the park" serves a fine-dining breakfast by candlelight. Located in Greensboro's finest historic district, it serves upscale traditional American dishes with European touches and offers private baths and an in-ground pool. $$.

O. Henry Hotel. 624 Green Valley Rd.; (800) 965-8259; www.ohenryhotel.com. Look for the rise of red brick conveniently located near Friendly Center. The stately AAA

good to be green

A visit to the country's first LEED Platinum hotel means your daytrip or overnight can help the planet too. The US Green Building Council awarded **The Proximity Hotel,** *704 Green Valley Rd., with the highest recognition in the Leadership in Energy and Environmental Design (LEED) rating system, the nationally accepted benchmark for the design, construction and operation of high performance green buildings.*

The Proximity is built to use forty percent less energy and thirty percent less water than a comparable hotel, but the local ownership didn't spare luxury. The hotel received a four diamond AAA rating because of its custom furnishings and detail, commissioned art, and innovative, stylish design complemented by abundant natural light and carefully-selected, green construction materials.

Print Works Bistro, the hotel's European-influenced restaurant, is worth the stop on its own. Built with the same sorts of green practices, the restaurant also uses local produce in dishes served on reclaimed walnut tabletops. In the kitchen, geothermal energy and sensor-controlled ventilation do their part to conserve.

The Proximity, named for a local mill, has 147 guest rooms, ten suites, and all the amenities expected of this level of hotel. Rates start at about $200 per night and Bistro entrees average $20 for dinner. Hotel packages include a restaurant voucher, and the hotel has partnered with AMTRAK by offering packages to travelers who want a completely green trip. For more, log on to www.proximity-hotel.com or call (336) 379-8200 or (800) 379-8200.

four-diamond hotel evokes the grandeur of the original O. Henry, which stood in downtown Greensboro from 1919 until it was demolished in 1978. The new hotel was designed, as were hotels at the turn of the 20th century, to be a part of the community and blend into its surroundings. A great restaurant and lounge are on premises (see Green Valley Grill under "where to eat"). $$$.

Sheraton Greensboro Hotel/Joseph S. Koury Convention Center. 3121 High Point Rd.; (336) 292-9161 or (800) 242-6556; www.sheratongreensboro.com. Rooms have 13-foot ceilings, extra-large bathrooms complete with whirlpool tubs, and a separate living area with pull-down bed. Six restaurants, four lounges, indoor/outdoor pool, health club, racquetball court, sauna and whirlpool, in-room voice mail with two-line telephone, in-room high-speed Internet access, satellite TV, pay-per-view movies, and more. The Sheraton is adjacent to the Four Seasons Town Centre Shopping Mall. $$$.

julian

If you want to explore some of the towns adjacent to Greensboro head onto US 421 south to the town of Julian. There's not much in this small, rural town, but residents have learned how to entertain themselves.

where to go

Piedmont Dragway. 6750 Holt's Store Rd.; (336) 449-7411; www.piedmontdragway .com. If you live for the smell of scorched rubber, the whine of a turbocharger, and the roar of a high-performance engine, then this popular drag strip is your ticket for one-on-one racing excitement. During its busy Mar through Dec season, you'll see funny-car, Harley-Davidson motorcycle, and souped-up dragster competitions. Call for specific dates and ticket prices. The dragway is 6 miles southeast of Greensboro off I-85 exit 132.

oak ridge

Oak Ridge remained a farming community from its founding in 1852 until the last decade. Now, developers are beginning to buy and develop much of the farmland here. The area's heritage can still be found, however, by the astute day-tripper. Just head out on US 421 out of Julian, westward on I-85, and then north on Highway 68.

where to go

Old Mill of Guilford. 1340 SR 68 North; (336) 643-4783; www.oldmillofguilford.com. This water-powered gristmill with the sights and smells of another era and listed on the National Register of Historic Places, is still working after nearly 250 years. The gift shop has a wide variety of stone-ground meals, honey, ham, and North Carolina pottery and crafts. Open daily 9 a.m. to 5 p.m. Free.

day trip 06

west

>>> **moravian village tour:**
winston-salem

winston-salem

In 1874 Richard Joshua Reynolds arrived here on horseback from Virginia to establish a tobacco factory, which later became the R. J. Reynolds Tobacco Company. But more than a century before the tobacco baron set up shop here, the region was home to German-speaking Moravians.

Members of the persecuted Protestant sect came from Germany by way of Pennsylvania to settle in an area they called Die Wachau, later called Wachovia, where they established the villages of Bethabara and Bethania. You still can see how these thrifty people lived at Historic Bethabara Park, site of the area's first Moravian settlement, and at Old Salem, founded as a town and backcountry trading center in 1766.

With good reason, Winston-Salem's dominant tourism attraction today is Old Salem, a straight shot from Raleigh-Durham on I-40 west. The historic district near downtown is one of the most authentic restorations in the United States. No visit to Winston-Salem would be complete without a stroll along Old Salem's cobblestone streets, but there is much to see beyond Old Salem as well.

When Forsyth County was formed in 1849, Salem was chosen to be the county seat. Moravian leaders, however, sold the new county a parcel of land for a town a mile north of Salem Square, that two years later, was named Winston.

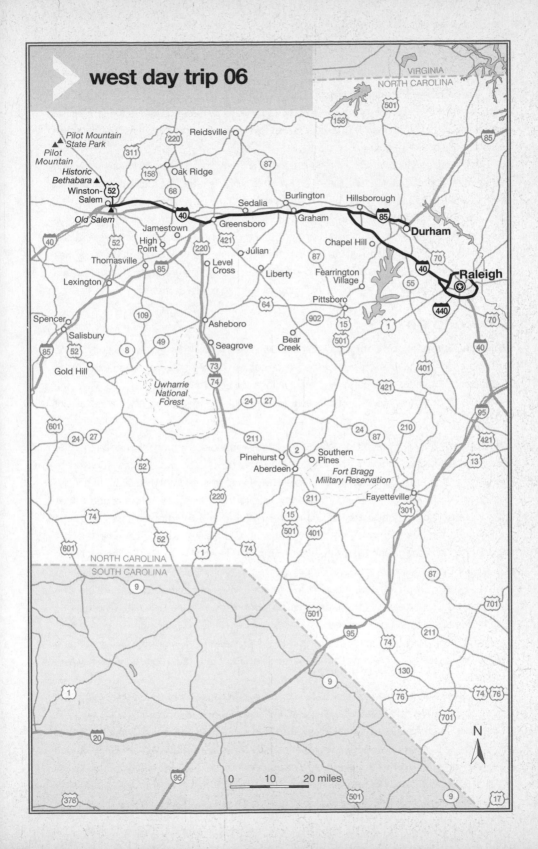

Enter Richard Joshua Reynolds. Tobacco ruled, and as it ascended to the throne, the stature of Winston was raised along with it. In 1913 Winston merged with Salem to become the largest city in North Carolina. Tobacco and textiles were huge industries that attracted large populations of people.

But tobacco is no longer king, and textiles are now produced elsewhere. Although recent census data put Winston-Salem as the state's fifth largest city, it still has the cultural legacy left by the Moravians and by philanthropists such as Reynolds.

From the 1960s on, the city billed itself as the "City of the Arts," thanks in part to the goodwill of the Reynolds family. Winston-Salem not only boasts the nation's first arts council, but also ranks first nationally in per capita contributions to the arts. The city has impressive art galleries, museums, and performance centers. The renowned North Carolina School of the Arts is here, as well as a symphony and an opera company.

where to go

Winston-Salem Visitor Center. 200 Brookstown Ave.; (866) 728-4200; www.visitwinston salem.com. Begin your excursion at the visitor center, either at the physical facility or on the Internet. At either, you can make reservations for accommodations or check out the schedule of performances at the Stevens Center. Pick up maps and ask for restaurant recommendations.

Old Salem. 601 Old Salem Rd.; (336) 721-7350; www.oldsalem.org. Founded in 1766 as a Moravian church town and backcountry trading center, Salem has survived to become one of America's most authentic and well-documented colonial sites. In this living-history town costumed interpreters demonstrate the household activities and trades that were part of the daily lives of European-American and African-American residents of Salem in the late 18th and early 19th centuries. Old Salem, which welcomes visitors into its homes, shops, and gardens year-round, is also home to St. Philips Moravian Church, the state's oldest standing African-American church, along with several museum shops, Salem Tavern restaurant, and the famous Winkler Bakery, all accessible free of admission. Old Salem is the birthplace of modern-day Winston-Salem. The historic district features about one hundred restored and reconstructed buildings. Tours are self-guided, but guides and costumed staff aid in the process of viewing and understanding the town's buildings, operations, and the people who made this community grow and prosper.

Highlights of the paid tour include a number of buildings, such as T. Vogler Gunsmith Shop, Shultz Shoemaker Shop, Single Brothers' House, and Salem Tavern.

Jan through Oct, Old Salem is open Tues through Sun plus Memorial Day and Labor Day. It is open seven days a week in Nov and Dec. Hours of individual buildings and shops may vary slightly. Staff may close tour buildings periodically for maintenance. The Visitor Center, 900 Old Salem Rd., is open Tues through Sat (and Mon in Nov and Dec) 8:30 a.m.

to 5:30 p.m., and Sun 12:30 to 5:30 p.m. Old Salem Interpretive Buildings are open Tues through Sat 9:30 a.m. to 4:30 p.m. and Sun 1 to 5 p.m.

Admission to Old Salem includes a self-guided tour of all the site's buildings, the Museum of Early Southern Decorative Arts, and the Toy Museum, with an option of a one-day ticket or a two-day ticket. Old Salem's one-day admission tickets are $21 for adults and $10 for children ages six to sixteen. Two-day tickets are $24 for adults and $10 for children ages six to sixteen.

The Gallery at Old Salem. 924 South Main St.; (888) 348-5420; www.oldsalem .org. Opened in 1996, the Gallery at Old Salem, located in the MESDA building, features changing exhibits. It provides additional space for art and historical exhibits throughout the year. Some come from MESDA collections while other exhibits feature other artists.

Museum of Early Southern Decorative Art (MESDA). 924 South Main St., Old Salem; (888) 348-5420; www.oldsalem.org. MESDA is the only museum dedicated to exhibiting and researching the regional decorative arts of the early South. With its twenty-four period rooms and seven galleries, MESDA showcases the furniture, paintings, textiles, ceramics, silver, and other metalwares made and used in Maryland, Virginia, the Carolinas, Georgia, Kentucky, and Tennessee through 1820. Guided tours begin on the hour and half hour, and last about eighty minutes. Open Tues through Sat 10 a.m. to 5 p.m. and Sun 1 to 5 p.m. The last tour is at 4 p.m. each day. Admission is $10 for adults, $5 for children ages five to sixteen and includes admission to the Toy Museum.

Old Salem Toy Museum. (336) 779-6140. The Old Salem Toy Museum houses a vast collection of antique toys. Many come from a personal collection donated by Anne and Thomas Gray. Dolls, dollhouses, board games, parlor games and puzzles, and planes, trains, and automobiles from North America and Europe provide an interesting look for the child in all of us. Special focus is given to the toys that belonged to the Moravian children who lived here. Hours are Tues through Sat 9:30 a.m. to 4:30 p.m. and Sun 1 to 5 p.m.

Salem Tavern. 800 South Main St., Old Salem. This original Salem Tavern was built in 1771 and was one of the first public buildings built in Salem. In 1784, it was destroyed by fire but quickly rebuilt using materials left over from constructing the Single Sisters' House. It reopened in 1785 and was restored to that condition in 1956. The tavern included two front rooms for gathering and a gentlemen's room for private dining. Guests could rent rooms upstairs for overnight stays. The tavern's most important guest was President George Washington, who stayed from May 31 to June 2, 1791. He arrived in a cream-colored coach with his secretary, several outriders, and servants, and was greeted by a brass band and a cheering crowd.

Single Brothers' House. 600 South Main St., Old Salem. This example of a Germanic half-timbered construction (1768–86) in the Moravian planned community of Salem was used as a trade school for Moravian boys beginning at around age fourteen. It also served as a dormitory for master craftsmen, journeymen, and apprentices. The first building of the Single Brothers' House (the half-timbered part) was built in 1769; the brick structure was added in 1786. The building has been restored to its original condition.

Delta Fine Arts Center. 2611 New Walkertown Rd.; (336) 722-2625; www.deltafinearts .org. The arts center hosts events and activities year-round to emphasize the contributions of African Americans to the arts and humanities. The center, now in its permanent home, presents regularly changing exhibits by Hispanic and black artists. Open Tues through Fri 10 a.m. to 5 p.m. and Sat 11 a.m. to 3 p.m.

Historic Bethabara. 2147 Bethabara Rd.; (336) 924-9148; www.bethabarapark.org. The first colonial townsite established in the Carolina Piedmont, Bethabara was intended to be a temporary town from which the central Moravian town of Salem and outlying farming communities would be developed within the Moravian lands of Wachovia. However, Bethabara continued in operation as a Moravian community long after Salem was established. Set in a beautiful 175-acre park, Bethabara was the only "house of passage" built by the Moravians at any of their colonial settlements in the New World. Archaeological investigations have demonstrated that the Bethabara archaeological remains at the townsite are intact; this work has contributed to a significant understanding of the Moravian culture, in particular the manufacture of Moravian pottery. A National Historic Landmark, this 1753 site of the first Moravian settlement in North Carolina was the area's frontier trade and religious center until 1772. Tour the 1788 congregation house known as the Gemeinhaus, visit the archaeological remains in the reconstructed palisade fort, and stroll through the historic gardens. Exhibit buildings are open for guided tours April 1 through December 15, except for Thanksgiving Day, Tues through Fri 10:30 a.m. to 4:30 p.m. and Sat and Sun 1:30 to 4:30 p.m. Admission is $2 for adults and $1 for children. Grounds, gardens, and trails are open free of charge, all day, all year.

Reynolda House, Museum of American Art. 2250 Reynolda Rd.; (888) 663-1149; www.reynoldahouse.org. An impressive collection of American masterpieces is scattered throughout the gracious, sixty-four-room estate where R. J. and Katherine Reynolds lived. The architecture, furnishings, and costume collection reflect their tastes. The artwork, on the other hand, reflects three centuries of major American paintings, prints, and sculptures by the likes of Jacob Lawrence, Jasper Johns, Stuart Davis, and Georgia O'Keeffe. The works are regarded as one of the finest collections of American art in North America. A National Historic Property, Reynolda House adjoins its original formal gardens and the estate's support buildings, now converted to specialty shops, offices, and restaurants. Open Tues through Sat from 9:30 a.m. to 4:30 p.m., Sun from 1:30 to 4:30 p.m. Closed on Monday,

Thanksgiving, Christmas, and New Year's Day. Admission: adults $10; senior citizens $9, students and children free.

SciWorks. 400 Hanes Mill Rd.; (336) 767-6730; www.sciworks.org. A 120-seat planetarium, 25,000 square feet of exhibit space, and a multitude of programs and hands-on exhibits such as the Coastal Encounters lab tank appeal to both the young and the young-at-heart. At SciWorks you'll be able to wish upon a star in the planetarium and learn about the Earth and the solar system, watch chemicals fizz and react, and see a dinosaur from millions of years ago. There are picnic areas and an adjacent fifteen-acre environmental park with animals and nature trails. Open Mon through Fri 10 a.m. to 4 p.m. and Sat 11 a.m. to 5 p.m. The park and barnyard close thirty minutes before the museum. Admission is $10 for adults, $8 for seniors and students ages six to nineteen, and $6 for children ages two through five.

Southeastern Center for Contemporary Art (SECCA). 750 Marguerite Dr.; (336) 725-1904; www.secca.org. SECCA is a series of cascading galleries housed in the 1929 English hunting lodge home of the late industrialist James G. Hanes. The original structure has been enhanced with 20,000 square feet of exhibit space, where temporary exhibits change several times a year and represent the finest contemporary art both regionally and nationally. Be sure to visit Centershop at SECCA to browse and purchase handcrafted jewelry, home decor items, unique toys, and more. Open Wed through Sat 10 a.m. to 5 p.m., Sun 2 to 5 p.m., closed national holidays. Admission: adults, $5; students and senior citizens, $3; children under twelve, free.

Stevens Center. 405 West Fourth St.; (336) 721-1945; www.uncsa.edu/stevenscenter. A restored 1929 silent movie palace in downtown Winston-Salem, the center is part of the acclaimed North Carolina School of the Arts and regularly showcases student and faculty work, as well as a host of feature performances that include chamber music, jazz, ballet, the symphony, and films.

where to shop

Downtown Arts District. Meander along Trade and Sixth Streets near the Marriott Hotel for the eclectic mix of shops and galleries that make up the resurging arts district.

Artworks Gallery. 564 North Trade St.; (336) 723-5890. Established in 1984, this is an artist-run cooperative that exhibits members' works.

Earthbound Arts. 610 Trade St.; (336) 773-1043. This shop carries only locally made products, and bills itself as "a magical world of handcrafted soap, candles, stained glass, copperwork, natural herbs, cards, jewelry, gourmet pickles and jams, and much more."

Fiber Company. 600 North Trade St.; (336) 725-5277. A collective of fiber artists and designers established in 1987, this has a working studio complemented by a shop and gallery that offer the works of member artists as well as those of other craftsmen.

Urban Artware. 207 West Sixth St.; (336) 722-2345. This is an art gallery and retail store with a mix of art and fine-crafted items, including one-of-a-kind artwork by some of the Southeast's finest contemporary artists, handcrafted jewelry, furniture, ceramics, wood, and glass items.

Hanes Mall. 3320 Silas Creek Pkwy.; (336) 765-8321; www.shophanesmall.com. One of the largest malls between Washington, D.C. and Atlanta. It has more than 200 stores.

Historic Reynolda Village. 2201 Reynolda Rd.; (336) 758-5584. On the former estate of R. J. Reynolds, this shopping plaza has more than thirty upscale shops, including restaurants, art galleries, jewelry and antiques, fine gifts, and specialty items. Open Mon through Sat 10 a.m. to 5 p.m.

Piedmont Craftsmen Gallery. 601 North Trade St.; (336) 725-1516; www.piedmont craftsmen.org. The gallery showcases the work of more than 350 of the Southeast's finest craft artists. Open Tues through Fri 10:30 a.m. to 5 p.m. and Sat 10 a.m. to 5 p.m.

where to eat

Krispy Kreme. 259 South Stratford Rd.; (336) 724-2484. Winston-Salem is home to this doughnut giant, and the Stratford Road location is by far the most popular stop. Try to get there when the HOT DOUGHNUTS NOW sign is flashing and you can watch as these sugary, melt-in-your-mouth delights come off the conveyor belt. Glazed, cream-filled, or with sprinkles. $.

Little Richard's Lexington BBQ. 4885 Country Club Rd.; (336) 760-3457. Stop here at "the original" Little Richard's for some of the best barbecue this side of Lexington, North Carolina. Richard Berrier, who bills himself as "chef de swine," founded the restaurant with a partner in 1991 (the business appears to be older because the building was erected in 1968). The partner split and opened another Little Richard's just a few miles away in Clemmons. There are no bitter feelings, but Berrier wants folks to know that his location, identifiable by the three smoking chimneys, is the last one in Winston that still pit-cooks its barbecue over hickory and hardwood coals. Try the chopped plate for the fullest smoked flavor. It comes with fries, homemade slaw, hush puppies, and rolls. For dessert, pick up a B&G Homemade Pie, made in Winston-Salem. $–$$.

Mary's, Of Course! 301 Brookstown Ave.; (336) 725-5764. If it's Sunday brunch you are looking for, it's Mary's, of Course! Located in an artsy space in the Old Salem area, Mary serves great eggs Benedict and vegetarian dishes. $.

ghosts of salem tavern

*It was a cool, misty fall day. We had three hours to spend in Winston-Salem, so it was lunch at **Salem Tavern**. Leaves from the big maple, white oak, and birch trees formed a thin, slick layer over the 250-year-old cobblestone streets.*

As we stepped into the tavern, we could almost smell the spirit of the thousands of patrons who came before us, just beneath the warm, comforting scent of baking gingerbread. I can't remember who brought up the subject of ghosts, but I couldn't blame them. Our waiter couldn't either.

Dressed as if he were ready to head back into the field at harvest, he jumped quickly into the story after serving us. Indeed, the story of the "Talking Corpse" is confirmed in Nancy Roberts's famed book Ghosts of the Carolinas. *The story goes that after the tavern closed one rainy, fall night (see a pattern here?), a traveler stopped for help. Despite the best efforts of the staff, the unidentified man died. He was buried, his belongings put aside for claiming. And claimed they were.*

After much ado about spirits in the tavern, a "shadowy, faceless form" appeared before the keeper and instructed him to send the belongings to the deceased's brother in Texas. Indeed, the man in Texas received them for his brother.

This particular ghost hasn't made a sound since. Or has he? The staff at Salem Tavern frequently spin yarns about strange happenings. Napkins become misplaced. Lantern sconces inexplicably fall off the walls. The burned shape of a man's face appeared on the seat of a bench, then the bench mysteriously disappeared. Even guests on occasion hear voices come from people who aren't there.

Our waiter said he believes that he's seen the figure of a man in the upstairs window of the original tavern across the way. Whether the talking corpse causes these instances, no one will suggest. We will suggest, however, that you try the pork roast.

Old Fourth Street Filling Station. 871 West Fourth St.; (336) 724-7600. Originally a gas station, this restaurant offers the best patio dining in town, with a fireplace inside for chilly nights. Menu choices range from salads to filet mignon. Try the pan-seared filet mignon with cognac cream sauce over buttermilk mashed potatoes. Also popular is the broiled mahimahi with a crab stuffing. Open 11 a.m. to 11 p.m. Mon through Thurs, to midnight on Fri and Sat. Sun brunch from 10 a.m. to 3 p.m. $$–$$$.

Old Salem Tavern. 736 Main St.; (336) 748-8585. A costumed staff serves lunch and dinner Mon through Sat (plus lunch on Sun from Mar through Dec) in the 1816 tavern annex.

Some menu items are authentic Moravian fare. For lunch, try the Moravian chicken pie or the Moravian beef ragout. From 5 to 6 p.m., early-bird specials offer reduced rates on Moravian chicken pie and sauerkraut stew, which include a garden salad or cup of soup, vegetables, pumpkin muffins, rolls, and coffee or iced tea. Dinner reservations are recommended. Lunch reservations are accepted only for parties of six or more. $$–$$$.

Village Tavern. 221 Reynolda Village; (336) 748-0221. Enjoy delicious entrees in a warm, casual atmosphere. Treat yourself to a meal on the outdoor patio, then take a stroll through the many other shops and boutiques that make up Reynolda Village. Try the hot crab dip appetizer, which was created by the owner and hasn't changed in years. The Carolina burger, with homemade chili, is also another popular menu item. Open 11 a.m. to 11 p.m. Mon through Thurs, to midnight Fri and Sat, and 9 a.m. to 10 p.m. Sun. $$–$$$.

WestEnd Cafe. 926 West Fourth St.; (336) 723-4774; www.westendcafe.com. A trendy local favorite, the cafe serves salads, grinders, "heavy hoagies," reubens, and other sandwiches. Open Mon through Fri 11 a.m. to 10 p.m., Sat noon to 10 p.m. $.

Winkler Bakery. 525 South Main St.; (888) 348-5420; www.oldsalem.org. Established in 1800, this bakery still serves up its famous coffee cake and gingerbread hot from the wood-fired oven. Winkler's offers as much history as food. $.

Zevely House Restaurant. 901 West Fourth St.; (336) 725-6666. Located in the historic West End, this oldest house in Winston offers an exquisite dining experience in small, elegant dining rooms or on the covered garden patio. $$$.

where to stay

The Augus T. Zevely Inn. 803 South Main St.; (800) 928-9299; www.winston-salem-inn .com. As the only lodging in the Old Salem Historic District, this twelve-room bed-and-breakfast has been meticulously and accurately restored to its mid-19th century appearance. The "Winter Kitchen" suite accommodates four, great for families. A continental-plus breakfast is served during the week and a full buffet breakfast on weekends; fresh fruit, fruit juices, and Moravian baked goods are always offered at breakfast. Complimentary wine and cheese are served in the evening. $$–$$$.

Brookstown Inn. 200 Brookstown Ave.; (800) 845-4262; www.brookstowninn.com. A seventy-one-room property adjacent to the restored village of Old Salem, the Brookstown Inn bills itself as an elegant bed-and-breakfast–style hostelry. On the National Register of Historic Places, the inn was once a warehouse and Winston-Salem's oldest factory. One of the largest historic inns in North America, the Brookstown's guest rooms typically have exposed brick and original beams and/or rafters. Ceilings are 12 to more than 20 feet high, and rooms range from approximately 350 square feet to more than 1,100. Rates include a complimentary wine and cheese reception every evening from 5 to 7, and a complimentary continental breakfast each morning. $$$.

Henry F. Shaffner House. 150 South Marshall St.; (800) 952-2256; www.shaffnerhouse .com. Built in 1907 by one of the cofounders of Wachovia Loan and Trust Company, this Victorian-style mansion, a restaurant and B&B, is just blocks from historic Old Salem and downtown Winston-Salem. Amenities include evening wine and cheese and a complimentary breakfast. Lunch is available Mon through Fri from 11 a.m. to 2 p.m.; fine dining seven days a week from 6:30 to 8 p.m. The Shaffner House has six rooms with private baths, three suites with private baths. $$–$$$.

Marriott at Winston Plaza. 425 North Cherry St.; (336) 725-3500. Adjacent to the Benton Convention Center this hotel is in an area that's been developed as Twin City Quarter, which is quickly attracting new, trendy restaurants and shops. You have 603 rooms to choose from, but you might try to book your room on the upper floors with views of the distant mountains, including Pilot Mountain and Hanging Rock. Be sure to ask about specials that put you on the Club Level (available for an extra $25 per night), where you'll receive upgraded amenities and access to the staffed Club Lounge, which serves a complimentary continental breakfast and evening hors d'oeuvres. This downtown hotel has a glass-enclosed heated swimming pool with an outdoor sundeck, a dry sauna, an 1,800-square-foot health club, two lounges, and a restaurant. $$–$$$.

day trip 07

west

>>> mayberry:
mount airy, pilot mountain

On this day trip you're headed to Mayberry. The fictional TV town was fashioned after Mount Airy for *The Andy Griffith Show*. Griffith grew up in a small home here, and although the actor now lives in Manteo, on the coast, it is here in Mount Airy that you will find the world's largest collection of Andy Griffith memorabilia. Other well-known celebrities, including country music singer Donna Fargo and bluegrass legend Tommy Jarrell, are natives of Mount Airy. The original Siamese twins, Eng and Chang Bunker, lived in the nearby White Plains community. You'll learn more about them at the Mount Airy Visitors Center.

Be sure to stop at Pilot Mountain, which Andy referred to as "Mount Pilot" in numerous episodes of *The Andy Griffith Show*. Take a hike to the top of this landmark for gorgeous views of the Piedmont and, to your west, the Blue Ridge Mountains.

mount airy

Following I-40 west, exit on I-40 West Business past the Greensboro airport. In Winston-Salem, take US 52/SR 8 north toward Mount Airy. The town ranked number 36 in the 1996 edition of The 100 Best Small Towns in America, recognized for its quality of life.

where to go

Mount Airy Visitors Center. 200 North Main St.; (800) 948-0949 or (336) 786-6116. Stop in and say howdy to the friendly folks at the Mount Airy Visitors Center and let them help you

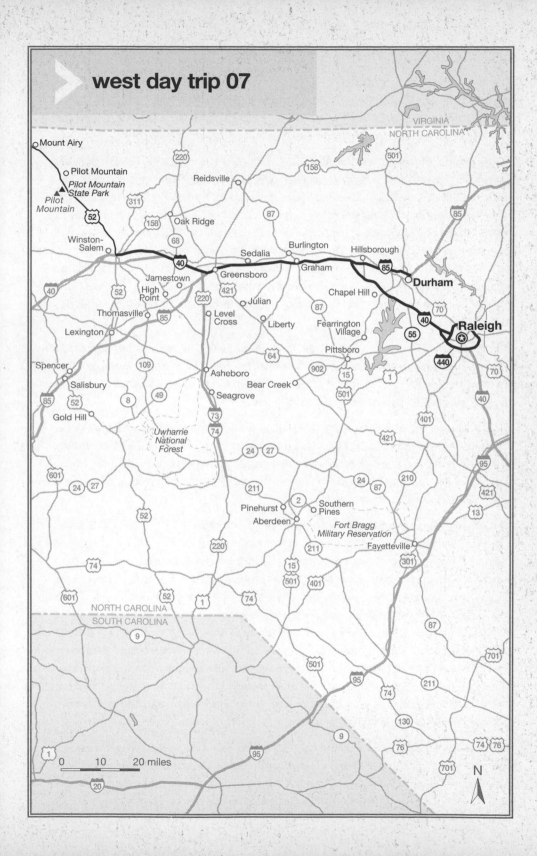

west day trip 07

Mount Airy

Pilot Mountain

Pilot Mountain State Park

Pilot Mountain

52

220

Reidsville

158

501

311

87

85

158

Oak Ridge

68

Winston-Salem

Burlington

Hillsborough

85

Sedalia

Graham

Durham

40

Greensboro

Jamestown

Chapel Hill

40

52

High Point

421

220

Julian

87

70

40

Thomasville

85

Level Cross

Liberty

Fearrington Village

55

Raleigh

Lexington

Pittsboro

440

64

902

15

1

70

Spencer

109

Asheboro

Bear Creek

40

Salisbury

24 27

Seagrove

501

85

52

8

49

Gold Hill

73

74

401

Uwharrie National Forest

421

95

601

24 27

24 87

210

421

52

211

13

Pinehurst

2

Southern Pines

Aberdeen

Fort Bragg Military Reservation

220

211

Fayetteville

301

74

15 501 401

601

52

1

74

NORTH CAROLINA

SOUTH CAROLINA

9

87

501

95

701

9

130

1

0   10   20 miles

95

76

74 76

20

701

N

get your bearings. They can give you directions to all the Mayberry sites, including Floyd's Barber Shop and Wally's Service Station, and set you straight on fact and fiction. Open Mon through Fri 8:30 a.m. to 5 p.m., Sat 10 a.m. to 4 p.m. and Sun 1 to 4 p.m.

Andy Griffith Museum. 218 Rockford St.; (336) 786-7998 or (800) 286-6193; www .andygriffithmuseum.org. The world's largest collection of Andy Griffith memorabilia, collected by Griffith's childhood friend and Mount Airy resident Emmett Forrest, are on display here. The collection contains everything from the chair Andy was rocked in as a baby to a Matlock suit. It's all located in the Andy Griffith Playhouse, ca. 1920, the first known site of a public school in Mount Airy. Andy Griffith attended elementary school and performed on stage here when the site was used as the Rockford Street Elementary School. Named for Griffith in the early 1970s, it now houses the Surry Arts Council's exhibits. Open Mon through Fri 9 a.m. to 5 p.m., Sat 11 a.m. to 4:30 p.m., and Sun 1:30 to 4:30 p.m. Admission is $3.

The Mayberry Jail. 215 City Hall; (336) 789-4636 or (800) 576-0231. At this re-creation of the jailhouse/police station seen in episodes of *The Andy Griffith Show,* a vintage 1962 Ford Galaxie squad car sits out front to let you know the defenders of Mayberry are never far away. Open Mon through Fri 8 a.m. to 4:30 p.m. Free.

Moore House. 202 Moore Ave.; (336) 786-4512; www.visitmayberry.com. Moore House, ca. 1862, is the oldest house in Mount Airy. Located in the front yard of the Moore House is a rustic hexagonal summerhouse with wood poles, intervening laurel root walls, and a wood shingle roof. The furniture inside the summerhouse includes a settee, a chair, and a table with a laurel root base and a plank top.

Mount Airy Museum of Regional History. 301 North Main St.; (336) 786-4478; www .northcarolinamuseum.org. More than 15,000 square feet of exhibits include a 100-foot mural of the surrounding mountains. Exhibits range from displays about the region's natural history to the world's largest open-face granite quarry, located in Mount Airy, and include an authentic reproduction of a log cabin, a turn-of-the-20th-century general store, a train room with a 70-foot scale model train exhibit, a gallery on fire fighters that features 1916, 1926, and 1946 fire trucks, all once used by the City of Mount Airy. The changing exhibits on the second floor focus on the early 1900s. A visit to the observation room, located on the fourth floor of the clock tower, provides an awesome view of the surrounding mountains. The Museum Gift Shoppe, located in the Main Gallery, has gift items related to exhibits, and local and regional history books are for sale. Open Tues through Sat 10 a.m. to 4 p.m. Admission is $4 for adults and $2 for students.

Siamese Twins Burial Site. 506 Old Hwy. 601; (336) 786-6116 or (800) 948-0949; www .visitmayberry.com. Eng and Chang Bunker, born in Siam, became circus performers who fathered twenty-two children. Known as "the original Siamese twins," they are buried outside the Mount Airy city limits in the White Plains Church community. To get there, take SR

601 south from Mount Airy past a Wal-Mart on the left. Turn left onto Old Highway 601, then travel 2 miles to pass over I-74 to White Plains Baptist Church on the right. The cemetery is behind the church.

where to eat

Snappy Lunch. 125 North Main St.; (336) 786-4931; www.thesnappylunch.com. In an early episode of *The Andy Griffith Show,* titled "Andy the Matchmaker," Andy suggested to Barney that they go to the Snappy Lunch to get a bite to eat. Griffith also mentioned the restaurant in his version of the song "Silhouettes." And in a television news interview, Griffith talked about getting a hot dog and a bottle of pop for 15 cents at the Snappy Lunch when he was a boy. Mount Airy's oldest restaurant, ca. 1923, is famous for the pork chop sandwich, which was created by owner Charles Dowell, who has been at Snappy Lunch for more than fifty years. $$.

where to stay

Andy's Homeplace. 711 East Haymore St.; (336) 789-5999. Spend the night in the home where Andy lived with his mother and father until he graduated from high school. Furnished with all the comforts of home, it has two bedrooms, a kitchen, a living room, and one bath. Rollaway beds are available for families or groups. Andy's Homeplace is located near the Andy Griffith Playhouse and Historic Downtown Mount Alry. Enjoy a continental breakfast provided by your host or have breakfast at Snappy Lunch. $$$.

Maxwell House Bed and Breakfast. 618 North Main St.; (336) 786-2174 or (877) 786-2174; www.bbonline.com/nc/maxwellhouse/index.html. Located in Historic Downtown Mount Airy, the Maxwell House is a three-story, Victorian-style home with a towerlike front and an inviting wraparound porch. Rates include a complimentary homemade breakfast and an afternoon or evening refreshment. $$–$$$.

The Mayberry Motor Inn. 501 Andy Griffith Pkwy. North; (336) 786-4109; www.mayberry motorinn.com. A gazebo off Fife Street (named for the famed TV deputy Barney Fife) gives a great view of Pilot Mountain. Guests can walk along Thelma Lou's trail or check out the Andy Griffith and Donna Fargo memorabilia that adorns the inn's office. A 1963 Ford squad car and Emmet's fix-it truck sit in the driveway of the inn. $.

pilot mountain

12 miles south of Mount Airy and 26 miles north of Winston-Salem on US 52, Pilot Mountain offers views of the Winston-Salem skyline and the Blue Ridge Mountains. Stop here on the way to or from Mount Airy to get a feel for the high country.

where to go

Pilot Mountain State Park. 1792 Pilot Knob Park Rd., Pinnacle; (336) 325-2355; www
.ncparks.gov. Pilot Mountain's solitary peak, rising more than 1,400 feet above the rolling
countryside of the upper Piedmont plateau, is the centerpiece of the state park. Divided into
two sections, with 1,000 acres on the Yadkin River, the park offers hiking trails, scenic overlooks, picnicking, family and group camping, and a climbing area. It's an excellent place to
observe wildlife, including the fall migration of raptors. Pilot Mountain was named a National
Natural Landmark in 1976. Free.

where to stay

Flippin's Bed and Breakfast. 203 West Main St.; (336) 368-1183. Situated in the picturesque setting of Pilot Mountain State Park, this Victorian-style bed-and-breakfast is lavishly
furnished with antiques. A dog kennel and meal plan are available. $$–$$$.

Scenic Overlook Bed and Breakfast. 144 Scenic Overlook Lane; (336) 368-9591; www
.scenicoverlook.com. Situated on fifty acres, this bed-and-breakfast has large, luxurious
suites, all with a view of the lake and Pilot Mountain. Rooms have fireplaces and Jacuzzis;
a meal plan, nonsmoking rooms, and boating are available. A complimentary full breakfast
is served in suite. $$$.

day trip 08

west

>>> **crossroads of furniture and barbecue:**
jamestown, high point, thomasville,
lexington

Southwest of Greensboro on I-85, Jamestown, High Point, Thomasville, and Lexington beckon the day visitor with their superlatives. What do we mean? Well, High Point claims the world's largest chest of drawers. Standing 32 feet high, the restored 19th-century dresser banishes any doubt that High Point is the undisputed furniture capital of the world. Thus, one reason to visit High Point is to shop for furniture.

Nearby Thomasville boasts the state's oldest railroad depot and the world's largest chair, a 30-foot-high monument that sits square in the heart of downtown. The Duncan Phyfe chair rises 18 feet above its base and has seated President Lyndon B. Johnson, Robert Redford, and several Miss Americas.

Lexington, farther south on I-85, is famous worldwide for its barbecue. Nearly twenty restaurants serve pork that is cooked in time-honored ways with secret sauces, served chopped or sliced. Lexington-style barbecue, recognized far and wide (except in eastern North Carolina) as the nation's best pork barbecue, is the highlight of the annual Barbecue Festival on the last Saturday in October.

jamestown

With a population scarcely over 3,000 residents, this small town probably gains more prominence from its namesake in Virginia than anything else. The visitor does, however, have a chance here to visit an unusual Quaker plantation, which played an interesting role in the

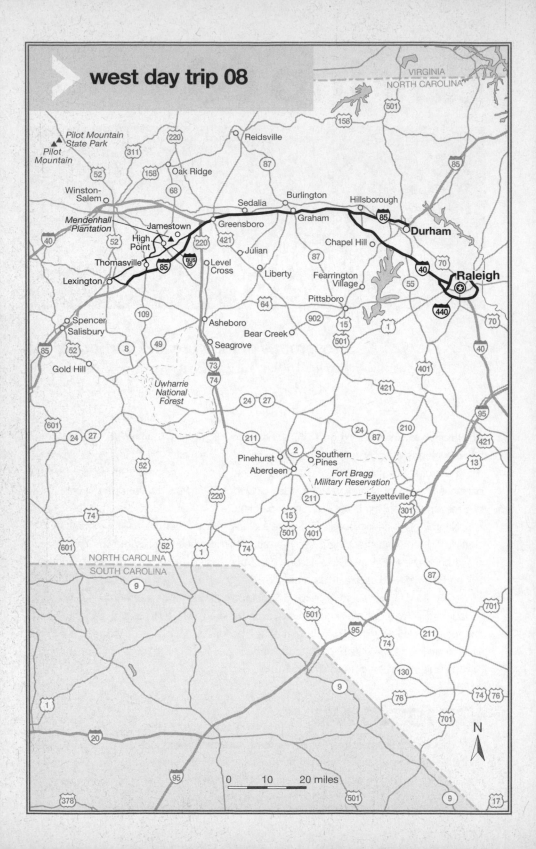

Underground Railroad, as well as a great small-town park. Head here on I-40 west out of Raleigh and then onto I-85 Business (locally referred to as "Business 85").

where to go

Castle McCulloch and the Crystal Garden. 3925 Kivett Dr.; (336) 887-5413; www .castlemcculloch.com. Just a ten-minute drive south of Greensboro, the castle is a restored gold refinery listed on the National Register of Historic Places. Built in 1823 and restored in the 1980s, the granite structure has a drawbridge, a moat, and a 70-foot tower. The Crystal Garden, built in 1997, is reminiscent of Victorian times, with beveled glass walls, a crystal chandelier, and a lovely veranda with a commanding view of the castle across the lake. Popular for weddings and receptions, the castle is open Mon through Fri 9 a.m. to 5 p.m. A mining operation gives guests the opportunity to pan for gold, emeralds, rubies, garnets, amethysts, crystals, and more. Mining is offered Sundays 11 a.m. to 5 p.m. and Mon through Wed 2 to 4 p.m. in summer. The castle also conducts seasonal events throughout the year.

City Lake Park. 602 West Main St.; (336) 883-3498. Just a short drive outside the city limits and across the street from Mendenhall Plantation, this 969-acre park, situated along High Point Lake, has picnic areas, amusement rides, miniature golf, fishing and boating, and a swimming pool and water slide. The park's amphitheatre is the site of numerous concerts and other events throughout the year.

Mendenhall Plantation. 603 West Main St.; (336) 454-3819; www.mendenhallplantation.org. This early 19th-century Quaker plantation includes many unique outbuildings, a museum, and one of two existing false-bottom wagons used to transport runaway slaves during the time of the Underground Railroad. The Quakers were actively opposed to slavery and worked to create a peaceful community wherever they lived. Open Tues through Fri 11 a.m. to 3 p.m., Sat 1 to 4 p.m., and Sun 1 to 4 p.m. Admission is $2 for adults and $1 for children and seniors.

high point

In 1859, when High Point was named after the "highest point" on the North Carolina Railroad, city founders knew that its central location would attract industry and commerce. Today High Point draws visitors from all fifty states and more than one hundred countries for the biannual International Home Furnishings Market, the largest event of its kind in the world. Day-trippers come to explore the region's rich history, distinctive cultural events, and diverse shopping selection. For furniture shoppers, High Point offers more than eighty retail furniture outlets. It is minutes from Jamestown via Business 85 (I-85).

where to go

Doll and Miniature Museum of High Point. 101 West Green St.; (336) 885-3655. Among the more than 2,500 dolls and miniatures from around the world is a nativity scene with fifty rare crèche dolls, plus a Shirley Temple collection and Bob Timberlake dolls. Open Tues through Sat 10 a.m. to 4 p.m., and Sun 1 to 4 p.m. Admission is $5 for adults, $4 for seniors, $2.50 for ages six through fifteen and free for children under six.

High Point Museum and Historical Park. 1859 East Lexington Ave.; (336) 885-1859; www.highpointmuseum.org. Exhibiting the development of High Point from a small Quaker village to the furniture capital of the world, the historical park is home to the Hoggatt House (1754), the Haley House (1786), and a working blacksmith shop. The museum is open Tues through Sat 10 a.m. to 4:30 p.m. and Sun 1 to 4:30 p.m. The historic park is open Tues through Sat 10 a.m. to 4:30 p.m. and Sun 1 to 4 p.m. Tours by costumed guides are offered Sat 10 a.m. to 4 p.m. and Sun 1 to 4 p.m. Free.

Piedmont Environmental Center. 1220 Penny Rd.; (336) 883-8531. Adjacent to High Point City Lake, 375 glorious acres include hiking trails, a nature preserve, a nature store, small animal exhibits, the North Carolina Mapscape (you can walk across the entire state in a few steps), and access to the 6-mile Greenway Trail. The center is open Mon through Fri 9 a.m. to 5 p.m. Trails are open sunrise to sunset daily. Free.

World's Largest Chest of Drawers. 508 Hamilton St.; (336) 887-7170. This unusual but beautiful 19th-century dresser was known as the Bureau of Information in 1926. It also once housed the local Jaycees and later the chamber of commerce. Orginally twenty feet tall, it was renovated in 1996 to 38 feet tall.

where to shop

For a free guide to furniture shopping at more than eighty retail furniture outlets in High Point and the surrounding communities, contact the **High Point Convention and Visitors Bureau,** (800) 720-5255; www.highpoint.org. It features familiar names like Boyles, Ashley and Drexel Heritage and even salvaged and office furniture.

High Point Farmers' Market. Roy B. Culler Senior Center; (336) 883-3584. Fresh fruit and vegetables, baked goods, flowers, and plants are available every Wednesday and Saturday through mid-October.

where to eat

The Dog House. 662 North Main St.; (336) 886-4953. A local favorite for nearly sixty years, the Dog House features lunch-counter dining for hot dogs and hamburgers. Open for lunch only, Mon through Sat. $.

Kepley's Barbecue. 1304 South Main St.; (336) 884-1021. The best barbecue north of Lexington, Kepley's serves barbecue sandwiches, plates, trays, hush puppies, and vinegar-based barbecue slaw. Open daily for lunch and dinner. $–$$.

Liberty Steakhouse and Brewery. 914 Mall Loop Rd.; (336) 882-4677. Great beef selections range from prime rib to filet mignon. Enjoy brick-oven specialty pizzas and, with a microbrewery on premises, eight beers on tap all the time. Open for lunch and dinner Mon through Sat. $$–$$$.

Plaza Cafe. 336 South Main St.; (336) 886-5271. A local favorite for breakfast and lunch, the diner-style cafe specializes in omeletes and fabulous Greek salads. Open daily for breakfast and lunch. $–$$.

Steak Street. 3915 Sedgebrook St.; (336) 841-0222. With "outdoor dining inside," according to the owners, the wrought iron furniture, outdoor lighting, and brick inlays on the main dining room floor give this restaurant a cafe feel. The restaurant's Cajun-Creole menu features select cuts of meat, as well as pasta, seafood, and large salads. Open for lunch and dinner daily. $$–$$$.

where to stay

Biltmore Suites Hotel. 4400 Regency Dr.; (336) 812-8188 or (888) 412-8188; www.bilt moresuiteshotel.com. The Biltmore is an all-suite hotel offering a deluxe continental breakfast, evening reception, fitness center, and surrounding-area destination shuttle. $$–$$$.

JH Adams Inn. 1108 North Main St.; (336) 882-3267 or (888) 256-1289; www.jhadamsinn .com. The Italian Renaissance–style inn was built in 1918 as a private residence for John Hampton Adams of Adam-Millis Hosiery Corporation. Today, the inn serves as a stately reminder of a bygone era. Located in the heart of downtown High Point, the restored home is now a thirty-room property with Jacuzzi tubs, fireplaces, and king-size beds in many rooms. A full breakfast buffet is served. $$$.

Toad Alley Bed and Bagel. 1001 Johnson St.; (336) 886-4773 or (800) 409-7946; www .toadalley.com. This 1924 Victorian home is located in High Point's Johnson Street Historic District. Renovated in 1987, the three-story home has a wraparound front porch with a swing, rocking chairs, and private sitting areas. Each of the five charming bedrooms has 9-foot ceilings, ceiling fan, private bath, and TV. $$–$$$.

thomasville

After North Carolina state senator John W. Thomas helped push through a $3 million state tax to build a railroad system, he settled in an area near the proposed route. Thomas built a depot, general store, and home, and the area became known as "Thomas's Depot." In

1852, the area officially took the name Thomasville by merging Thomas's name with that of local Rounsaville. Continue on the southbound Business 85 route to get to Thomasville.

where to go

North Carolina's Oldest Railroad Depot. 44 West Main St.; (336) 472-4422 or (800) 611-9907; www.thomasvilletourism.com. The oldest remaining railroad depot in North Carolina, built in 1870, houses the Thomasville Visitors Center. The restored structure is on the National Register of Historic Places. Open Mon through Fri 9 a.m. to 5 p.m., Sat 9 a.m. to 1 p.m. Free.

World's Largest Chair. Intersection of Main Street and SR 109. A symbol of Thomasville's furniture heritage, the fifty-year-old, 30-foot-high monument stands in the heart of downtown Thomasville. The first "big chair" was built in 1922 for the Thomasville Chair Company. In 1936 the old wooden chair was scrapped, and in 1951 ground was broken for a new chair. Recently refurbished, the present structure is a mix of cement, granite dust, and iron, but it appears to be wooden.

where to eat

Safari Big Game Steakhouse Restaurant. 15A Laura Lane; (336) 472-3274. The owners claim to offer "big steak food at little steak prices." The 32-ounce porterhouse, for example, goes for $25. The menu also includes such exotic fare as frog's legs, alligator meat, buffalo, ostrich, wild boar, pheasant, and venison. $$–$$$.

lexington

Settled in 1775 and incorporated in 1828, Lexington was named in honor of the Revolutionary War battle in Massachusetts. Lexington is the county seat of Davidson County, named for Revolutionary War General William Lee Davidson. Uptown is listed on the National Register of Historic Places. Lexington is home to Bob Timberlake, internationally renowned artist and home furnishings designer, and the Bob Timberlake Gallery. But the town is perhaps best known for its pork barbecue. The drive on Business 85 south from Thomasville to Lexington will take about twenty minutes. When you've eaten your fill in Lexington, hop off Business 85 and take I-85 east to return to Raleigh-Durham.

where to go

Lexington Tourism Authority. 114 East Center St.; (336) 236-4218 or (866) 604-2389; www.visitlexingtonnc.org. Stop here to begin a self-guided walking tour of Historic Uptown Lexington. The guide, which you can print out from the Web site or pick up here, highlights forty-one historic properties in a five-block National Register Historic District plus fringe sites dating from 1824 to 1948. You will want to stop at The Candy Factory and listen to the player piano and browse Lanier Hardware.

Childress Vineyards. 1000 Childress Vineyards Rd.; (336) 236-9463; www.childress vineyards.com. The striking Italian Renaissance building and the beautiful rolling hills of this world-class vineyard are more than welcoming. *Wine Enthusiast* magazine has named this NASCAR team owner's facility as one of the top twenty-five tasting rooms in America. Take a tour, have a spectacular meal, and most importantly taste wine here. The tasting room is open Mon through Sat 10 a.m. to 6 p.m. and Sun noon to 5 p.m. Winery tours are offered Mon through Fri at noon, 2, and 4 p.m. and on Sat and Sun at noon, 1, 2, 3, and 4 p.m.

Davidson County Historical Museum. 2 South Main St.; (336) 242-2035. The museum's permanent and changing exhibits spotlight the history of the area. It's housed in the old Davidson County Courthouse on the square, which was completed in 1858 and damaged in an 1865 fire during Union General Judson Kilpatrick's occupation. Open Tues through Fri 10 a.m. to 4 p.m.

Richard Childress Racing. 180 Industrial Dr., Welcome; (336) 731-3389 or (800) 476-3389; www.rcrracing.com. Visitors can tour behind the scenes of some of RCR's successful NASCAR teams. Located just ten minutes north of Lexington, the museum and gift shop display a variety of racecars, trophies, photos, and video of RCR's thirty-plus years in the sport. The museum includes cars and other items from the career of the late, great Dale Earnhardt. Hours are Mon through Fri 9 a.m. to 5 p.m. and Sat 9 a.m. to 3 p.m. Admission is $12 for adults, $8 for seniors, $5 for age seven and older, and is free for children six years and younger.

where to shop

The Bob Timberlake Gallery. 1714 East Center St.; (336) 249-4428 or (800) 244-0095; www.bobtimberlake.com. This gallery, retail store, and museum that features the art, home furnishings, and accessories of internationally recognized artist and designer Bob Timberlake is located just off I-85 at exit 94 in Lexington. Special events throughout the year highlight Timberlake and other North Carolina artists. Open Tues through Sat 10 a.m. to 5 p.m.

The Country Store. 6031 Old US 52, Welcome; (336) 731-2211. Ten minutes north of Lexington, the Country Store is noted for its handmade quilts, tables, chairs, crafts, and canned foods. Local senior citizens make all the items. Open Thurs through Sat.

Historic Uptown Lexington and Visitors Center. 220 North Main St.; (336) 249-0383; www.uptownlexington.com. Historic Uptown Lexington contains antiques stores, the state's largest True Value hardware store (Lanier's), bridal shops, a dress fabric store, an old-fashioned candy store, bakeries, an art and history museum, consignment shops, an old-fashioned grocery store known for homemade pimento cheese and chicken salad, a toy store, restaurants, and more.

where to eat

Lexington Area Barbecue Restaurants. Internationally known for pork shoulders slow-cooked over hot hickory coals, eighteen barbecue restaurants in the small town of Lexington are indeed an attraction for visitors, travel writers, and food editors. The typical cuisine is sliced or chopped pork, served with barbecue slaw (a tomato-vinegar dressing—no mayonnaise), hush puppies, and sweet tea. At last count, the visitor's authority listed twenty-one such restaurants in the area. All are easily accessible from Lexington but may be located in other towns as noted. The following, delivered without editorial comment, critique or debate, are priced $–$$.

Backcountry Barbecue. 4014 Linwood Southmont Rd.; (336) 956-1696.

The Barbecue Center. 900 North Main St.; (336) 248-4633.

Barbecue Shack. 706 Randolph St., Thomasville; (336) 472-8566.

Cook's Barbecue. 366 Valient Dr.; (336) 798-1928.

Henry James Family Dining. 283 Talbert Blvd.; (336) 243-2534.

Jed's BBQ. 709 National Hwy., Thomasville; (336) 475-5806.

Jimmy's Barbecue. 1703 Cotton Grove Rd.; (336) 357-2311.

Kerley's Barbecue. Old Hwy. 52, Welcome; (336) 731-8245.

Lexington Barbecue. Business I-85; (336) 249-9814.

Lexington Style Trimmings. 1513 East Center St.; (336) 249-8211.

Rick's Smokehouse. 6043 Hwy. 8 North, Welcome; (336) 731-4060.

Smiley's Barbecue. 917 Winston Rd.; (336) 248-4528.

Smokey Joe's Barbecue. 1101 South Main St.; (336) 249-0315.

Speedy's Barbecue. 1317 Winston Rd.; (336) 248-2410.

Speedy Lohr's BBQ. 8000 North Hwy. 150; (336) 764-5509.

Stamey's Barbecue of Tyro. 4524 South Hwy. 150, Tyro; (336) 853-6426.

Tar Heel Q. 6835 US 64 West; (336) 787-4550.

Terry House Barbecue. 947 Fisher Ferry St., Thomasville; (336) 475-1628.

Tommy's Barbecue. 206 National Hwy., Thomasville; (336) 476-4322.

Troutman's Barbecue. 18466 South Hwy. 109, Denton; (336) 859-2206.

Whitley's Restaurant. 3664 Hwy. 8,Lexington; (336) 357-2364.

day trip 09

west

>>> **all aboard!:**
salisbury, spencer, gold hill

From Raleigh-Durham travel on I-40 west to Greensboro to pick up I-85 south and a straight shot into Salisbury. Former Senator Elizabeth Dole was born here, as was the burgundy-red, bubbly cherry concoction known as Cheerwine, first formulated in 1917 in the basement of L. D. Peeler's wholesale grocery store.

The town of Spencer, just 2 miles north of Salisbury, was once the site of the largest steam locomotive servicing station operated by Southern Railway. Built in 1896 and now known as the North Carolina Transportation Museum, the site presents exhibits on the development of various modes of transport. Here you can see an old roundhouse and ride a steam locomotive.

Complete your day trip by heading to the site of the richest gold mining property east of the Mississippi in the aptly named town of Gold Hill. Once a thriving, rough, and rowdy mining town in the eastern part of Rowan County, Gold Hill is now a quaint, restored "Western primitive" village of homes and stores.

On the return trip from Gold Hill to Raleigh, take SR 49 north through Asheboro (see West Day Trip 10 if you'd like to extend your trip), and US 64 east into Raleigh.

salisbury

No one knows whether the town was named for Salisbury, England, or Salisbury, Maryland, where the earliest settlers of Rowan County originated. Nonetheless Salisbury shares sister-city status with the town in England.

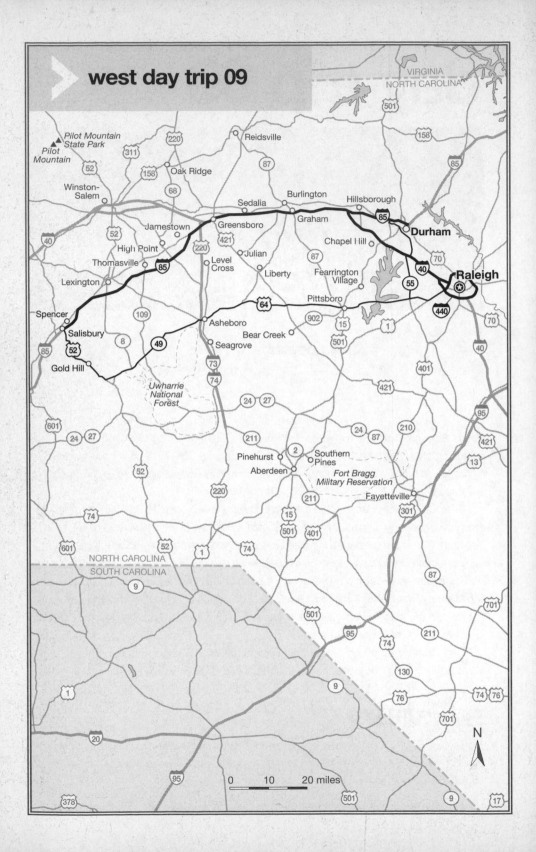

What is known about Salisbury is that Daniel Boone once roamed the region and Andrew Jackson practiced law here. During the conflict that some Southerners still refer to as the "War of Northern Aggression," Salisbury was home to one of the Confederacy's largest prison camps, the only such camp in North Carolina. Five thousand Union troops were buried nearby in a plot of land now designated a National Cemetery.

The thirty-square-block historic district consists of downtown Salisbury and the West Square residential district. Listed on the National Register of Historic Places, this area includes the Dr. Josephus Hall House, which was built in 1820 as the Salisbury Female Academy and later became the home of physician Josephus Hall. Also in the historic district is the Utzman-Chambers House, an 1819 Federal town house constructed by master builder Jacob Stirewalt.

where to go

Rowan County Convention and Visitors Bureau. 204 East Innes St.; (800) 332-2343 or (704) 638-3100; www.visitsalisburync.com. Stop here to pick up a narrative cassette tape for touring the Historic National Cemetery and Confederate Prison Site. A tape and player can be rented for $2. Also pick up maps and brochures or buy a $5 CD for the Salisbury Heritage walking tour. Trolley tours, departing from here, are also offered Saturdays at 11 a.m. and 1 p.m. Open Mon through Fri 9 a.m. to 5 p.m., Sat 10 a.m. to 4 p.m., and Sun 1 to 4 p.m.

Dan Nicholas Park and Campground. 6800 Bringle Ferry Rd.; (704) 216-7800; www .dannicholas.net. Located 8 miles southeast of Salisbury, this 425-acre park has a ten-acre lake for paddleboating and fishing, plus live animal exhibits, tennis courts, picnic shelters, a playground, volleyball, horseshoes, ball fields, an outdoor theater, miniature golf, a carousel, gem mining, and a miniature train ride for children. The eighty-site family campground is open year-round and the park facilities are typically open during daylight hours.

Dr. Josephus Hall House. 226 South Jackson St.; (704) 636-0103; www.historicsalisbury .org. This impressive museum was once home to Dr. Josephus Hall, chief surgeon at the Salisbury Confederate Prison during the Civil War. Built in 1820 in the Federal style, the house includes additions from 1859 and 1900 that have given the house Greek Revival and Victorian features. The interior has painted ceilings, original fixtures, and an impressive collection of mid-Victorian furnishings and decorative accessories belonging to the Hall family. Docents in period costume conduct guided tours. Open Sat and Sun 1 to 4 p.m.

Historic National Cemetery and Confederate Prison Site. 204 East Innes St.; (800) 332-2343 or (704) 638-3100; www.visitsalisburync.com. This self-guided driving tour is a must for Civil War buffs. Although nothing remains of the Salisbury Prison, the tour provides insights into this period of history. Three monuments erected by the State of Maine, the Commonwealth of Pennsylvania, and the U.S. government stand in the Salisbury National Cemetery as a tribute to the 11,700 Union soldiers who died while at the prison.

Old Stone House. Old Stone House Road, Granite Quarry; (704) 633-5946. Built by German immigrant Michael Braun in 1766, this two-story Georgian-style house is the oldest structure in Rowan County. The dry-stacked stones on the front of the house were carefully shaped and matched, creating an impressive facade. 3 miles from downtown Salisbury, the house is open Sat and Sun 1 to 4 p.m.

Rowan Museum. 202 North Main St.; (704) 633-5946. This 1854 courthouse, which survived famed 1865 raid by Union General George Stoneman, is one of the finest examples of pre–Civil War architecture in the state. The museum artifacts and displays depict the life and history of Rowan County.

Salisbury Heritage Walking Tour. (800) 332-2343 or (704) 638-3100; www.visitsalisburync.com. A perfect way to see Historic Salisbury at your own pace, this 2-mile walking tour provides a personal glimpse into the history and architecture of historic downtown Salisbury and the stately homes of the West Square District. The brochures, tapes, and tape players for the tour are loaned for $2 and can be obtained at the Visitor Information Center.

Utzman-Chambers House. 116 South Jackson St.; (704) 633-5946. This 1819 Federal town house was constructed by Jacob Stirewalt, master builder of the period, and reflects the lifestyle of the more affluent citizens of the early 1800s with its unique curved staircase, exquisite interior moldings and details. One of the few surviving Federal period town houses in Piedmont, North Carolina, its period rooms are furnished with Hepplewhite and Chippendale as well as furniture made by Rowan County craftsmen. The house and gardens are open Thurs through Sun from 1 to 4 p.m.

Waterworks Visual Arts Center. 123 East Liberty St.; (704) 638-1882; www.waterworks.org. Originally located in the city's first waterworks building, the center moved across the street from the police station into another refurbished building in 2002. The center offers regional and national gallery exhibitions, studio classes, workshops, and lectures, as well as outreach programs. The sculpture gallery invites visitors to participate in the art experience through touch, sound, fragrance, and sight. Visitors are welcome to read or do research in the Dula Art Library. The center is open Mon through Fri 10 a.m. to 5 p.m. (until 7 p.m. on Thursdays) and Sat 11 a.m. to 3 p.m. Free. Donations are accepted.

where to shop

Okey Dokey and Company. 126 East Innes St.; (704) 645-8744. Located in what operated as O.O. Rufty's General Store for nearly one hundred years, Okey Dokey has kept the charm of the bygone era, including the high tin ceilings. Located in the historic downtown Salisbury area, the store has changed its merchandise ever so slightly since it changed names. Hundreds of items from candy to hardware pack the shelves, but the serious antiques shopper may come across some great finds too. The store is open Mon through Sat 9 a.m. to 5 p.m.

The Salisbury Emporium. 230 East Kerr St.; (704) 642-0039. The Salisbury Emporium is a collection of shops and galleries located in a renovated historic landmark adjacent to the architecturally acclaimed Salisbury Train Station. The Emporium contains more than 15,000 square feet of gifts, antiques, home accessories, Christmas items, fine art, handcrafts, and more. Open Tues through Sat 10 a.m. to 6 p.m. and Sun 1 to 5 p.m.

Salisbury Square Antiques and Collectibles. 111 South Main St.; (704) 633-0773. This antiques mall in historic downtown Salisbury has more than ninety dealers and more than 43,000 square feet of antiques, glassware, and collectibles. Open daily.

The Stitchin' Post and Gifts. 104 South Main St.; (704) 637-0708; www.spgifts.com. This historic 1879 shop has high ceilings, original wood floors, and exposed brick walls. The renovated storefront gives you the warm feeling of walking into history. Unusual gifts for every season can be found here in the heart of downtown Salisbury just off the square. Open Mon through Sat 10 a.m. to 5:30 p.m. Also open Sun afternoons between Thanksgiving and Christmas.

where to eat

The Checkered Flag Barbecue. 1530 South Main St.; (704) 636-2628. Popular among the breakfast crowd, the Checkered Flag also serves barbecue and sandwiches during lunch. $–$$.

Sweet Meadow Cafe. 118 West Innes St.; (704) 637-8715. Serving contemporary cuisine with a twist, the restaurant has an eclectic menu that includes crab cakes—crispy on the outside, nice and soft on the inside—red beans and rice, and other items. Fresh breads are made daily. Works by local artists are on display. $–$$.

The Wrenn House. 115 South Jackson St.; (704) 633-9978; www.thewrennhouse.com. Pull up a chair for the city's namesake dish, Salisbury steak. The menu also features blue-plate specials that offer a meat and two vegetables. $–$$.

where to stay

Mama Josephine's Country Cottage. 601 West Innes St.; (704) 490-2001. Mama Josephine's has twelve cozy rooms and a nearby 1870s cottage for rent. The Country Cottage is located within walking distance of the historic district. $$.

Rowan Oak House Bed and Breakfast. 208 South Fulton St.; (704) 633-2086 or (800) 786-0437; www.rowanoakbb.com. An elegant Queen Anne Victorian in the historic district of downtown Salisbury, Rowan Oak has a wraparound porch, leaded and stained-glass windows, original gas and electric fixtures, seven fireplaces, antiques-filled large rooms, and luxurious bathrooms. This smoke-free property is just three blocks from downtown shopping, antiquing, and fine restaurants. $$.

Turn of the Century Victorian Bed and Breakfast. 529 South Fulton St.; (704) 642-1660 or (800) 250-5349; www.turnofthecenturybb.com. This bed-and-breakfast mixes 1890s elegance with contemporary comforts and amenities. The business suite includes a private office/sitting room. The home has a welcoming wraparound front porch, and complimentary gourmet breakfast is served. $$$.

spencer

Because it sat halfway between Atlanta and Washington, D.C., Spencer was chosen as Southern Railway's repair facility location. The town of Spencer and the shops were named for Southern Railway's first president, Samuel Spencer. To get to Spencer head out on SR 150 north out of Salisbury.

where to go

North Carolina Transportation Museum. 411 South Salisbury Ave.; (704) 636-2889 or (877) 628-6386; www.nctrans.org. Located on the site of what was once Southern Railway Company's largest steam locomotive repair facility, the museum has thirteen buildings, including a restored roundhouse, on fifty-seven acres. Exhibits on early transportation allow you to visit antique automobiles at Bumper to Bumper and trace the history of transportation in Wagons, Wheels, & Wings. Experience days of the working railroad repair shop in the restored 1924 Robert Julian roundhouse. Enjoy seasonal train rides, an audiovisual show, and the visitor center and gift shop. Hours May 1 through Oct 31 are Mon through Sat 9 a.m. to 5 p.m. and Sun 1 to 5 p.m. Hours Nov 1 through Apr 30 are Tues through Sat 9 a.m. to 5 p.m. and Sun 1 to 5 p.m. Free admission; there is a charge for train rides, turntable rides, and guided tours.

Spencer Historic District. (704) 633-2231; www.ci.spencer.nc.us. Adjacent to the North Carolina Transportation Museum, the Spencer National Historic Register District is the largest contiguous district in North Carolina. It contains 322 residential and commercial buildings constructed primarily between 1905 and 1920 to provide support and housing for the workers of Southern Railway's former steam locomotive repair facility.

where to shop

The Little Choo Choo Shop. 500 South Salisbury Ave.; (704) 637-8717. Across the street from the North Carolina Transportation Museum, this well-stocked model-railroad shop is a must–see for train enthusiasts. Open Tues through Sat 10 a.m. to 5:30 p.m.

where to eat

Pinocchio's. 518 South Salisbury Ave.; (704) 636-8891; www.pinocchiosofspencer.com. Home-style Italian fare, made to order from scratch, includes seafood, pasta, pizza, and even homemade gelato. Guests are invited to join in Thurs family game night. Live music is scheduled periodically. Open for lunch Mon through Fri and dinner Tues through Sat. $$.

gold hill

"The richest mining property east of the Mississippi" was the message sent to England after gold was discovered in this part of Rowan County in 1824. Here, vertical shaft mines ran eighty stories deep. With its boardwalks and narrow streets connecting places that were here as early as the 1840s, Gold Hill feels like the set of a Western movie. There are few formal attractions here, but there are ample opportunities to hike, picnic, and visit a time gone by. It's only about twenty minutes south on US 52.

where to shop

E. H. Montgomery Store. 770 Saint Stephens Church; (704) 279-1632. Aside from being a general store, E. H. Montgomery's has "the best hot dogs in three counties," according to the owner. Order milkshakes or soft drinks or pick up some old-fashioned candy at the counter. The store opened in this building in 1850. Open Wed through Sun.

Mauney's 1840 Store and Museum. 775 Saint Stephens Church; (704) 279-1632. Opened in 1840, Mauney's was the first store in Gold Hill. The town was named right inside this store by a group of prospectors. Offering Victorian-era antiques, the store doubles as a museum that displays photos from the days when Gold Hill was emerging as a mining town. Open Wed through Sun.

where to eat

Miss Ruby's Restaurant. 840 Saint Stephens Church; (704) 209-6049. An upscale country inn that offers such items as filet topped with rosemary goat cheese and a balsamic reduction, served with horseradish, mashed potatoes, and steamed asparagus. Try the "Stick to Your Innards" creamy cheddar cheese grits topped with shrimp and maple country ham. Open Wed through Sun for lunch and dinner, and Sun for brunch. $$–$$$.

day trip 10

west

>>> **on safari:**
randleman, asheboro, seagrove

While in Randolph County, consider yourself on safari. This day trip could be composed of the traditional kind of safari on the plains of the African Serengeti in the county seat of Asheboro, or it could be an expedition to find the king—the king of NASCAR, that is—in the town of Randleman. A trip to the county's southern town of Seagrove might simply be a quest to find that perfect gift or mantle display. To begin your adventure, head west on I-40 toward Greensboro, where you'll pick up US 220 south toward Asheboro.

The first stop along the way is Level Cross in Randleman, where NASCAR legend Richard Petty and the Petty Racing Team make their home. From Petty's shop and museum, it's only fifteen minutes to Asheboro, where you'll visit one of the South's finest collections of vintage Harley-Davidson motorcycles. Nearby is the North Carolina Aviation Museum, home to vintage military aircraft.

Of course, Asheboro's big drawing card is the North Carolina Zoo. The nation's largest and perhaps finest walk-through natural-habitat zoo has more than 1,100 animals and 60,000 plants in its African and North American sections. After visiting the zoo, make your way to Seagrove, which bills itself as the "pottery capital of the world." Try to schedule your trip around the kiln openings, traditionally in the spring, or the pottery festival the weekend before Thanksgiving. Along the way, visit Pisgah Bridge, one of only two covered bridges in North Carolina.

As you head home by way of US 64 north, you could stop at the gravesite of Frances Bavier, who played Aunt Bee on *The Andy Griffith Show*. Bavier is buried in Siler City's

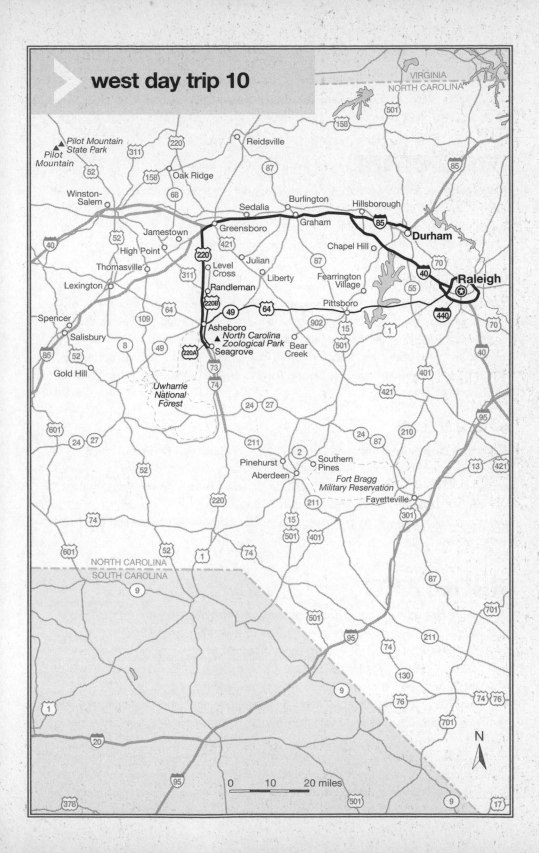

west day trip 10

Oakwood Cemetery. If you are a huge fan of the old Andy Griffith episodes, be sure to see our West Day Trip 07 to Mount Airy, the town that fictional Mayberry was based on.

randleman

With Greensboro and Asheboro only 14 miles in opposite directions, the community of Level Cross in Randleman is a convenient stop for day-trippers visiting either destination. There are two reasons to park your car here: to visit the Richard Petty Museum and to have lunch where the shop mechanics do, at Frank and Larry's Breakfast and Lunch.

where to go

Richard Petty Museum. 142 West Academy St., Randleman; (336) 495-1143; www .heartofnorthcarolina.com. Racecars, awards, and photos honor this seven-time Winston Cup Series champion. See highlights of "The King's" thirty-five-year career in a full-length movie in the mini theater, and take home gifts for a favorite race fan. Open Wed through Sat 9 a.m. to 5 p.m. Admission is $8 for adults, $5 for children ages seven and up, and free for children six and under.

where to eat

Frank and Larry's Breakfast and Lunch. 5624 Randleman Rd., Randleman; (336) 674-9177. This is the spot where the locals and the Petty shop mechanics gather for breakfast and lunch. The restaurant has been here as long as Richard has, the owners proudly boast. Offering daily blue plate lunch specials, Frank & Larry's is popular for hot dogs, hamburgers, and barbecue as well as breakfasts that include homemade biscuits and gravy and homemade sausage. $.

asheboro

In 1701 explorer John Lawson crossed the Uwharrie River into a Keyauwee Indian village. "Nature hath so fortify'd the Town with Mountains, that were it a Great Seat of War, it might easily be made impregnable, having large cornfields joining to their cabins, and a Savanna near the Town, at the foot of these Mountains, that is capable of keeping some hundreds of heads of Cattle," Lawson wrote in *A New Voyage to Carolina,* published in 1709.

The mountains and rolling hills where the Keyauwee made their home are now the domain of a species more ancient than man, a species whose denizens make up kingdom Animalia.

Six miles southeast of Asheboro, the North Carolina Zoological Park sits on 1,450 acres skirting the eastern edge of the Uwharries,where Native Americans once walked, exotic animals now roam, and more freely than in most other zoos in the world. That's because Randolph County's rolling hills make for ideal natural habitats, where animals move about unrestricted by obvious fences and steel bars.

Although a visit to the zoo can take the better part of the day, you will want to allow time to visit the other sites in Asheboro. They include the American Classic Motorcycle Museum, with its more than six decades of motorcycle history, and for classic aircraft enthusiasts and World War II buffs, the North Carolina Aviation Museum.

Finally, if you just want to get away from it all, there's the Uwharrie National Forest, which occupies 50,189 acres west of Asheboro. You're not likely to run up on any of the Keyauwee that John Lawson encountered in those old mountains, but all that mesmerized him is still there, and almost as pristine as it was when he first laid eyes on it. For more information, call (800) 626-2672 or visit www.cs.unca.edu/nfsnc/recreation/uwharrie/index.htm.

where to go

American Classic Motorcycle Museum. 1170 US 64 West. (336) 629-9564; www.heartofamerica.com. One of the South's finest collections of antique and classic Harley-Davidson motorcycles, the museum has more than thirty bikes dating from 1936 through 1972, and an authentic 1948 Harley dealership/repair shop. Open Mon 6 a.m. to 2 p.m., Tues through Fri 6 a.m. to 5:30 p.m. and Sat 6 a.m. to 4 p.m. Free.

North Carolina Aviation Museum. 2222–6 Pilotsview Rd., Asheboro Regional Airport; (336) 625-0170; www.ncairmuseum.org. This museum, created for the preservation of military aircraft, is home to an impressive collection of airworthy vintage military aircraft. The museum also houses exhibits of World War II military uniforms and a collection of WW II–era newspaper features. Open Mon through Sat 10 a.m. to 5 p.m. and Sun noon to 5 p.m. with some reduced hours in winter. Admission is $8 for adults and $5 for students.

North Carolina Zoological Park. 4401 Zoo Pkwy.; (336) 879-7000 or (800) 488-0444; www.nczoo.org. This facility was the first American zoo designed from its inception around the "natural habitat" philosophy, presenting animals and plants in exhibits that closely resemble the habitats in which they would be found in the wild.

The zoo's African habitats stretch over 300 acres and contain nine large outdoor exhibits for animals such as lions, zebras, ostriches, baboons, chimpanzees, rhinos, and elephants. It also includes the African Pavilion with lush plantings of tropical plants. The 200-acre North American habitat is home to alligators, bison, roadrunners, rattlesnakes, and tarantulas. The streamside exhibit re-creates North Carolina's stream wildlife, from the mountains through the Piedmont region and coastal plain. Visitors can also walk through the Sonoran Desert or see polar bears play on the arctic coast.

The best way to see the zoo is on foot, so you can explore the exhibits and trails. An internal tram is available to transport visitors between exhibit areas, but most animals are not visible from the trams. You can enter or exit by either the North American or African gate; a shuttle bus transports visitors to the parking areas. Zoo officials recommend taking a minimum of five hours to explore all that the park offers at a comfortable pace.

The zoo is open Apr 1 to Oct 31 daily 9 a.m. to 5 p.m., Nov 1 to Mar 31 daily 9 a.m. to 4 p.m., and closed Christmas Day. There are additional hours during special events and reduced hours during inclement weather. Admission is $10 for adults, $8 for seniors and $6 or children.

Pisgah Covered Bridge. Take exit 49, just south of Asheboro off US 220 Business. Look for the historical markers that will direct you to the covered bridge, one of only two in North Carolina, which was built around 1910. Hiking trails, picnic tables, and parking are available.

where to shop

Collector's Antique Mall. 211 Sunset Ave.; (336) 629-8105; www.collectorsantiquemall .com. More than 125 dealers offer antiques and collectibles in more than 35,000 square feet of retail space in the downtown antiques district of Asheboro. Open daily.

where to eat

Blue Mist Barbecue. 3409 US 64 East; (336) 625-3980. Blue Mist serves the area's finest barbecue plates and sandwiches. Open daily. $$.

Rock-Ola Café. 1131 East Dixie Dr.; (336) 626-4001. This family-oriented, casual dining establishment serves pork, chicken, ribs, certified Angus beef, pasta, and seafood. Try the handmade onion rings or loaded cheese fries for starters. Open daily. $$.

Sir Pizza. 813 East Dixie Dr.; (336) 629-2874. Sir Pizza has been an Asheboro favorite for pizza, pasta, and sandwiches since 1969. The locals tell us that when people who have moved from Asheboro return home, this is the first place they want to return to. Open daily. $$. (Second location at 724 North Fayetteville St.; 336-629-9101.)

Taste of Asia. 127 East Taft Ave.; (336) 626-7578. Serving such popular Thai and Cambodian dishes as curries and seafood stir-fry. Open daily. $$.

where to stay

Asheboro has several major chain hotels, including Comfort Inn, Days Inn, Hampton Inn, Holiday Inn Express, Jameson Inn, and Super 8 Motel. In addition, there is one bed-and-breakfast situated on a 128-acre farm, twenty minutes north and another country lodge just east of town.

Hunter's Run Lodge Bed & Breakfast. 1245 Mount Tabor Church Rd.; (336) 302-4107 or (336) 629-3074; www.bbonline.com/nc/huntersrun. Located just outside Asheboro is a traditional country inn on sixty-eight acres of rolling green hills. Stroll by the lake, wet a line, sit by the fireplace, or unwind in a Jacuzzi. A stay here also features complimentary continental breakfast on weekdays and a full breakfast on weekends. The lodge also offers two cabins for rent. $$.

The Inn at Rising Meadow Farm. 3750 Williams Dairy Rd., Liberty; (336) 622-1795. If animals were your reason for this day trip, then you'd do well to travel twenty minutes north of Asheboro for an overnight stay in this two–guest room bed-and-breakfast. Spend some time fishing in the pond (or just toss in some feed), catch lightning bugs, or acquaint yourself with the sheep (raised for wool products sold here), cows, goats, horses, and donkey that live here. If you want to lend a hand, there may be eggs to gather or kittens to hold. $$.

seagrove

Fifteen minutes south of Asheboro, Seagrove, named for a railroad official, invites visitors to discover one of the finest sources of decorative pottery on the East Coast. What you'll find here is not just handmade ashtrays and such. Seagrove pottery passes for museum-quality art, with some pieces going for as much as $12,000. Some of the more than one hundred potters who work in the area have garnered national and worldwide attention. Take US 220 south to begin your search for the perfect piece of pottery.

where to go

North Carolina Pottery Center. 233 East Ave.; (336) 873-8430; www.ncpotterycenter .com. Seagrove pottery is showcased at the North Carolina Pottery Center's museum, gallery, and learning center. The facility presents permanent displays that include Native American pieces as well as current works and changing exhibits. Open Tues through Sat 10 a.m. to 4 p.m. Adults, $2, students in grades nine through twelve, $1, and free for children through grade eight.

where to shop

For a guide to the potteries and galleries in the Seagrove area, order the free brochure from the **Randolph County Tourism Development Authority,** (800) 626-2672 or download it from the Web site, www.heartofnorthcarolina.com, yourself. Another helpful website is www .discoverseagrove.com, maintained by the **Seagrove Area Potter Association.** Following is a sampling of some of our favorite potteries.

King's Pottery. 4905 Reeder Rd.; (336) 381-3090; www.kingspottery.com. Operated by the King family, this pottery specializes in wheel-thrown and hand-built utilitarian pottery. The wood-fired and salt-glazed items include folk art, face jugs, and specialty pieces. Open Mon through Sat 9 a.m. to 5 p.m. and Sun noon to 5 p.m., but the owners suggest calling first if you "are coming some distance."

Phil Morgan Pottery. 966 SR 705; (336) 873-7304. Morgan specializes in quality crystalline-glazed porcelain, reflecting 1,500-year-old techniques from China's Chung Dynasty. Morgan's pieces are in collections worldwide, including those of heads of state in the United States, Argentina, and China. His shop, established in 1973, also sells hand-painted decorative and utilitarian pieces. Open Tues through Sat.

Pott's Pottery. 630 East Main St.; (336) 873-9660; www.pottspotteryinseagrove.com. Opened in 1991, Pott's Pottery specializes in wheel-thrown utilitarian ware. Open Mon through Sat.

Seagrove Pottery. 106 North Broad St.; (336) 873-7280. This gallery represents more than fifty potters and artists from the Seagrove region, offering a wide variety of face jugs, utilitarian and decorative pottery, basketry, candles, and hand-painted garden accessories. Open Mon through Sat 9 a.m. to 9 p.m. and Sun 11 a.m. to 5 p.m.

Turn and Burn. 124 East Ave.; (336) 873-7381. Operating since 1985, Turn and Burn specializes in traditional Seagrove salt glaze in utilitarian and decorative pottery, wood–fired stoneware, contemporary and traditional folk art, raku, and fire pit. Open 9 a.m. to 5 p.m. daily.

where to eat

Jugtown Cafe. 7042 Old US Hwy. 220; (336) 873-8292. Stop by for blue-plate specials, breakfast with biscuits, gravy, grits and sausage, and great homemade pies. Try the "huge" cookies, reasonably priced at 80 cents each. Open Mon through Wed 6 a.m. to 2 p.m., Thurs through Sat 6 a.m. to 8 p.m., Sun 7 a.m. to 2 p.m. $–$$.

Westmoore Family Restaurant. 2172 SR 705 South; (910) 464-5222. A full line of fried and broiled seafood, steaks, salads, and sandwiches is available plus pit-cooked barbecue and daily blue plate specials. This place is popular for its charcoal-grilled burgers, clubs, and seafood. $–$$.

where to stay

The Duck Smith House Bed and Breakfast. 465 North Broad St.; (336) 873-7099 or (888) 869-9018; www.ducksmith.com. This beautifully restored historic farm house has four guest rooms. The full country breakfast includes freshly picked fruits and items that range from blueberry pancakes to country ham, eggs, and cheese grits, all served with homemade breads. Homemade jams and cobblers are made from fifty-year-old fruit trees on the property. This B&B is within walking distance of the Seagrove potteries and North Carolina Pottery Center. $$.

festivals and celebrations

january

Cape Fear Model Railroad Show & Sale, Wilmington. Lionel, N-Scale, and HO-Scale trains are on exhibit at the American Legion Post. (910) 270-2696.

february

Anniversary Battle of Moore's Creek Bridge, Currie. The battle here in 1776 that effectively ended British rule, is remembered. (910) 283-5591; www.nps.gov/mocr/index.htm.

Carolina Jazz Festival, Chapel Hill. This festival on the campus of UNC and throughout the town features big and small names in jazz. (919) 962-1039; www.unc.edu/music/jazzfest/.

march

Anniversary of the Battle at Guilford Courthouse, Greensboro. The commemoration of this battle includes a week full of events. (336) 288-1776; www.nps.gov/guco.

april

Dogwood Festival, Fayetteville. Three days of events include concerts, family fun, and more. (910) 323-1934; www.faydogwoodfestival.com.

North Carolina Azalea Festival, Wilmington. One of the state's largest and longest running events features garden tours and festival activities. (910) 794-4650; www.ncazaleafestival.org.

North Carolina Pickle Festival, Mount Olive. Pet animals, eat pickles, and have some fun at this festival. (919) 658-3113; www.ncpicklefest.org.

may

Buggy Festival, Carthage. Buggies have been big business in Carthage since the middle of the 19th century and this festival celebrates that. www.thebuggyfestival.com.

Sanford Pottery Festival, Sanford. This largest of the state's pottery festivals includes family activities and pottery for sale. www.sanfordpottery.org.

Tanglewood Cup Steeplechase, Tanglewood. This steeplechase has run since 1965. (336) 712-4426; www.tanglewoodpark.org.

june

Benson State Singing Convention, Benson. For nearly a century gospel music has taken center stage for three days in Benson. (919) 894-4389; www.gospelsingingconvention.org.

NC Blueberry Festival, Burgaw. Although second in the state's blueberry production, Pender County hosts this festival of art, music, and more than a little pie. (910) 300-6116; www.ncblueberryfestival.com.

Spivey Corner National Hollerin' Contest, Dunn. A car show, kids' corner, food, and more accompany four categories of hollerin' contests. (910) 567-2600; www.hollerincontest .com.

july

NC Fourth of July Celebration, Southport. This is the state's most prominent Independence Day Celebration. (910) 457-6964; www.nc4thofjuly.com.

Robbin's Farmer's Day, Robbins. Since 1955 the town has paid tribute to the simple life and the family farm. www.robbinsfarmersday.com.

august

Crape Myrtle Festival, Scotland Neck. This daylong festival celebrates the trees that accent the town of Scotland Neck. (252) 826-3152; www.townofscotlandneck.com.

NC Watermelon Festival, Murfreesboro. There are several festivals of the mighty melon in the Carolinas but this one claims the state name. (252) 398-5922; www.murfreesboronc .org/watermelon.htm.

Wyndam Championship, Greensboro. This PGA tournament has been going on in Greensboro in one form or another since 1928. (336) 379-1570; www.wyndhamchampion ship.com.

september

Collard Festival, Ayden. An eating contest and cooking contest for this leafy green vegetable are just part of the fun of this festival. (252) 746-7080; www.aydencollardfestival.com.

International Folk Festival, Fayetteville. This weekend includes music, a parade, food, and more. (910) 323-1776; www.theartscouncil.com.

Mayberry Days, Mount Airy. From a golf tournament to a gospel singing, this event recognizes the prominence the popular television series brought the town of Mount Airy with stars of the show, look-alikes, and various events. (336) 786-7998; www.mayberrydays.org.

Mule Days, Benson. A mule pulling contest, a rodeo, and bluegrass are blended with traditional festival fun. (919) 894-3825; www.bensonmuledays.com.

october

Barbecue Festival, Lexington. Crafts, entertainment, and of course, the best in barbecue make this festival tops in the state. (336) 956-1880; www.barbecuefestival.com.

NASCAR Day Festival, Randleman. The town of Randleman partners with the Richard Petty Museum to put on this show of speed, history, and festival fun. (336) 495-1100; www.randlemanchamber.com/nascar.htm.

NC Seafood Festival, Morehead City. For three days Morehead City puts on one of the state's biggest beach parties of the year that includes music, dancing, family entertainment, and practically every kind of seafood imaginable. (252) 726-6273; www.ncseafoodfestival.org.

november

Fort Branch Battle Re-enactment, Hamilton. Since access to Fort Branch is limited, this is an excellent time to visit. The event includes full three days of events. (252) 792-6605; www.fortbranchcivilwarsite.com.

Seagrove Pottery Festival, Seagrove. Just about all the potters in the Seagrove area turn out for this event to sell their wares. (336) 873-7887; www.seagrovepotteryheritage.com.

december

Santa Train and Jingle Bell Express, Spencer. Santa spreads holiday cheer at the NC Transportation Museum. (704) 636-2889; www.nctrans.org.

Tanglewood Festival of Lights, Clemmons. This spectacular drive-through display includes a million lights and is one of the biggest holiday displays in the state. (336) 778-6300; www.tanglewoodpark.org.

>> a taste of the vine: north carolina wine listings

After spending any amount of time at all in North Carolina you are likely to begin to notice wineries beckoning you to have a taste.

North Carolina's history in the wine business goes back to Sir Walter Raleigh's arrival here in the 16th century as his men discovered a vine (the mother vine) on the state's Outer Banks. It wasn't long before grape cultivation and wine production began. In the early 1800s, Thomas Jefferson noted North Carolina taking the lead with wine culture, and the 1840 Federal Census listed the state as the number one wine producer in the country. Then came prohibition in 1919, and wine bottles were exchanged for mason jars that held a certain more potent, clear potable.

It would be almost a century before wine would really make a comeback. Prior to the 21st century, there weren't many more than a dozen wineries in North Carolina. A decade later the state boasts nearly 100, ranking it seventh among all states and establishing wineries as a bonafide contributor to the state's tourism industry.

While some wineries produce Cabernet Sauvignon, Cabernet Franc, Merlot, Syrah, Chardonnay and Viognier from the more familiar European vinifera grape, others produce varieties from the sweeter, more unusual muscadine grapes, the official state fruit also known as the Scuppernong. It's popular not necessarily as much for its taste as for its benefits as an antioxidant.

The following list is a guide, cross-referenced with our day trips, to all the wineries located within about two hours of the Raleigh-Durham area. While most are in the Yadkin Valley near the Triad area, wineries have popped up in most every part of the state. Most offer specific tasting room hours, many offer eating establishments with outstanding views, and some present entertainment, special events, and even a place to lay your head.

east day trip 03

Adams Vineyards, John Adams Rd., Willow Spring; (919) 567-1010; www.adamsvineyards.com.

Hinnant Family Vineyards & Winery, 2603 Hospital Rd., Goldsboro; (919) 965-3350; www.hinnantvineyards.com.

Secret Garden Winery, 1018 Airport Rd., Pikeville; (919) 734-0260; www.asecretgardenwinery.com.

southeast day trip 01

Bannerman Vineyard, 5608 Oak Bluff Lane, Wilmington; (910) 259-5474; www.banner manvineyard.com.

Lumina Winery, 6620 Gordon Rd., Suite H, Wilmington; (910) 793-5299; www.lumina wine.com.

Noni Bacca Winery, 420 Eastwood Rd., #108, Wilmington; (877) 397-7617, (910) 397-7617; www.nbwinery.com.

south day trip 01

Enoch Winery & Vineyard, 7778 Meadowbrook Rd., Benson; (919) 207-0100; www .enochwinery.com.

Country Squire Winery, 748 Hwy. 24/50, Warsaw; (910) 296-1727; www.country squirewinery.com.

Duplin Winery, 505 N. Sycamore St., Rose Hill; (910) 289-3888; www.duplinwinery.com.

south day trip 02

Lac Belle Amie Vineyard & Winery, 195 Vineyard Dr., Elizabethtown; (910) 645-6450; www.lacbelleamie.com.

Lu Mil Vineyard, 438 Suggs Taylor Rd., Elizabethtown; (800) 545-2293, (910) 866-5819; www.lumilvineyard.com.

Cypress Bend Vineyards, 21904 Riverton Rd., Wagram; (910) 369-0411; www.cypress bendvineyards.com.

west day trip 01

Rock of Ages Winery and Vineyard, 1890 Charlie Long Rd., Hurdle Mills; (336) 364-7625; www.rockofageswinery.com.

Grove Winery, 1129 Pinehurst Dr., Chapel Hill; (336) 584-4060; www.grovewinery.com.

west day trip 02

Horizon Cellars, 466 Vineyard Ridge, Siler City; (919) 742-1404; www.horizoncellars.com.

SilkHope Winery, 701 Duncan Farm Rd., Siler City; (919) 545-5696; www.silkhopewinery .com.

Wolfe Wines, 8973 Old Plank Rd., Snow Camp; (336) 376-1401; www.wolfewines.com.

west day trip 04

Benjamin Vineyards & Winery, 6516 Whitney Rd., Graham; (336) 376-1080; www.ben jaminvineyards.com.

Glen Marie Vineyards & Winery, 1838 Johnson Rd., Burlington; (336) 578-3938; www .glenmariewinery.com.

Iron Gate Vineyards, 2440 Lynch Store Rd., Mebane; (919) 304-9463; www.irongate vineyards.com.

Autumn Creek Vineyards, 364 Means Creek Rd., Mayodan; (336) 548-9463; www .autumncreekvineyards.com.

west day trip 05

Stonefield Cellars Winery, 8220 SR 68 North, Stokesdale; (336) 644-9908; www.stone fieldcellars.com.

west day trip 06

Germanton Vineyard and Winery, 3530 SR 8-65, Germanton; (336) 969-2075; www .germantongallery.com.

Weathervane Winery, 484 Hartman Rd., Winston-Salem; (336) 793-3366; www.weather vanewinery.com.

Divine Llama Vineyards, 3524 Yadkinville Rd., Winston-Salem; (336) 699-2525; www .divinellamavineyards.com.

Westbend Vineyards, 5394 Williams Rd., Lewisville; (336) 945-5032; www.westbend vineyards.com.

Hanover Park Vineyard, 1927 Courtney-Huntsville Rd., Yadkinville; (336) 463-2875; www .hanoverparkwines.com.

Allison Oaks Vineyards, 1213 Henry St., Yadkinville; (336) 677-1388; www.allisonoaks vineyards.com.

Brandon Hills Vineyard, 1927 Brandon Hills Rd., Yadkinville; (336) 463-9463; www.brandon hillsvineyard.com.

Cellar 4201, 4201Apperson Rd., East Bend; (336) 699-6030; www.cellar4201.com.

Flint Hill Vineyards, 2153 Flint Hill Rd., East Bend; (336) 699-4455; www.flinthillvineyards .com.

Dobbins Creek Vineyards, 4430 Vineyard View Lane, Hamptonville; (336) 468-4770; www.dobbinscreekvineyards.com.

Laurel Gray Vineyards, 5726 West Old Hwy. 421, Hamptonville; (336) 468-9463; www .laurelgray.com.

Buck Shoals Vineyard, 6121 Vintner Way, Hamptonville; (336) 468-9274; www.buck shoalsvineyard.com.

Shadow Springs Vineyard, 5543 Crater Road, Hamptonville; (336) 468-5000; www .shadowspringsvineyard.com.

west day trip 07

RagApple Lassie Vineyards, 3724 RagApple Lassie Lane, Boonville; (336) 367-6000; www.ragapplelassie.com.

Sanders Ridge Vineyard and Winery, 3200 Round Hill Rd., Boonville; (336) 677-1700; www.sandersridge.com.

Shelton Vineyards, 286 Cabernet Lane, Dobson; (336) 366-4724; www.sheltonvineyards .com.

Round Peak Vineyards, 765 Round Peak Church Rd., Mt. Airy; (336) 352-5595; www .roundpeak.com.

Old North State Winery, 308 North Main St., Mt. Airy; (336) 789-9463; www.oldnorth statewinery.com.

Hutton Vineyards, 103 Buck Fork Rd., Dobson; (336) 374-2621; www.huttonwinery.com.

Stony Knoll Vineyards, 1143 Stony Knoll Rd., Dobson; (336) 374-5752; www.stony knollvineyards.com.

McRitchie Winery & Ciderworks, 315 Thurmond PO Rd., Thurmond; (336) 874-3003; www.mcritchiewine.com.

Carolina Heritage Vineyard & Winery, 170 Heritage Vines Way, Elkin; (336) 366-3301; www.carolinaheritagevineyards.com.

Grassy Creek Vineyard & Winery, 235 Chatham Cottage Circle, Elkin; (336) 835-4230; www.grassycreekvineyard.com.

Elkin Creek Vineyard, 318 Elkin Creek Mill Rd., Elkin; (336) 526-5119; www.elkin creekvineyard.com.

Brushy Mountain Winery, 125 West Main St., Elkin; (336) 835-1313; www.brushymoun tainwine.com.

west day trip 08

Zimmerman Vineyards, 1428 Tabernacle Church Rd., Trinity;. (336) 861-1414; www .zimmermanvineyards.net.

Childress Vineyards, 1000 Childress Vineyards Rd., Lexington; (336) 236-9463; www .childressvineyards.com.

Junius Lindsay Vineyard, 385 Doctor Zimmerman Rd., Lexington; (336) 764-0487; www .juniuslindsay.com.

RayLen Vineyards & Winery, 3577 US Hwy. 158, Mocksville; (336) 998-3100; www .raylenvineyards.com.

Misty Creek Farm & Vineyards, 710 Wyo Rd., Mocksville; (336) 998-3303; www.misty creekwines.net.

Garden Gate Vineyards, 261 Scenic Dr., Mocksville; (336) 751-3794; www.gardengate vineyards.com.

west day trip 09

Old Stone Vineyard and Winery, 6245 US 52 South, Salisbury; (704) 279-0930; www .osvwinery.com.

Uwharrie Vineyards, 28030 Austin Rd., New London; (704) 982-9463; www.uwharrie vineyards.com.

Stony Mountain Vineyards, 26370 Mountain Ridge Rd., Albemarle; (704) 982-0922; www .stonymountainvineyards.com.

Dennis Vineyards, 24043 Endy Rd., Albemarle; (800) 230-1743, (704) 982-6090; www .dennisvineyards.com.

index